WORKING WITH CRITICAL REALISM

This international and interdisciplinary collection gathers stories from researchers and research students about their methodological encounters with critical realism. Whether the contributors are experienced or novice researchers, they are predominantly new to critical realism. For various reasons, as the contributors detail, they have all been drawn to critical realism.

It is well known that critical realism can be bewildering and even overwhelming to newcomers, especially to those unfamiliar with language of, and without a grounding in, philosophy. While there are now numerous and important introductory and applied critical realist texts that make critical realism more accessible to a broader audience, stories from newcomers have been absent – especially as part of a single collection.

The significance and uniqueness of this collection lies in its documentation of first-hand reflective insights on the practical use and implementation of critical realism. The contributors feature critical realist inspired research journeys in Australia, England, Scotland, Belgium, Sweden, and Spain.

The hope of this book is that the stories and accounts presented in it will inspire – or at least sufficiently arouse – the curiosity of others to explore critical realist possibilities, which we believe offer enormous value to serious researchers across and within all disciplines and subjects who are interested in rigorous intellectual work with a socially progressive purpose.

Alpesh Maisuria is Associate Professor of Education Policy in Critical Education, University of the West of England, Bristol, UK. Through underlabouring Marxism, his work examines the ideological and political drivers of policy decisions to critique the role and function of education in (re)producing forms of inequality. He has an extensive publications record, including the *Encyclopaedia of Marxism and Education* (Brill 2022). Alpesh is the Joint Deputy Editor of *Journal for*

Critical Education Policy Studies (JCEPS) and is the co-convenor of the Marxism and Education: Renewing Dialogues (MERD) seminar series (see the Facebook group). He is also Academic Parliamentary Fellow for the House of Commons Library in the UK Parliament, and the American Education Research Association (AERA) Marxian and Society SIG Programme Chair.

Grant Banfield is Adjunct Lecturer, University of South Australia. He has been a teacher and university researcher/academic in Australian secondary schools and universities for over 40 years. His commitment throughout has been to the advancement of education as an emancipatory and revolutionary project. Grant's research, writing, and scholarship centre on exploring the relationship between realist philosophy of science and Marxian social theory and the possibilities this brings for ethical and transformative praxis. He is the author of *Critical Realism for Marxist Sociology of Education* (Routledge 2016).

Routledge Studies in Critical Realism

Critical Realism is a broad movement within philosophy and social science. It is a movement that began in British philosophy and sociology following the founding work of Roy Bhaskar, Margaret Archer and others. Critical Realism emerged from the desire to realise an adequate realist philosophy of science, social science, and of critique. Against empiricism, positivism and various idealisms (interpretivism, radical social constructionism), Critical Realism argues for the necessity of ontology. The pursuit of ontology is the attempt to understand and say something about 'the things themselves' and not simply about our beliefs, experiences, or our current knowledge and understanding of those things. Critical Realism also argues against the implicit ontology of the empiricists and idealists of events and regularities, reducing reality to thought, language, belief, custom, or experience. Instead Critical Realism advocates a structural realist and causal powers approach to natural and social ontology, with a focus upon social relations and process of social transformation.

Important movements within Critical Realism include the morphogenetic approach developed by Margaret Archer; Critical Realist economics developed by Tony Lawson; as well as dialectical Critical Realism (embracing being, becoming and absence) and the philosophy of meta-Reality (emphasising priority of the non-dual) developed by Roy Bhaskar.

For over thirty years, Routledge has been closely associated with Critical Realism and, in particular, the work of Roy Bhaskar, publishing well over fifty works in, or informed by, Critical Realism (in series including Critical Realism: Interventions; Ontological Explorations; New Studies in Critical Realism and Education). These have all now been brought together under one series dedicated to Critical Realism.

The Centre for Critical Realism is the advisory editorial board for the series. If you would like to know more about the Centre for Critical Realism, or to submit a book proposal, please visit www.centreforcriticalrealism.com.

Ethical Consumption: Practices and Identities
A Realist Approach
Yana Manyukhina

The Subject of Human Being
Christopher W. Haley

Religious Education from a Critical Realist Perspective
Sensus Fidei and Critical Thinking
Johnny C. Go

Explaining Society
Critical Realism in the Social Sciences
Berth Danermark, Mats Ekström and Jan Ch. Karlsson

Social and Ethnic Inequalities in the Cypriot Education System
A Critical Realist View on Empowerment
Areti Stylianou and David Scott

The Space that Separates: A Realist Theory of Art
Nick Wilson

Critical Realism, Feminism, and Gender: A Reader
Michiel van Ingen, Steph Grohmann and Lena Gunnarsson

The Morphogenesis of the Norwegian Educational System
Emergence and Development from a Critical Realist Perspective
Margaret S. Archer, Unn-Doris K. Bæck and Tone Skinningsrud

Explaining Morality
Critical Realism and Moral Questions
Steve Ash

Big Picture Perspectives on Planetary Flourishing
Metatheory for the Anthropocene Vol 1
Nicholas Hedlund and Sean Esbjörn-Hargens

Working with Critical Realism
Stories of Methodological Encounters
Alpesh Maisuria and Grant Banfield

A Critical Realist Theory of Sport
Graham Scambler

For more information about this series, please visit: https://www.routledge.com/Routledge-Studies-in-Critical-Realism-Routledge-Critical-Realism/book-series/SE0518

WORKING WITH CRITICAL REALISM

Stories of Methodological Encounters

Edited by Alpesh Maisuria and Grant Banfield

Routledge
Taylor & Francis Group
LONDON AND NEW YORK

Designed cover image: *Eagle at the Speed of Light* by Grant Banfield

First published 2023
by Routledge
4 Park Square, Milton Park, Abingdon, Oxon OX14 4RN

and by Routledge
605 Third Avenue, New York, NY 10158

Routledge is an imprint of the Taylor & Francis Group, an informa business

© 2023 selection and editorial matter, Alpesh Maisuria and Grant Banfield individual chapters, the contributors

The right of Alpesh Maisuria and Grant Banfield to be identified as the authors of the editorial material, and of the authors for their individual chapters, has been asserted in accordance with sections 77 and 78 of the Copyright, Designs and Patents Act 1988.

All rights reserved. No part of this book may be reprinted or reproduced or utilised in any form or by any electronic, mechanical, or other means, now known or hereafter invented, including photocopying and recording, or in any information storage or retrieval system, without permission in writing from the publishers.

Trademark notice: Product or corporate names may be trademarks or registered trademarks, and are used only for identification and explanation without intent to infringe.

British Library Cataloguing-in-Publication Data
A catalogue record for this book is available from the British Library

Library of Congress Cataloging-in-Publication Data
Names: Maisuria, Alpesh, author. | Banfield, Grant, author.
Title: Working with critical realism : stories of methodological encounters / Alpesh Maisuria, Grant Banfield.
Description: Abingdon, Oxon ; New York, NY : Routledge, 2023. | Series: Routledge studies in critical realism | Includes bibliographical references and index. |
Identifiers: LCCN 2022030635 (print) | LCCN 2022030636 (ebook) | ISBN 9781032045634 (hbk) | ISBN 9781032045610 (pbk) | ISBN 9781003193784 (ebk)
Subjects: LCSH: Critical realism--Methodology.
Classification: LCC B835 .M335 2023 (print) | LCC B835 (ebook) | DDC 149/.2--dc23/eng/20220824
LC record available at https://lccn.loc.gov/2022030635
LC ebook record available at https://lccn.loc.gov/2022030636

ISBN: 978-1-032-04563-4 (hbk)
ISBN: 978-1-032-04561-0 (pbk)
ISBN: 978-1-003-19378-4 (ebk)

DOI: 10.4324/9781003193784

Typeset in Bembo
by KnowledgeWorks Global Ltd.

CONTENTS

Acknowledgements   *x*
Foreword   *xi*
Notes on Contributors   *xiii*

1 Introduction: Journeying through Critical Realism   1
 Alpesh Maisuria and Grant Banfield

2 A Detective, Physicist, and Historian Walk into a Bar: Abduction, Retroduction, and Retrodiction in Critical Realist Evaluations   14
 Didier Boost, Björn Blom, and Peter Raeymaeckers

3 Bridging the Gap Between Philosophy and Empirical Research: A Critical Realist Methodology Using Quantitative Methods   29
 Catherine Hastings

4 Parent Engagement in Student Learning: Using Critical Realism to Uncover the Generative Mechanisms Needed for Teachers to Embrace Parent Engagement in Their Teaching Practice   41
 Catherine Mary Quinn

5 On the Anti-Imperialist Possibilities of Critical Realism   51
 Omar Kaissi

6 Cobbling Together Methods for a Coherent Critical Realist
   Methodology: Searching for Mechanisms   63
   Bree Weizenegger

7 A Critical Realist Perspective on the 'Quality and
   Reform Dance' in the Australian Vocational Education
   and Training (VET) Sector: The Road Less Travelled   77
   Deborah Johnson

8 The Utility of Critical Realism in Indigenous Research   89
   Cassandra Diamond

9 The Spatiality of School Choice: A Critical Realist
   Quantitative Geography of Education?   97
   Anna-Maria Fjellman

10 Real Men, Real Violence: Critical Realism and the
   Search for the Masculine Subject   107
   Ben Wadham

11 The Critical Realist Toolkit   121
   Ellenah Mackie

12 Journeys to Critical Realism: A Conversation
   about Spirituality, Love, and Human Emancipation   130
   Loretta Geuenich, Celina Valente, and Grant Banfield

13 A Kind of Conclusion: Against Full-Stops and Bookends?   145
   Alpesh Maisuria and Grant Banfield

Index   *158*

BE-COMING, BE-GOING

If I were ...

An Eagle at the Speed of Light

    ... what would I be?

If we were ...

Lightning at the Speed of the Heart

    ... what could we be?

ACKNOWLEDGEMENTS

All edited works are the result of a collective endeavour, and this volume represents the efforts and excellence of 16 authors in five countries – to all those, thank you. We would also like to thank Routledge and the Routledge Studies in Critical Realism board for all their help and encouragement. The editorial task has been made more challenging because of a pandemic and times zones differences, but this has been made easier by the assistance from Tessa Podpadec, Vera Fernandes, and Lauren Wilce during the final stages of the book. We appreciate their support in the production of this volume.

FOREWORD
– *by Leigh Price*

When I first came to critical realism over 20 years ago, no one at my university had heard of it or of Roy Bhaskar, and I had never heard his name spoken out loud by anyone. At that time there was very little applied research using critical realism and the philosophy was still struggling for recognition within academia. This book is therefore an incredible illustration of how far critical realism has come since then. It is a wide-ranging collection of critical realist research stories not only from mainly Australia but also from Sweden, Belgium, Scotland, and England. What delights me about this book, and other similar collections, is that they demonstrate not only that critical realism has a global reach, but also that critical realism is inherently useful. Without exception, these researchers are striving for social justice. Their aim is to make the world a better place, one in which children can grow up safely and where people need not fear discrimination based on aspects of who they are. Therefore, the authors of these chapters are hoping to counter such social ills as racism (Cassandra Diamond), sexism (Bree Weizenegger), classism (Alpesh Maisuria and Grant Banfield), homelessness (Catherine Hastings), male violence (Ben Wadham), oppression in the educational contexts (Anna-Maria Fjellman, Ellenah Mackie, and Catherine Quinn), and social deprivation and abuse (Björn Blom, Didier Boost, and Peter Raeymaeckers).

Roy Bhaskar was himself motivated to carry out social justice-style research; in his case, he wanted to find out why there was so much poverty in developing countries. However, he was not able to carry out this research because he realised that the philosophy of science that existed at that time was inadequate to the task. As a result, he dedicated the rest of his career to developing a philosophy that could guide emancipation (Bhaskar 2016, 5). Therefore, books such as this are, in a way, the fruition of Roy Bhaskar's work; they represent exactly where he hoped his philosophy would lead.

I am pleased to see that the editors of *Working with Critical Realism: Stories of Methodological Encounters* have included discussions about the value of spirituality in the process of emancipation (see Chapters 11 by Ellenah Mackie and 12 by Loretta Geuenich, Celina Valente, and Grant Banfield). I agree with Roy Bhaskar that, without spirituality, emancipatory projects are likely to fail, and I see a great deal of value in meta-Reality as a resource for activists. However, as an atheist of sorts, I tend towards a secular version of spirituality. It is a remarkable characteristic of Roy Bhaskar's work that it manages to provide a way to identify 'goodness' that is acceptable to religious, spiritual, and atheistic people alike.

Finally, I am also pleased to see the explicitly Marxist discussion brought to the book in particular by Alpesh Maisuria and Grant Banfield in their fascinating dialogue in the final chapter. Roy Bhaskar was thoroughly committed to political activism and as such he could be described as a Marxist, albeit a reformist one. Most of his friends were Marxists and in the early part of his life he was not just an armchair activist but joined the revolution personally. For example, as he told Savita Singh in their book *Reality and its Depths*, he and his wife, Hilary Wainwright, travelled to Mozambique to spend time with the liberation movement there as guests of the MPLA (Movimento Popular de Libertação de Angola [Popular Movement for the Liberation of Angola]). One of his first acts of political identification was to join a Frantz Fanon study group; and he became very active in movements in solidarity with the campaign against the war in Vietnam and the USA's blockade of Cuba.

In summary then, anyone reading this book, who is interested in critical realism, will find a wealth of valuable information inside it. I especially recommend the brief introduction to key critical realist concepts provided by Alpesh Maisuria and Grant Banfield in Chapter 1. However, if you read this book, also expect to be inspired to help change the world for the better. Aluta continua!

Leigh Price, General Editor of the Journal of Critical Realism.
Recipient of the Cheryl Frank Memorial Prize for exemplifying the best new writing in the tradition of critical realism.

Reference

Bhaskar, R. 2016. *Enlightened Common Sense – The Philosophy of Critical Realism*. London: Routledge.

NOTES ON CONTRIBUTORS

Björn Blom is Professor of Social Work at Umeå University, Department of Social Work, Sweden. His research areas are organisation of social services and client work; social workers' knowledge and professional practice; evaluation, quality, and results in social work. He has co-authored several books on different topics in social work. Most recent books in English are *Social and Caring Professions in European Welfare States: Policies, Services and Professional Practices* (Policy Press 2017) and *Theory for Social Work Practice* (Studentlitteratur 2019).

Didier Boost is Researcher at the Centre for Research on Environmental and Social Change and Teaching Assistant in the Master of Social Work and Welfare Studies at the University of Antwerp, Belgium. A common thread between his previous and current research is the notion of evidence-based practice and the search for ways to adequately assess the impact of social work interventions. His PhD focusses on critical realism as a philosophy of science and the application of 'realist evaluation' in the context of social work.

Cassandra Diamond is Torres Strait Islander woman who grew up on the Darling Downs in Queensland, Australia. She completed a Bachelor of Arts in Justice Administration at Griffith University before embarking on career that would encompass youth work, community development, Indigenous community engagement, child protection, and other related fields. Cassandra spent 12 years working across a variety of portfolios with the Queensland Government before leaving to work for the CSIRO (Commonwealth Scientific and Industrial Research Organisation), where she now manages a national STEM education programme aimed at young Indigenous women. Cassandra has recently completed a Bachelor of Education (Honours) and is looking to continue her academic career.

Anna-Maria Fjellman is Senior Lecturer at the University of Gothenburg, Sweden. In 2019, Fjellman finished her doctoral thesis entitled *School choice, space and the geography of marketisation – Analyses of educational restructuring in upper secondary education in Sweden*. Fjellman has a background as a teacher in Swedish and Social Studies for upper secondary school although she has primarily worked in adult education. Fjellman's research interests include marketisation, school choice, school markets, space, mobility, spatial analysis, and investigating structural patterns and changes in educational opportunities and consequences for equity in the Swedish school system.

Loretta Geuenich has a background in human services, adult education, international development, and community-based research and evaluation. She currently works in the public sector on child and family services systems reform, and evaluation capacity building. She completed doctoral studies in 2019 with a thesis titled *Towards greater social and ethical response-ability? Practicing contemplative higher education in times of uncertainty and change*. Loretta is interested in how critical realism helps frame a deeper understanding of what it means to be human, and how to harness inherent human capacities for personal and social change.

Catherine Hastings is Adjunct Fellow in the Department of Sociology at Macquarie University, Australia. In 2020, she received her PhD for a thesis titled 'Family Homelessness in Australia: A Quantitative Critical Realist Study'. Catherine has an established applied social research and evaluation consultancy which she pursues alongside scholarly research on homelessness, disadvantage, and legal need.

Deborah Johnson is Social Worker and Educator in Sawtell, Australia. Deborah began as a Community Worker and counsellor in programmes designed to support individuals and communities to address issues of social disadvantage and abuse. Recognising the role that education can play as an agent for change and empowerment, Deborah's doctoral focus is on notions of quality and power and how these concepts drive reform in Australia's vocational and education training sector. Deborah is employed as a Senior Education Officer for the largest vocational training provider in the southern hemisphere. As an educator, Deborah is tasked to support educational excellence in this large and complex bureaucracy.

Omar Kaissi is Teaching Fellow in Education at Moray House School of Education and Sport, The University of Edinburgh, Scotland. His research interests include the sociology of education, sociology of knowledge and knowledge production, sociology of civil societies, and civil society organisation. Omar comments regularly on contemporary political, social, and educational affairs in Lebanon, the MENA region, and beyond. His writing is published both on his personal blog and Arabic media outlets.

Ellenah Mackie has held leadership positions across a wide range of portfolios in successive Queensland Governments. She holds university qualifications in psychology, criminology, business, and education and has spent most of her adult life working on issues of social and economic justice. Ellenah's doctoral research employs Roy Bhaskar's Philosophy of Meta-Reality to examine the Fourth Industrial Revolution and the role of an 'enabling state' to ensure positive social impact.

Catherine Quinn specialises in professional development for principals, teachers, and parents, in Australia, in the area of parental engagement in their child's learning. A dedicated teacher with a decade of experience as a secondary school principal, Cathy moved out of the Principal role and became aware of developments regarding parental engagement in schools. Quinn has devoted the past 15 years to refining strategies for parental engagement and developing a comprehensive programme with emphasis on meeting the Australian Professional Standard for Principals and Teachers. Now a full-time educational consultant and completing a Doctorate in this area.

Peter Raeymaeckers is Professor at the Department of Sociology, University of Antwerp, Belgium. He conducts research on social work practice and non-profit governance. He supervises projects on network governance, strategies of advocacy, faith-based organizations, evaluation of social work practices, and other topics related to the current societal challenges that non-profit organizations face. Raeymaeckers teaches in social work and innovation and policy practice.

Celina Valente has a PhD from Flinders University in South Australia. Her research gravitates around critical realism, activism, and reflexivity. Celina was born in Argentina but now lives in Adelaide with her husband and two children. She has a background in sociology, research, and teaching. She is currently working in the public sector doing research and evaluation of social justice projects.

Ben Wadham is a criminologist of the military in Australia. He researches violence among men in institutional settings. Ben is conducting the first independent national study into institutional abuse in the Australian Defence Force. Ben is the Director of Open Door: Veteran transition Integration and Wellbeing research centre at Flinders University. His work also extends to developing young men stopping violence programmes for South Australian schools and community organisations. Ben uses critical social theory to make sense of culture, power, and identity, hence a strong focus on men and masculinities.

Bree Weizenegger is PhD candidate in the Department of Social Work at The University of Melbourne, Australia, conducting research into the mechanisms of change in feminist-informed, sexual assault counselling. Bree has a long history of trying to understand how humans make meaning of their suffering and has studied comparative religion, sociology, gender studies, social work, and psychotherapy to engage with this question. Bree has worked in the fields of women's health and sexual assault counselling, and she now works in private practice with clients whose life difficulties have often emerged from trauma histories.

1
INTRODUCTION

Journeying through Critical Realism

Alpesh Maisuria and Grant Banfield

This book has been a long time in the making. It is the outcome of over 13 years of discussions and collaborations between us that, in part, are told in Chapter 13. Like all the contributors to this volume, we have stories of coming to critical realism. In some ways, as you will read, these stories are remarkably similar, but there are nuances as well. We think valuable lessons can be drawn from all these encounters.

One thing all our stories tell is of a steep intellectual climb that critical realism demands. However, from our experiences, we unequivocally say that the vistas gleaned along the way make that climb well worth it. If you are reading this, you might be someone on that climb. You already may have decided on a critical realist ascent. You've opened this book in the hope it might be a guide, or even an inspiration, for what you anticipate is ahead. Alternatively, you may simply be curious to know what critical realism might offer you. For you, this book will be like a travel brochure. Or maybe you have opened these pages because you have been encouraged (or even pushed?) by, for example, a research supervisor to embark on a critical realist journey. You have put yourself in the hands of a trusted other. Not fully aware of what is ahead, your emotions are probably a mixture of excitement and anxiety. All the contributors to this book know these emotions well.

The contributors to this volume tell their stories of hands and heads-on engagement with critical realism. They share their accounts of working with critical realism to tackle theoretical methodological and ethical issues that, through prior experience, they already knew to be problematic. This is not to say that such knowing represented a fully cognisant recognition of the issues. However, they were aware, at some level, of a theory-practice inconsistency that bothered them. As you will see, the contributors come from a variety of backgrounds and possess varying degrees of research experience.

DOI: 10.4324/9781003193784-1

It is well known that critical realism can be bewildering and even overwhelming to newcomers – especially for those without a formal grounding in philosophy. Reading the work of 'experts' well versed in the language, history, and arguments of critical realism can be daunting. Against this, it is to be kept in mind that the writings of experts are the outcome of hard work. What we read must be understood as the relating of vistas glimpsed at particular points in an intellectual journey. We all have those glimpses no matter how insignificant we might think them to be. But once they are shared, we can find that others too have made similar observations or even that the way we have grasped things is not so insignificant after all. For these reasons alone, sharing personal stories is useful. The paucity of narratives in a single and coherent collection telling of coming to critical realism is conspicuous in its absence. The contributors to this volume are experienced or novice researchers, working in a very wide range of fields. They tell of what drew them to critical realism in the first instance and share their accounts of success, frustration, and insight.

While there are now many useful introductory, and also methods, texts that make critical realism more accessible to a broader audience, this book foregrounds accounts of journeys and experiences, which in turn are used to animate the way that critical realism has been practically and intellectually used to develop research and scholarship that is grounded with a rigorous philosophy of science. Our objective is that this book will inspire – or at least sufficiently arouse – the curiosity of others to explore critical realist possibilities. We hope the book will be a cross-disciplinary resource for researchers, students, and academics interested in rigorous intellectual work with a socially progressive purpose.

The objective that we have set for this opening chapter is to provide an outline of the conceptual architecture of critical realism. We think this is important for two reasons. First, in anticipating that many readers will be unfamiliar with the theoretical structure and philosophical language of critical realism, a general orientating frame is vital. Second, the architecture will serve as the necessary conceptual scaffolding on which the content of the chapters that follow can meaningfully hang.

Critical Realism and a Mapping of Its Conceptual Architecture

If it is possible to identify a point in time marking the birth of critical realism, then it would probably be 1975 with the publication of *A Realist Theory of Science*. This was Roy Bhaskar's first book. Its aim is clearly stated "to be a philosophy for the sciences (and against the ideologies that threaten them)" (Bhaskar 1975, 262). The central target of *A Realist Theory of Science* was the Humean account of causal laws, i.e., the philosophical foundation of 'normal' or positivist science. As one "of the most hallowed doctrines of received philosophy of science" (Bhaskar 1975, 127) Humean causality was uncritically taken as not just sufficient but necessary for scientific explanation. In a full-frontal attack on positivism, original critical realism shows the purpose of science does not rest in uncovering laws relating atomistic events. Rather, it resides in *explaining* the nature of things and their constitutive causal powers. The scientific realism expressed in *A Realist Theory of Science* encompassed a dispositional (powers based) realism.

A Realist Theory of Science was also a near unchanged version of the PhD manuscript he submitted as a student at Oxford University under the supervision of realist philosopher Rom Harrè. Bhaskar twice submitted a manuscript for examination. On both occasions they were rejected by the examiners who insisted the work did not contain original content. One can only imagine how devastating this was for the young Bhaskar. But views from elsewhere were different. For example, historian Perry Anderson wrote to Bhaskar after reading the manuscript to tell him, "this is a work of the moment" and because of its radical implications should have expected it to be rejected! (Bhaskar 2010, 46).

There were no problems in finding a publisher for Bhaskar's thesis and now with numerous editions of *A Realist Theory of Science*, we can say: 'the rest is history'. Since *A Realist Theory of Science*, critical realism has grown, with the work of Bhaskar and others, into what can appropriately be called a philosophical movement. More specifically, it is a movement committed to social transformation and human flourishing in which it sees itself as a conceptual underlabourer. Bhaskar takes the idea of 'underlabouring' from British Enlightenment philosopher John Locke who said of philosophy that "it is ambition enough to be employed as an underlabourer in clearing the ground a little, and removing some of the rubbish that lies in the way to knowledge" (quoted in Bhaskar 2016, 2). Philosophy's role in bringing forth a better world and better lives is a modest one: that of the underlabourer working with and not the over-lord working on. In this regard,

> an underlabouring philosophy such as critical realism, seriously committed to the project of universal human flourishing, can aspire to be more than a nuisance, a Nietzschean gadfly on the neck of the powers that be; it can become a spark, a liberation, lifting the weight of the (Lockean) rubbish that mires us. This is philosophy as enlightened common sense and as midwife, an agent of emancipatory change.
>
> (Bhaskar 2016, 5)

Among critical realists the development of critical realism is generally understood to consist in three chronological phases: 'original', 'dialectical', and 'spiritual' (or the 'Philosophy of Meta-Reality'). Each phase is qualitatively different from, but an emergent development of, the previous. In other words, original critical realism grounds Dialectical Critical Realism which, in turn, founds the Philosophy of Meta-Reality. Before detailing each of the phases, we will provide a brief overall sketch of the critical realist system or, what we are calling, 'architecture'.

As we will see later, the 'original' phase of critical realism is a revindication of ontology. However, we will also see that ontological seriousness remains the grounding gravitas of critical realism throughout its development. Reflecting on his life's work, Bhaskar insisted that "the single a big idea in critical realism is the idea of *ontology*" (2016, 112). The dominant ontological motif of original critical realism is that of *difference*: the natural and social worlds are *structured, differentiated*, and *emergent*. Original critical realism is described as consisting in three moves: the development of a (i) philosophy of natural science (Bhaskar 1975), (ii) philosophy of social science (Bhaskar 1979), and (iii) theory of explanatory critique (Bhaskar 1986). In the dialectisation of critical realism (Bhaskar 1993, 1994), original critical realism is embraced as the First Moment (1M) and becomes one side of a four-sided dialectic. The other three are: (i) a Second Edge (2E) emphasising absence and processes of *be-coming and be-going*, (ii) a Third Level (3L) of *totality* stressing openness and possibility, and (iii) a Fourth Dimension (4D) of *transformative praxis*. Dialectical Critical Realism carries the acronym of 'MELD'. Completing the chronological development of critical realism are the three moves of Bhaskar's 'spiritual turn' (Bhaskar 2000, 2002a, 2002b). The Fifth Aspect (5A) emphasises *reflexivity*, the Sixth Realm stresses *re-enchantment* and Seventh Zone or Awakening prioritises, in contrast to 1M, *identity* over difference. Taken together, the three phases of critical realism are known by the acronym MELDARA/Z and are summarised in Table 1.1.

As we have already noted, original critical realism came into being with the publication of *A Realist Theory of Science* and its bold critique of positivism. However, it was not just Humean empiricism that Bhaskar had in his sights. Counterposed to empiricism, Bhaskar placed Kantian idealism arguing that both share the meta-theory "that ontology was impossible, a mistake" (Bhaskar 2016, 6). Underlabouring Hume and Kant, Bhaskar posits a transcendental realist philosophy emphasising ontological depth realism. His critique begins with a realist interrogation of Kant's transcendental idealism. He agrees with Kant's move against Humean (empiricist) scepticism and insists that knowledge acquisition is possible via transcendental deduction, i.e., that thought can be derived from scientific knowledge. However, Bhaskar rejects the Kantian phenomenal-noumenal split that denies the possibility of knowing the 'thing-in-itself' and ultimately prioritises epistemology over ontology. Bhaskar's transcendental realism establishes

TABLE 1.1 MELDARA/Z: The Global Architecture of Critical Realism

1M (First Moment)	Difference	The natural and social worlds are differentiated, stratified, and emergent
2E (Second Edge)	Absence	Being as processes of be-coming (absenting absences) and be-going (absenting)
3L (Third Level)	Totality	Being as, and within, an open whole
4D (Fourth Dimension)	Praxis	Being as transformative depth praxis
5A (Fifth Aspect)	Spirituality	Being as reflexivity
6R (Sixth Realm)	Re-enchantment	Being as intrinsically valuable
7Z/A (Seventh Zone/Awakening)	Identity	Being as non-dual asserting the primacy of identity over difference

that while scientific knowledge is fallible, it does, nevertheless, provide rigorous criteria for judgement of truth claims about a mind-independent (objectively real) world. In short, the natural world is understood to consist in causality itself and not in causal *laws*.

In carving a path between scientism and historicism, transcendental realism reveals a scientism-historicism (Humean/Kantian) partnership. Wary of science, the tendency of historicism is to replace science with history. In its post-positivist enthusiasm, historicism conjures a 'speculative illusion' that reality is socially constructed and that concepts can be the judges of concepts. While the positivist and speculative illusions appear as antagonists, Bhaskar argues they are actually allies in their promulgation of an erroneous view of the nature of science and its practice. In contrast to the view that science is a search for concepts, Bhaskar's transcendental realism reveals that scientific practice is the *ontological* search for causality. Ontology trumps epistemology. This is why scientists do experiments, they isolate the workings of 'things' in order to observe their unhindered natures. The actual practice of science reveals the world consists in the nature of things and that not all things are directly observable or open to first-hand experience. In short, for science to be possible, the world – as an open system – must consist in structured and stratified relations between different kinds of things.

While critical realists distinguish *essence* from *appearance* and prioritise the former over the latter, they insist that transcendental realism does not collapse to reductive realism. Bhaskar's ontology may be naturalist and essentialist, but it does not entail essential*ism*. His revindication of ontology comes via an emergentist depth realism where the properties of higher order strata are formed in non-predictable ways from the properties of lower, more basic, strata. For explanatory purposes Bhaskar depicts his emergentist ontology consisting in three levels or domains: the 'Real', 'Actual', and 'Empirical' (see Table 1.2):

The three domains are said to comprise the intransitive (ontological) dimension of science – as distinct from science's intransitive (epistemological) dimension. Transcendental realist ontology distinguishes generative mechanisms, the events they realise, and the experiences in which they are captured. All three domains are real such that D_r = Mechanisms + Events + Experiences. By recognising D_r natural necessity as causally generative enabled Bhaskar to identify a fundamental problem of western philosophy resting in the pairing of ontological actualism (the reduction of the real to what is only actual) and the epistemic fallacy (the reduction of *what is* to *what is known*). But what of *social* science?

TABLE 1.2 Domains of Reality

	Domain of real (D_r)	*Domain of actual (D_a)*	*Domain of empirical (D_e)*
Mechanisms	X		
Events	X	X	
Experiences	X	X	X

Source: Adapted from (Bhaskar 1975, 13).

Transcendental Realism was brought to the social sciences in 1979 with the publication of *The Possibility of Naturalism* (Bhaskar 1979). It begins by asking the transcendental question: 'Is scientific knowledge of society possible?'. Answering in the affirmative, Bhaskar showed that social objects can be studied *scientifically* in the same way as natural ones. While social and natural objects are different *kinds* of things with different causal powers, they both can be examined via retroductive (naturalist) methods: an explanatory search for underlying mechanisms. Bhaskar's exploration of the possibility of naturalism specifically in the social sciences signals the move to critical naturalism. It also sets the philosophical foundations of a naturalist critique of the social sciences and the workings of the social world.

The foundations of naturalist critique are presented in *The Possibility of Naturalism* as an immanent critique of the two existing dominant but opposed positions on naturalism. One is hyper-naturalist. Drawing on the likes of Hume and the Vienna Circle hyper-naturalism carries positivism to, and through, the doors of the social sciences. The other is anti-naturalist. Founded on the dialectics of Hegel and Kant, its philosophical heritage is anti-positivist hermeneutics. Bhaskar offers Durkheimian structuralism as the hyper-naturalist exemplar and Weberian interpretivism to represent anti-naturalism. With the former tending to structural determinism and the latter to agential voluntarism, Bhaskar argues that both are inadequate for scientific practice. Crucially, both accept the legitimacy of positivism. Where Durkheimian structuralism gives it general legitimacy across the natural and social sciences, Weberian interpretivism endorses positivism by quarantining it to natural science. Bhaskar puts forward a third possibility for naturalism: a *qualified* emergentist naturalism. Starting from premise that objects of the natural and social worlds are *qualitatively* different, there are limits to how they can be studied. The crucial limit resides in the fact that, unlike the natural world, the social world consists of human beings and their casual powers. Bhaskar's qualified naturalism demands that scientific explanation of society accounts for what the social world means to actors. By emphasising social life as deeply meaning- and concept-dependent, critical naturalism aligns with hermeneutics. However, critical naturalism rejects the anti-naturalist tendencies of hermeneutics that ultimately endorse positivism.

The essence of critical naturalism is captured in Bhaskar's 'transformational model of social activity' (TMSA), which depicts society and individuals as mutually dependent and also ontologically distinguishable. British sociologist, Margaret Archer, has been significant in operationalising the TMSA. She was the first to point out that Bhaskar was wrong to equate his TMSA with Anthony Giddens' theory of structuration (Giddens 1984). In her morphogenetic approach to the structure-agency problematic, Archer (1995, 2000) argues the structure-agency relation must be grasped as an analytic dualism. Giddens couldn't do this because, without a sense of dispositional realism, he conflated structures and agents so they were analytically indistinguishable. Archer pointed out that the separation of structures and agents is vital if Bhaskar's qualified naturalism is to hold.

If human agency is a critical limit to naturalism, then social science must include causally real explanations of human consciousness. From this logic, Bhaskar (1986) embarks on his third original critical realist move: the development of *explanatory critique*. This move directly challenges another plank of the positivism: the separation of *facts and values*. Against Hume's law that an 'ought' cannot be derived from an 'is', Bhaskar argues that, when a social ill is identified, action ought to follow. Explanatory social science and emancipatory practice depend upon action. Reasons have causal powers - they provide reasons for action. Of course, reasons can emerge from illusory beliefs with their origins in mechanisms maintaining structures and practices of oppression. Explanatory critique is directed to bring the workings of those mechanisms to the surface of attention to reveal possibilities for "reflection on the presuppositions of the pathology of everyday life" (Bhaskar 1993, 15).

Explanatory critique can be understood as a prelude to 4D Dialectical Critical Realism and Bhaskar's 'spiritual turn'. To this point we have seen ontology expressed as difference with *non-identity* afforded priority over *identity*. In the dialectisation of critical realism, things begin to shift. Where original critical realism focuses on the ontology of natural necessity or 'being', Dialectical Critical Realism focuses on 'be-coming' and 'be-going'. The fundamental concept of Dialectical Critical Realism is *absence*. Emphasis is given to change. Of course, change is implied in original critical realism via, for example, the concept of emergence. But in Dialectical Critical Realism it is made explicit describing causality as a rhythmic tensed spatialising process (Bhaskar 1993, 106; 250). Absence is given priority over presence (Bhaskar 1993, 301). Change is the outcome of real determinant processes of deep real causality.

The dialectisation of critical realism is a critical engagement with the dialectical systems of Hegel and Marx. More particularly, it is what Bhaskar refers to as a 'materialist diffraction' of Hegel in which Bhaskar proceeds "on the basis as of aligning himself with Marx" (Norrie 2020, 82). Bhaskar understood Marx as an ontological materialist and a practical materialist "asserting the constitutive role of transformative agency in the reproduction and transmission of social forms" (1991, 369) it is the species being characteristics grounded non-reductively in physiological and neurological structures of human beings, from which human agency emerges. In the Hegelian dialectic, the drive is to rationally close and complete itself. Dialectical Critical Realism is different. It expresses an open totality: the world is dynamic, forever emerging and incomplete. At 3L totality, openness prevails. It also invites the possibility of an enduring human agency. This is taken further in 4D: totalising depth praxis. Human powers include the materially grounded capacities for reason, emotion, and imagination that emerge as critique, solidarity, and transformative action.

The entire weight of critical realism has pushed itself to spirituality (Bhaskar 2000) and the Philosophy of Meta-Reality (Bhaskar 2002a, 2002b) – as resources to "strengthen the cultural resources of the left" (Bhaskar 2010, 148). For Bhaskar, the human spirit is the living expression of dialectics: the pulse of freedom.

Importantly, in this respect, openness is not restricted to an 'outer world' but also includes an 'inner world'. We can say that totality moves both ways. Non-Identity and Identity meet with the coming together of 1M and 7Z/A such that "identities and unities are … presupposed by basic critical realism at 1M" (Bhaskar 2016, 146). Even in original critical realism, being was both difference and unity. Ontologically, there can be no closure. It is an artificial imposition on the world driven by the necessity to pause it, briefly, so we might be able to (only ever partially and fallibly) know it. Closure is only ever temporary.

Introducing the Chapters to Come

The contributors to this volume demonstrate the need to share stories to provide impetus and motivation to critical realist undertakings. We hope that this book provides stimulation and encouragement for others to go on this journey that has much reward.

A key feature of early critical realism was *explanation* and *abstraction*. In Chapter 2 – *A Detective, Physicist and Historian Walk into a Bar: Abduction, Retroduction, and Retrodiction in Critical Realist Evaluations* – Didier Boost, Björn Blom, and Peter Raeymaeckers show abstraction to be like the meeting of three characters – the *detective*, *physicist*, and *historian*. These characters represent different roles a researcher takes consisting of journeying through six stages for abstractive reasoning. The authors 'illustrate the dynamic relation between the *detective, physicist* and *historian*' and show their experience of being each of these when analysing empirical data and their own evaluations of social work programmes in Belgium and Sweden.

Catherine Hastings focusses Chapter 3 – *Bridging the Gap between Philosophy and Empirical Research: A Critical Realist Methodology Using Quantitative Methods* – on the causal explanations of homelessness and extreme poverty through critical realism's ontological, epistemological, and axiomatic presuppositions. While dealing with the common structure/agency problematic in interdisciplinary social science enquiry, Hastings's chapter also demonstrates her experience of operationalising critical realist philosophy in quantitative empirical research. Importantly, Hastings draws the reader's attention to the importance of 'the basis upon which a researcher incorporates methods into a methodology'.

Researchers often begin their studies meandering through various intellectual positions without a deep awareness of philosophy of science and its importance for serious research. In Chapter 4 – *Parent Engagement in Student Learning: Using Critical Realism to Uncover the Generative Mechanisms Needed for Teachers to Embrace Parent Engagement in Their Teaching Practice* – Catherine Quinn describes her encounter with critical realism as an 'awakening' that was facilitated by her supervisor, which is a theme in this book of journeys. In her study of the need for teachers to embrace parent engagement in their teaching practice for student learning, Quinn shows how the approach of philosophical *underlabouring* became so crucial to find a way through a journey – from constructivism to Bourdieu finally arriving at critical realism to make judgements between differing explanations about what could make the world a better place.

The diversity of researchers using early critical realism is characterised by Omar Kaissi in Chapter 5 – *On the Anti-imperialist Possibilities of Critical Realism*. Kaissi describes his journey of using critical realism for his research on gender, boys, and masculinities in four western contexts. He discusses the possibilities of doing analytical anti-imperialism, working with concepts of structure, agency, and causality while being mindful of the specificities of context. The end-game with critical realism, for Kaissi, was countering the desire for ontic closure evident in both positivist and interpretivist social science. Using empirical examples, he demonstrates what it means and entails to think about critical realist-informed methodology as anti-imperialist. His journey represents 'critical realist research as a type of high-risk, albeit educative, research, whose methodological buttressing requires activism (progress *for* methodology) as much as practice (progress *through* methodology)'.

One of Bhaskar's accomplishments in early critical realism was to offer a way through postmodernism and social constructionism, which are problematic when they have an ontological shyness and deny material reality and experiences in the real world. In Chapter 6 – *Cobbling Together Methods for a Coherent Critical Realist Methodology: Searching for Mechanisms*, Bree Weizenegger accounts her experiences of research into the causes of change for victim/survivors engaging in feminist-informed sexual assault counselling. Weizenegger discusses the 'happy accident' of discovering critical realism. She describes her attraction to critical realism because of its revindication of ontology and its concomitant capacity 'to research those things which occupy many feminist counsellors' minds: structures of oppression, their internalisation, and a non-reductive understanding of their impact on the experience of being human'. For Weizenegger, it felt like there was a fundamental incompatibility between the ontological shy philosophy of post-positivist methodological approaches and the lived experience of victims of sexual violence. This is where critical realism has most purchase for Weizenegger, who was most attracted to the offer of depth ontology and the possibility of researching the structures of both the social world and also minds – as *real*.

Explanatory social science research is also the focus of Deborah Johnson's chapter (Chapter 7) – *A Critical Realist Perspective on the 'Quality and Reform Dance' in the Australian Vocational Education and Training (VET) Sector: The Road Less Travelled*. The author uses depth ontology and develops a fact-value argument in the process of retroduction to examine her experience of researching the Australian Vocational Education and Training sector (VET). This chapter explains her choice of critical realism, highlighting the benefit of a depth ontology which brought explanatory power to her research. It provided 'conceptual and methodological strategies to expose the often-hidden dynamics in the Australian VET sector'. This chapter establishes why no other approach offered the same opportunities to understand the sector. Johnson concludes the chapter by offering four insights to new researchers who are curious about how to be post-positivist and want to avoid a hard relativist non-real meta-philosophy.

One of the cornerstones of the very first phase of critical realism development was the epistemological fallacy – the subsuming of ontology into epistemology. This was the point of departure for Cassandra Diamond's foray into critical realism. In Chapter 8 – *The Utility of Critical Realism in Indigenous Research* – Diamond describes an interest in research on young Aboriginal and Torres Strait Islander women, studying STEM, and their experiences of racism. Diamond identifies many resonances between indigenous research methods and approaches, and critical realism's stratified ontology and human emancipation. The author tells of the way that these research methods were complimentary, partly because 'Aboriginal and Torres Strait Islander people are very aware of their ontology and understand its nature and origins'. Diamond also covers the importance of the end goal of human emancipation projects discussing resistance, political integrity, and privilege.

When considered a meta-theory, critical realism can be pivoted to any type of data gathering approach – quantitative or qualitative. Critical realism is also compatible with any critical macro theory. In Chapter 9 – *The Spatiality of School Choice – A Critical Realist Quantitative Geography of Education?* – Anna-Maria Fjellman describes her experience of using critical realism in a critical quantitative spatial inquiry. Her focus was on 'analysing students attending Swedish upper secondary education drawing on Doreen Massey's theoretical concept of space'. After describing 'an academic identity crisis (is this what I am supposed to do with my life?) together with severe methodological difficulties', Fjellman shares her re-imagining and exploring the assumptions of an analysis through a critical realist rationale. The agility of the critical realism concepts of reality and causality is highlighted in this chapter, where the author draws on her journey of asking critical questions in quantitative research and the difficulties of doing this, including academic identity.

Chapter 10 – *Real Men, Real Violence: Critical Realism and the Search for the Masculine Subject* – is authored by Ben Wadham. Wadham describes his journey as a researcher interested in masculinity, manhood, subjectivity, and violence. Wadham describes coming to critical realism after Adorno's negative dialectics, which is obtuse and difficult to apply. A key question that this researcher engages with is, 'what are the generative mechanisms of men's violence?' Wadham describes how a broader question stared back at him: 'how can we understand and reduce men's use of violence on the streets, against their families and upon themselves? How can we change the way men, and the culturally produced masculinities embody violence from the local to the global?' To do this, he turned to critical realism to reassess what the journal-based literature had said and moved beyond models to *explanations*.

The third phase of development in critical realism – TDCR, also known as Philosophy of Meta-Reality, is a matter of controversy. This development in Bhaskar's trajectory is known among critical realists as his 'spiritual turn' or, simply, his move to 'meta-reality'. The key texts here are: *From East to West* (Bhaskar 2000), *Reflections on Meta-Reality* (Bhaskar 2002a), and *The Philosophy of Meta-Reality* (Bhaskar 2002b). These texts have been the entry point into critical realism for Ellenah Mackie. In Chapter 11 – *The Critical Realist Toolkit* – Mackie has contributed a critical realism toolkit to explain real-world problems. It is grounded on the critical realism concept of *concrete universal* with the notion of utopia. Her journey with critical realism has enabled her to make sense of the connection between universality, singularity, social being, and utopia. Mackie describes a journey beginning with philosophy of meta-reality, which is unconventional as it is the final phase of Bhaskar's development of critical realism, but it was ideal for Mackie because it provided the basis of hope at a time of desperation and also the tools to live a meaning-filled life via making sense of real-world problems.

Also contextualised within this turn to spirituality and human emancipation is Chapter 12 by Loretta Geuenich and Celina Valente with Grant Banfield – *Journeys to Critical Realism: A Conversation about Spirituality, Love and Human Emancipation*. So many students have come to critical realism and journey through it with the encouragement of a significant person, this is usually a supervisor or a mentor. This chapter is a dialogue between two research students – Geuenich and Valente with their supervisor (Banfield). The chapter covers a wide scope, including life histories/experiences, and importantly what attracted them to critical realism. Both students came to critical realism expressing frustration with the inadequacy of contemporary social science (and western theory more generally) to not only explain but also guide the absenting of the ills of current times. They explore the nature of their emancipatory commitments as part of their intellectual and personal lives – and the central place that love and ground state spirituality have to those commitments.

The final chapter (Chapter 13) – *A Kind of Conclusion* – *Against Full-Stops and Bookends?* – has a focus on Marxism, which takes the form of a dialogue. Maisuria and Banfield engage each other in a conversation about the way that they were able to exploit critical realism to support their respective Marxist doctorates and subsequent scholarly thinking and practice. A provocative focal point of the discussion revolves around the spiritual development of Bhaskar's work in TDCR as potentially undermining its function as meta-theory that philosophically underlabours (see Banfield 2016; Maisuria 2017). There is a problematisation of critical realism becoming a macro-theory that offers a critical realism as an applied theory for social transformation. In other words, critical realism becomes an alternative to Marxism rather than in the service of it. This conversation follows those like Creaven who take it as a decisive turning away from Marxism in its "abstract unhistorical moralism" (Creaven 2007, 54). However, others like Margaret Archer, Andrew Collier, and Douglas Porpora (see Archer, Collier, and Porpora 2009) welcome the introduction of a spiritual dimension of Bhaskar's work as a means to further developing a critical realist understanding of Marxism. A theme that emerges in this chapter is the power of collaborative working when on the margins of the mainstream academic domains – both as Marxists and also as engaged in critical realism. Like several of the preceding chapters, discussion focuses on the importance of having a supportive supervisor and being part of networks, and part of the *raison d'être* of this book is to contribute to this.

Without the critical realism and other networks that give rise to informal and formal discussions, the relationship with critical realism becomes that much more difficult. We hope this recommendation words move all supervisors reading this work to encourage and cajole their students towards critical realism and learn together. We also hope that the stories have encouraged critical realism-curious folk, and even those who are already immersed, to work together, especially for work of a progressive kind.

Critical realism is establishing itself in the social sciences as an explanatory and emancipatory approach, but there is a long way to go before it figures alongside the interpretivist and constructivist alternatives to positivism in method(ology) training. The contributors to this volume have demonstrated the need to share stories to provide impetus and motivation to critical realist undertakings. We hope that this book provides stimulation and encouragement to others to go on this journey that has much reward.

References

Archer, M. 1995. *Realist Social Theory: The Morphogenetic Approach.* Cambridge: Cambridge University Press.
Archer, M. 2000. *Being Human – The Problem of Agency.* Cambridge: Cambridge University Press.
Archer, M., A. Collier, and D. Porpora, eds. 2009. *Transcendence: Critical Realism and God.* London: Routledge.
Banfield, G. 2016. *Critical Realism for Marxist Sociology of Education.* London: Routledge.
Bhaskar, R. 1975. *A Realist Theory of Science.* London: Verso.
Bhaskar, R. 1979. *Possibility of Naturalism: Philosophical Critique of the Contemporary Human Sciences.* Brighton: Harvester Press.
Bhaskar, R. 1986. *Scientific Realism and Human Emancipation.* London: Verso.
Bhaskar, R. 1991. *Philosophy and the Idea of Freedom* Oxford: Basil Blackwell.
Bhaskar, R. 1993. *Dialectic: The Pulse of Freedom.* London: Verso.
Bhaskar, R. 1994. *Plato Etc.: The Problems of Philosophy and Their Resolution* London: Verso.
Bhaskar, R. 2000. *From East to West: Odyssey of a Soul.* London: Routledge.
Bhaskar, R. 2002a. *Reflections on Meta-Reality – Transcendence, Emancipation and Everyday Life.* New Delhi: Sage.
Bhaskar, R. 2002b. *The Philosophy of Meta-Reality, Volume 1, Meta-Reality: Creativity, Love and Freedom.* New Delhi: Sage
Bhaskar, R. 2010. *The Formation of Critical Realism – A Personal Perspective.* London: Routledge.
Bhaskar, R. 2016. *Enlightened Common Sense – The Philosophy of Critical Realism.* London: Routledge.
Creaven, S. 2007. *Emergentist Marxism – Dialectical Philosophy and Social Theory.* Milton Park: Routledge.

Giddens, A. 1984. *The Constitution of Society – Outline of the Theory of Structuration.* Cambridge: Polity Press.

Maisuria, A. 2017. *Class Consciousness and Education in Sweden: A Marxist Analysis of Revolution in a Social Democracy.* London: Routledge.

Norrie, A. 2020. *Dialectic and Difference – Dialectical Critical Realism and the Grounds of Justice* London: Routledge.

2

A DETECTIVE, PHYSICIST, AND HISTORIAN WALK INTO A BAR

Abduction, Retroduction, and Retrodiction in Critical Realist Evaluations

Didier Boost, Björn Blom, and Peter Raeymaeckers

Introduction

As discussed in the introductory chapter of this book, critical realism proposes a meta-theoretical position that combines a realist ontology with a relativist epistemology (Bhaskar 1998). Critical realism, thus, acknowledges the existence of an objective – yet stratified and emergent – reality, while upholding that our knowledge of it is socially constructed. When it comes to understanding society, critical realism opposes the empiricist notion of causality as the constant conjunction of empirical events and presents a non-deterministic alternative that focuses on underlying generative mechanisms. Put differently, sociological inquiry should take a leap beyond the empirical level, unravel the complexities of the social world, and unearth how events are the result of causal structures operating in particular contexts. This ambition has steadily been converting scholars since the late 1970s. Given the paradigm's tendency to prioritise ontology over epistemology and research methods, however, there is a lack of guidelines to assist researchers – both old and new – with realising the emancipatory social science that Roy Bhaskar envisioned (Hammersley 2002). This perfectly reflects our personal experience. On the one hand, the abundance of complex philosophical texts filled with transcendental arguments on ontology and meta-reality has been the foremost reason why our initial encounters with critical realism felt like jumping down the rabbit hole. While we strongly believe in the importance of ontological debates to question, modify, and reinforce one's own assumptions, we feel it is necessary to develop a more 'hands-on approach' for researchers starting with empirical research using concepts and theories derived from critical realism. On the other hand, the promise of bringing forth progressive change by uncovering mechanisms that lead to human suffering and oppression has exactly been what motivated us to work our way through the seminal literature, try to

DOI: 10.4324/9781003193784-2

understand the philosophical premises, and, above all, consider their practical implications.

This chapter therefore fills the gap between the vast literature on the philosophical cornerstones of critical realism and studies reporting the findings of critical realist analyses. We shed light on what is often not explicitly discussed in theoretical and empirical publications, namely: the process of translating meta-theoretical principles into practical conduct during hands-on research. This chapter specifically focuses on the process of abstraction through abductive, retroductive, and retrodictive reasoning and presents some clear-cut questions to keep in mind during the analysis of empirical data. To put flesh on the bones of the philosophical and methodological debates, we use examples from our own evaluations of social work programmes in Belgium and Sweden. As the critical realist notion of 'epistemic humility' befits, however, we are not asserting to hold the absolute truth nor to provide guidelines which fit the work and context of all potential readers. Our foremost ambition is to provide a transparent account of our own thought processes and hopefully inspire other researchers to overcome some of the hurdles associated with applying a complex philosophical stance such as critical realism. Before turning to these insights, however, we first situate our own research and – given the interdisciplinary audience of this book – briefly introduce social work and the importance of evaluation research in this context.

Social Work and Evaluation Research

Social work is globally defined as a practice-based profession and an academic discipline that promotes social change and development, social cohesion, and the empowerment and liberation of people (IFSW 2014). Behind this overarching conception, we can find a vast variety of settings that social workers operate in and ways they intervene at the individual, community, and societal level (Vandekinderen et al. 2020). All of these different traditions of social work are increasingly challenged and pressured to demonstrate their impact, effectiveness, and efficiency (Blom 2009). In this context, where the profession is no longer taken for granted (Parton 1994), evidence-based practice is seen as a way to substantiate and broaden our understanding of social work with regard to both its content and results (Gambrill 2006; Gilgun 2005; Morén and Blom 2003). The idea of evidence-based practice dictates that interventions should be grounded on empirical findings that show which actions are likely to produce predictable, beneficial, and effective results (Cournoyer and Powers 2002). This growing emphasis on clinical effectiveness inherently ascribes an important role to evaluation research (Powell 2002). Evaluation research, however, can be conducted with different motives in mind: either aiming to (de)legitimise the existence of interventions by providing evidence on their effects or striving to improve practice itself by deepening our understanding of the underlying mechanisms. As previous research has shown, it is very hard – if not impossible – to delineate the causal relationship between what social workers do and the effects of their interventions, because their practices are complexly shaped by various factors at different levels (Ebrahim 2019). It will therefore come as no surprise that we have found inspiration not only in the ontological and epistemological underpinnings of critical realism but also in the applied realism of 'realist evaluation' (Pawson 2013) to unravel this complexity. In doing so, we invigorate the argument of other authors who stress the compatibility between critical realism, realist evaluation, and social work (Kjørstad and Solem 2017). Although there has been no collaboration between the authors of this chapter from Belgium[1] and Sweden[2] in terms of empirical research, this chapter is the result of our exchanges and discussions on adopting a critical realist perspective in social work research. This chapter should be read in the light of these ongoing debates and reflections.

Abstraction

The unique selling point of critical realism is the focus on generative mechanisms to explain how events are the results of causal structures operating in particular contexts. This ambition, however, is not easily achieved as mechanisms are hidden beneath the empirical level and cannot be observed directly through our own senses. Although we need to acknowledge mechanisms as ontologically *real* entities because of the outcomes they generate, we can only approximate them through concepts and theories (Morén and Blom 2003). The analysis of social phenomena, thus, always involves abstraction. In the remainder of this chapter, we therefore share our own experience with this conduct and provide practical guidelines to assist researchers with explaining phenomena through the lens of critical realism. More specifically, we imagine abstraction as a gathering of three characters – the *detective*, *physicist*, and *historian* – which explains the different roles a researcher takes on throughout this complicated process. We situate these characters in the model of *explanatory research based on critical realism* of Danermark, Ekström, and Karlsson (2019) and reconceptualise the six stages according to our own experience with abstractive reasoning. Our foremost ambition is not only to illustrate the dynamic relation between the detective, physicist, and historian but also to show how abstraction can be translated into clear-cut questions to ask yourself during the analysis of empirical data. In other words, we explicate how empirical observations can be transformed into a critical realist understanding of phenomena. For each of the six stages we provide examples based on our evaluation of 'Integrated Rights-Practices' where social workers strived to realise the social rights of vulnerable citizens through inter-organisational collaboration and proactive, outreaching, generalist, and relation-based interventions. We were commissioned to study the pilot-projects experimenting with this approach, unravel if, how and why they realised social rights and, ultimately, formulate recommendations to revise the Decree on Local Social Policy. Given our particular focus on the process of abstraction, we only present empirical findings to illustrate our arguments. For those interested in a full overview of our study, we refer to Boost et al. (2021).

Stage 1: Description

Even though social scientists are rarely concerned with discovering what happened in a bloodstained hotel room, we can draw an interesting parallel between how a detective approaches a murder mystery and how social phenomena are studied by critical realists. The model of Danermark et al. (2019) argues that an explanatory analysis takes the concrete as the point of departure and focuses on describing complex phenomena based on the interpretations and accounts of those involved. This is quintessential detective work. To solve a case, a detective indeed starts with gathering evidence at the crime scene and interviews victims, suspects, and eyewitnesses. In critical realist terms, this first stage thus limits itself to the empirical domain whereby the researcher's role remains descriptive in nature, depicting the transitive knowledge and relative accounts that different people hold over the subject under study. In other words, this is not yet a move of abstraction or interpretation. Even though abductive and retroductive inferences – which play a central role in the later stages – can be drawn from data which has not been collected with a critical realist perspective in mind, we believe that this first descriptive stage can be organised in ways that attempt to optimise such an analysis. For our own work, we have found inspiration in the idea of 'realist evaluation' introduced by Pawson and Tilley (1997). The central premise of this approach is that social programmes are theories incarnate which "begin in the heads of policy architects, pass into the hands of practitioners and, sometimes, into the hearts and minds of programme subjects" (Pawson 2006, 28). These different stakeholders often hold a different perspective on the desired outcomes, the ways to achieve them, and, above all, the (implicit) theories on how change is realised (Rogers 2008). Similar to the detective's interest in victims, suspects, and eyewitnesses, we have experienced the distinction between *designers*, *implementers*, and *target-group* helpful to ensure that most relevant actors in the context of social interventions are included in the research design. These different perspectives are fundamental to develop evaluations with the potential to impact further decision-making, policy, and practice (Patton 2008). Put differently, to achieve the emancipatory and explanatory ambition of critical realism, we need to collaborate with a variety of actors as they provide a unique access point to reality. This also means that researchers need to be aware of and reveal mechanisms of power between policy actors and other stakeholders in their research setting (Feagin 2001). In that regard, we strongly believe in giving a voice to vulnerable communities and consulting those with a lived experience of the phenomena we study (Blom and Morén 2019; Emmel et al. 2007; Jackson and Kolla 2012).

Example

The policy framework of the 'Integrated Rights-Practices' was rather descriptive in nature and mostly focused on demarking the goals and overarching strategies. As a result, the pilot-projects needed to translate these general guidelines into social work programmes and interventions that fitted their local contexts. During the first stage of our analysis, we therefore took on the role of the detective and followed the pilot-projects to gain a better understanding of their content. In other words, our initial task was to learn about the various ways the idea of Integrated Rights-Practices was put into practice. Throughout this process, the policymakers and designers of the interventions were the most important informants. Once the pilot-projects became operational, however, we shifted our focus towards the experience of social workers and vulnerable citizens and organised interviews and focus groups with them as the respective implementers and target-group.

Stage 2: Analytical Resolution

In the model of Danermark et al. (2019), the second stage is presented as analytical resolution whereby components, aspects, and dimensions of interest are identified and separated. This strongly reflects how scientific analysis starts with data reduction and organisation (Miles and Huberman 1994). In other words, given that it is practically impossible to study phenomena in their full complexity, we must confine ourselves to certain elements but not others. This process of focusing is an inherent part of qualitative detective work that determines which observations, clues, and testimonies are relevant to pursue. In our personal experience, however, this stage does not end with identification and separation but rather with connecting the different components of interest. This step in the process of abstraction is not that different from how detectives – at least in movies – clutter their walls with relevant bits of evidence, connect the different clues with pieces of string and pushpins, and then take a step back to see the greater whole. Similar to the detective, this stage remains focused on events in the empirical domain, but rather than merely describing the relevant occurrences, the attention is now turned to reconstructing the chain of events and discovering patterns in the data. In critical realism, these patterns are understood as demi-regularities or the occasional, but less than universal, actualisations of tendencies over a definite region of time and space (Lawson 1997). The discovery of these patterns is of utmost importance, because demi-regularities are evidence of relatively enduring and identifiable mechanisms operating at the deeper levels of reality (Næss 2019). In other words, the process of interpreting the connections between empirical events through the question, 'what patterns can be observed in the data?', prepares the ground for later abduction and retroduction.

Example

The diversity between the pilot-projects was fundamental not only to determine what components to focus on but also to discover demi-regularities across the different contexts and local strategies. Throughout the analysis and interpretation of interviews with social workers and citizens, we found some reoccurring trends or demi-regularities in the empirical data. First and foremost, the various approaches of the Integrated Rights-Practices resulted in more rights being realised. Citizens consistently stressed that the sudden realisation of multiple rights, which had previously been left unclaimed, significantly ameliorated the financial situation of their household. There was, thus, a pattern that both confirmed the severity of the problem and the potential of social work interventions with a clear focus on realising rights. Moreover, the citizens explicitly reported being happy about these services and always drew a comparison between the Integrated Rights-Practice and their previous experience with the 'regular' practice of the involved organisations. These demi-regularities – which we discovered by interpreting the stories of social workers and citizens, and then taking a step back to see the greater whole – sparked a hunch that there must be something fundamentally different about the Integrated Rights-Practices. This confirms that the discovery of demi-regularities usually turns upon comparisons (Lawson 1998). In the metaphor of the detective, this demi-regularity helped us to draw an X on the map and locate where to focus our abduction and retroduction in the following stages.

Stage 3: Abduction

Abduction can generally be defined as redescribing and interpreting a single event or occurrence as an expression of a more general phenomenon (Danermark et al. 2019). In this sense, abduction provides epistemological guidance as it leads the inquirer to explore the empirical world in new and innovative ways (Jagosh 2020, 122). Because of this, abductive reasoning is a creative process that requires imagination, analogies, or metaphors. An often-used example to illustrate the outcome of abduction is Gilbert's idea to perceive earth as a giant magnet (Jagosh 2020; Merton 1967). These kinds of inferences provide a set of ideas or hypotheses that can be validated, refuted, or adapted through further research. Because of this, abduction has previously been compared to how a detective recontextualises clues within a frame of different possible scenarios of how the crime could have been committed. As Danermark et al. (2019) argue, however, whereas detectives may find a final solution to crimes, the abductive conclusions of social scientists are seldom of that absolute nature. The phenomena of our interest can indeed be recontextualised in different ways without being able to ultimately decide which one is truer than the other. In our personal experience, this stage of explanation building can therefore best be imagined as a meeting between the detective and the physicist. In their conversation, the former posits possible scenarios that stay close to the empirical observations and established demi-regularities, while the latter helps to reframe these as an expression of more general phenomena. It should be noted, however, that abductive reasoning does not require a continuous reinvention of the proverbial wheel. There are many established theories, concepts, and metaphors available – both inside and outside one's own discipline – which can help to *re*describe empirical findings

TABLE 2.1 Three Questions for Abductive Reasoning

Q1: Are there theories, concepts, or models – inside or outside my own discipline – that can be used to *re*describe the empirical observations?
Q2: Are there experiences – both as a researcher or practitioner – that can be used to *re*describe the empirical observations?
Q3: Are there analogies or metaphors – both established and new – that can be used to *re*describe the empirical observations?

in innovative ways. Because of this, the physicist's broad scientific knowledge and familiarity with more conceptual thought operations are indispensable to advance towards a deeper understanding of the phenomena under study. In practice, we propose three questions that allow for abductive reasoning (see Table 2.1). It is worth noting that they are not mutually exclusive, meaning that the process of abduction will often rely on a pragmatic combination of these questions. Moreover, the fact that the same event and occurrence can be *re*described and reinterpreted in different ways does not – as we further elaborate in Stage 5 – advocate for an extreme relativism where 'anything goes'. We should, however, acknowledge that the researcher's knowledge, experience, and interests influence what aspects are emphasised. Since there is no absolute right or wrong when it comes to abduction in critical realism, we should always be transparent about our own inferences and limitations.

Example

To contextualise the situation of the citizens as an expression of a more general phenomena, we found inspiration in the concept of *non-take-up* (Hernanz, Malherbet and Pellizzari 2004). More specifically, we adopted theories – from outside of our own field – to explain non-take-up as the consequence of how people weigh information, process, and social costs against the perceived benefits of claiming their rights. In other words, the metaphor of *a balancing scale* provided an established, but in our context refreshing perspective to understand this phenomenon. Unfortunately, it is not always possible to find existing theories and concepts that are fully suitable for the subject under study. In those instances, as shown in Table 2.1, one can either *re*describe events based on your own experiences or use imagination to develop analogies and metaphors themselves. In other words, there can always be room for new concepts and models. In a different project, we previously used these specific strategies to interpret how the interventions of social workers in Swedish foster homes can contribute to a sense of safety in children. Although we found inspiration in established theories of social relations and humans as narrative beings, they were too general to accurately reflect what was happening in the foster homes. To *re*describe the empirical data in more specific ways, the evaluator turned to his own frame of reference and experience. More specifically, he noticed a striking resemblance between the observations in the foster homes and his previous interactions with families in crisis as a professional social worker. This similar experience enabled him to explain how a sense of safety was established in the foster homes by comparing it by analogy to how small children develop trusting relationships with their parents.

Stage 4: Retroduction

Whereas abduction focuses on redescribing events and seeing them in a new light, retroduction is about reconstructing the basic conditions for these phenomena to manifest themselves in those specific ways. In other words, retroduction takes a leap beyond the empirical domain and focuses on explaining events by identifying their underlying mechanisms (Lawson 1997). Retroductive inference is, thus, about creating ontological depth (Jagosh 2020). Although physics and critical realism are respectively concerned with the natural and social world, there is a reason why textbooks on critical realism often explain mechanisms through examples such as magnetism and gravity. Both physicists and critical realists are trying to identify the basic elements, structures, and forces of reality. In that regard, the questions Newton asked himself when he witnessed the apple fall to the ground are not that different from the inferences made by critical realists to uncover generative mechanisms. Compared to the previous conversation with the detective, these questions are not focused on reconstructing what happened at the empirical level, but rather on discovering the mechanisms in the domain of the real. In other words, retroduction is about identifying conditions that are necessary for things to be the way they are and, thus, identifying conditions necessary for the demi-regularities discovered by the detective to manifest themselves. When critical realists take on the role of the *physicist*, they ask themselves questions like: 'what is fundamentally constitutive for the studied structures and/or relations to be the way they are?', 'how is X possible?', or 'what is it about X that explains Y?' (Danermark et al. 2019).

Example

Whereas the detective helped us to see patterns in the empirical data and his conversation with the physicist reconceptualised non-take-up as an imbalance between perceived benefits and costs, a deeper understanding of why the Integrated Rights-Practices were effective and experienced in such a positive way was still rather lacking. We therefore needed to ask the question, what was fundamentally different about the Integrated Rights-Practices compared to the regular practice and, thus, discover the underlying entities, processes, and/or (social) structures that gave rise to their outcomes (Astbury and Leeuw 2010). What was fundamentally constitutive to the Integrated Rights-Practices was that the responsibility and initiative to realise rights was explicitly shifted from the demand-side to the supply-side of the welfare state. This shift in responsibility was a decisive mechanism, because in the regular practice of social services, citizens are often considered rational consumers that are expected to independently approach the 'right' services for their problems (Clarke 2006; Hasenfeld and Garrow 2012). Now, social workers were expected to approach citizens and realise their rights, they became more aware about the potential thresholds and citizens were far less confronted with the information, process, and social costs associated to the take-up of rights. In our study, we further unravelled this overarching mechanism of a shifted responsibility and tried to explain what it was exactly about proactive, outreaching, generalist, and relation-based interventions that provided an answer to the determinants of non-take-up (Boost et al. 2021). In other words, we continued to ask ourselves retroductive questions to further specify how the shift in responsibility was connected to other mechanisms. This is strongly in line with how the social world is considered an open system where a multitude of possible mechanisms are cooperating.

Stage 5: Comparison between Different Abstractions

Critical realism's relativist epistemology implies that the theories we construct as detectives and physicists are always an approximation of reality and, thus, fallible. The idea that the ways in which we come to know the world are relative to the activities and belief systems of groups of people in time and space does not mean that it is impossible to decide between different accounts of the same phenomenon (Scott 2013). The fifth stage in the model of Danermark et al. (2019) is therefore about estimating the relative explanatory power of the mechanisms identified through the earlier abductive and retroductive thinking. The process of making these decisions and determining which mechanisms provide the best possible explanation of reality is coined as 'judgmental rationality' within critical realism. This is where the physicist and historian find themselves in deep conversation with each other. Whereas the first is mostly concerned with uncovering the underlying forces of reality, the latter emphasises the relative importance of particular incidents throughout the course of history. In doing so, the historian often adopts counterfactual methods and asks what would have happened if events had developed in alternative ways. This form of inference focuses on hypothesis testing – not empirical, but in the researcher's mind and/or conversation – and provides a convenient way to appraise the validity of the claims brought to the table by the physicist. More specifically, we can imagine the *historian* to challenge the *physicist* with 'open' counterfactual questions like, 'what would have happened if ...?'. Since it is always possible to come up with multiple answers to that question, they need to somehow determine which of the alternatives is the most plausible. In realist research, these judgement calls are often made by assessing the formulated theories for their consilience, simplicity, and analogy (Haig and Evers 2015). Consilience is about the theory being more explanatory coherent and explaining a greater range of facts compared to others. This is where the detective overhears the physicist and historian, takes an unsolicited seat at their table, and abruptly interrupts the conversation to make them evaluate whether their abstractions can fully explain the identified demi-regularities. Simplicity, in turn, states that theories with fewer special or ad hoc assumptions are preferred. In that regard, we can imagine the *detective* demanding the scholars to come down from their ivory tower, explain themselves in lay terms, and consider the real-world implications of their abstract reasonings. This is similar to the idea that mechanisms should be defined at the middle-range, striking a workable balance between non-testable grand theories and concrete descriptions (Van Belle, van de Pas and Marchal 2017). Analogy, lastly, considers theories more coherent when they are supported by established theories. This shows how abstraction is not a linear, but an iterative process where retroductive conclusions open the possibilities for new abductive thought operations and vice versa.

Example

In our evaluation, taking on the role of the historian, we questioned what would have happened if the responsibility was not shifted from the demand-side to the supply-side of the welfare state. After some thorough consideration, we concluded that every other mechanism – with regard to proactive, outreaching, generalist, and relation-based interventions – was dependent on social workers and their organisations taking the initiative to approach citizens, inform them and support them with realising their rights. Put differently, without shifting the responsibility, citizens would have remained ignorant about their own entitlements and would never have claimed them independently. After being convinced about the fundamental role of this overarching mechanism, we reflected upon the consilience, simplicity, and analogy of our analysis. With regard to consilience, the shift in responsibility provided a coherent explanation that was reflected in every pilot-project and could explain all of the other observations. Moreover, this explanation was rather simple in nature and required no ad hoc assumptions with the exception that realising rights is not the sole responsibility of social work practice and that social policies on multiple levels should enable citizens to obtain an acceptable standard of living. Lastly, we could find analogies between our own conclusions and previous debates on e-governance, where push and pull strategies were discussed (Linders et al. 2015). Our analysis was, thus, supported by previous research that advocates for proactive approaches. We abductively extended this argument to social work practice.

Stage 6: Concretisation and Contextualisation

The final stage of the abstraction process is about the concretisation and contextualisation of the established explanations or examining how different structures and mechanisms manifest themselves in concrete situations. More specifically, the attention is turned to not only how specific conditions trigger the identified mechanisms but also how mechanisms interact with mechanisms at different levels (Danermark et al. 2019). To analyse the contextual contingencies of social work interventions it is helpful to distinguish between three specific types of contexts, namely: the client's context, the intervention context, and the societal and cultural context (Blom and Morén 2010). At each of these levels, there is a potential for discovering elements that trigger and/or counteract the mechanisms under study. To further unravel how mechanisms interact with other mechanisms in the causation of actual events, critical realism refers to *retrodiction* as a specific mode of abstraction (Lawson 1998). Although retrodiction is often overlooked, it provides an explicit answer to an important limitation of retroduction, namely: the chaotic, emergent, and complex properties of our social world are often neglected by illuminating particular mechanisms and (re) describing them in those consilient, simple, and analogous manners. This echoes what critical realists call the multiple determination of actual events or the idea that to explain the world as it really is, we need to unravel how a multitude of causal powers interact and jointly contribute to occurrences manifesting themselves in their specific ways (Bhaskar and Danermark 2006). This emphasis on both context and retrodiction is fundamentally different from how the natural sciences strive to isolate individual causal powers and eliminate the effects of other mechanisms and contingencies in experimental settings (Elder-Vass 2015). For social scientists, the conditions that trigger or counteract mechanisms are an inherent part of the research agenda. With this in mind, we can imagine the historian leaving the bar, continuing to ponder over his conversation with the detective and physicist, and contemplating the contingencies of their collective explanations on his way home. Here, in relation to concrete situations the historian asks himself 'closed' counterfactual questions like, 'would this be possible if…?', 'could this happen in…?', or 'is this connected to…?' that lead to a more definitive yes or no answer. In other words, the historian uses his vast knowledge about the world to reintroduce complexity into the equation by situating the explanations in a broader, but concrete context of time and space. This way the historian brings the explanations to the actual domain. These reflections will ultimately lead to new hunches and hypotheses which may require a new round of data collection and the recommencement of working through the different stages.

Example

In our study of Integrated Rights-Practices, we have approached context as the underlying causes for non-take-up to suit our ambition of discovering mechanisms which explain how and why this problem can be overcome through social work interventions. This means that we have not fully studied or represented the complex, contingent, and emergent nature of events. Nevertheless, we acknowledge that a more detailed account of the influence of other context elements – such as the welfare system, location, types of rights and their regulations, involved actors, the circumstances of citizens and other factors – could advance and strengthen our understanding. For example, we presume that the towering workloads in social services and the increasing focus on performance under the flag of New Public Management (Van Berkel and Knies 2016) restrict social workers to more reactive and demand-driven approaches. In retrodictive terms, the mechanism of the shift in responsibility seems to be counteracted in a context where occupational professionalism has changed into organisational professionalism (Evetts 2015). Because of this, we expect that the creation of enabling conditions – in terms of time, trust, and autonomy – is a fundamental prerequisite to shift the responsibility from the demand-side to the supply-side of the welfare state. These are possible avenues to explore in future research that iteratively builds on earlier findings.

We summarise our reconceptualisation of Danermark et al.'s (2019) *explanatory research based on critical realism* model in Figure 2.1 and situate the role of the *detective*, *physicist*, and *historian* in the process of abstraction across the domain of the empirical, the actual, and the real.

Conclusion

In this chapter, our ambition has been to illustrate how the meta-theoretical principles found in critical realism can be translated into practical conduct during hands-on research based on our own experience with adopting this perspective in the context of evaluating social work practices. We are aware, however, that our depiction of the process of abstractive reasoning is, in itself, also an abstraction of reality. We therefore advise newcomers to critical realism to consider models like ours a starting point to their own journey. Especially for those with an interest in applied research, we have experienced that the overwhelming feeling of not fully understanding critical realism's philosophy of science is best managed by slowly trying to adopt different elements in your day-to-day practice. In other words, to realise the emancipatory potential of critical realism in practice, we should not get lost in the philosophical debates, but rather consider their implications and apply the central premises – such as a generative understanding of causation – in empirical research. As we have shown, the roles of the detective, physicist, and historian are co-productive and mutually reinforcing in that context and help to work across the domains of the empirical, actual, and real. Although we have presented their conversations as taking place inside of your own head, we would like to end by stressing the importance of real-life discussions with colleagues and research participants. Abstraction is seldomly a solitary act. In our past research projects, the best ideas were often the result of (informal) talks where the roles of the detective, physicist, and historian were unwittingly fulfilled and spontaneously exchanged between different individuals.

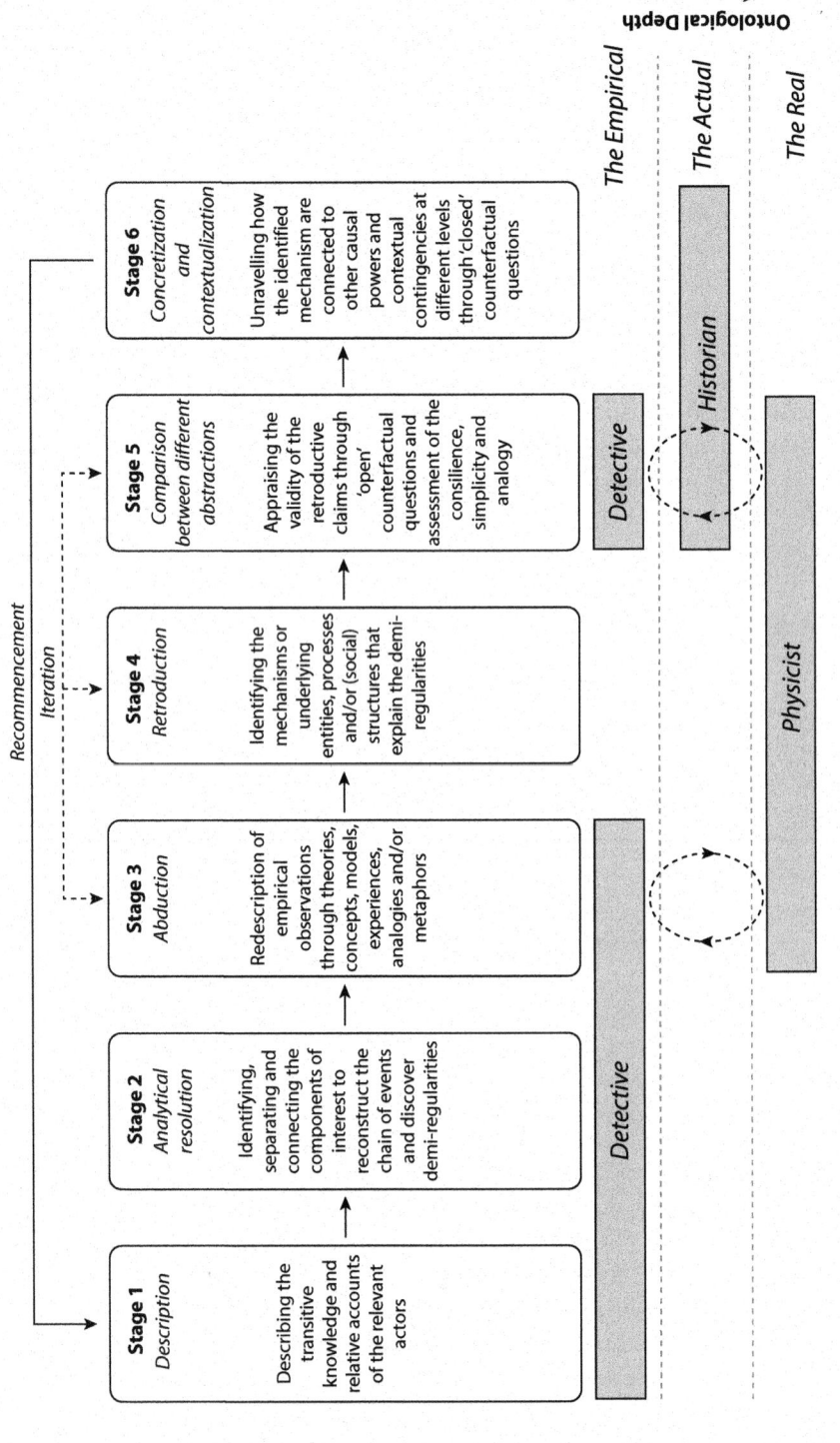

26 Didier Boost, Björn Blom, and Peter Raeymaeckers

FIGURE 2.1 Reconceptualisation of the Explanatory Research Model

Notes

1 Didier Boost and Peter Raeymaeckers.
2 Björn Blom.

References

Astbury, B. and F. L. Leeuw. 2010. "Unpacking Black Boxes: Mechanisms and Theory Building in Evaluation." *American Journal of Evaluation* 31 (3): 363–381. doi:10.1177/1098214010371972.
Bhaskar, R. 1998. *The Possibility of Naturalism: A Philosophical Critique of the Contemporary Human Sciences*. Abingdon: Routledge.
Bhaskar, R. and B. Danermark. 2006. "Meta-theory, Interdisciplinarity and Disability Research: A Critical Realist Perspective." *Scandinavian Journal of Disability Research* 8 (4): 278–297. doi:10.1080/15017410600914329.
Blom, B. 2009. "Knowing or Un-Knowing? That Is the Question: In the Era of Evidence-Based Social Work Practice." *Journal of Social Work* 9 (2): 158–177. doi:10.1177/1468017308101820.
Blom, B. and S. Morén. 2010. "Explaining Social Work Practice—The CAIMeR Theory." *Journal of Social Work* 10 (1): 98–119. doi: 10.1177/1468017309350661.
Blom, B. and S. Morén. 2019. *Theory for Social Work Practice*. Lund: Studentlitteratur.
Boost, D., P. Raeymaeckers, K. Hermans and S. Elloukmani. 2021. "Overcoming Non-Take-Up of Rights: A Realist Evaluation of Integrated Rights-Practices." *Journal of Social Work* 21 (4): 831–852. doi:1468017320948332.
Clarke, J. 2006. "Consumers, Clients or Citizens? Politics, Policy and Practice in the Reform of Social Care." *European Societies* 8 (3): 423–442. doi:10.1080/14616690600821966.
Cournoyer, B. R. and G. T. Powers. 2002. "Evidence-Based Social Work: The Quiet Revolution Continues." In *Social Workers' Desk Reference*, edited by A. R. Roberts and G. J. Greene, 798–807. New York: Oxford University Press.
Danermark, B., M. Ekström and J. C. Karlsson. 2019. *Explaining Society: Critical Realism in the Social Sciences*. Abingdon: Routledge.
Ebrahim, A. 2019. *Measuring Social Change: Performance and Accountability in a Complex World*. Stanford: Stanford University Press.
Elder-Vass, D. 2015. "Developing Social Theory Using Critical Realism." *Journal of Critical Realism* 14 (1): 80–92. doi:10.1179/1476743014Z.00000000047.
Emmel, N., K. Hughes, J. Greenhalgh and A. Sales. 2007. "Accessing Socially Excluded People – Trust and the Gatekeeper in the Researcher-Participant Relationship." In *Sociological Research Online* 12 (2):43–55. https://doi.org/10.5153/sro.1512.
Evetts J. 2015. "A New Professionalism? Challenges and Opportunities." *Current Sociology* 59 (4): 406–422. doi:10.1177/0011392111402585.
Feagin, J. R. 2001. "Social Justice and Sociology: Agendas for the Twenty-First Century." *American Sociological Review* 66 (1). https://doi.org/10.2307/2657391.
Gambrill, E. 2006. "Evidence-Based Practice and Policy: Choices Ahead." *Research on Social Work Practice* 16 (3): 338–357. doi:10.1177/1049731505284205.
Gilgun, J. F. 2005. "The Four Cornerstones of Evidence-Based Practice in Social Work." *Research on Social Work Practice* 15 (1): 52–61. doi:10.1177/1049731504269581.
Haig, B. D. and C. W. Evers. 2015. *Realist Inquiry in Social Science*. Thousand Oaks: Sage.
Hammersley, M. 2002. "Research as Emancipatory: The Case of Bhaskar's Critical Realism." *Journal of Critical Realism* 1 (1): 33–48. doi:10.1558/jocr.v1i1.33.

Hasenfeld, Y. and E. Garrow. 2012. "Nonprofit Human-Service Organizations, Social Rights, and Advocacy in a Neoliberal Welfare State." *Social Service Review* 86 (2): 295–322. doi:10.1086/666391.

Hernanz, V., F. Malherbet and M. Pellizzari. 2004. *Take-Up of Welfare Benefits in OECD Countries: A Review of the Evidence*. Paris: OECD Publishing. doi:10.1787/525815265414.

IFSW. 2014. Global Definition of Social Work. Retrieved from http://ifsw.org/policies/definition-of-social-work/.

Jackson, S. F. and G. Kolla. 2012. "A New Realistic Evaluation Analysis Method: Linked Coding of Context, Mechanism, and Outcome Relationships." *American Journal of Evaluation* 33 (3): 339–349. doi:10.1177/1098214012440030.

Jagosh, J. 2020. "Retroductive Theorizing in Pawson and Tilley's Applied Scientific Realism." *Journal of Critical Realism* 19 (2): 121–130. doi:10.1080/14767430.2020.1723301.

Kjørstad, M. and M. B. Solem. 2017. *Critical Realism for Welfare Professions*. Abingdon: Routledge.

Lawson, T. 1997. *Economics and Reality*. Abingdon: Routledge.

Lawson, T. 1998. "Economic Science without Experimentation/Abstraction." In *Critical Realism: Essential Readings*, edited by M. Archer, R. Bhaskar, A. Collier, T. Lawson and A. Norrie, 144–169. Abingdon: Routledge.

Linders, D., C. Z. Liao and C. Wang. 2015. "Proactive e-Governance: Flipping the Service Delivery Model from Pull to Push in Taiwan." *Government Information Quarterly* 35 (4): 68–76. https://doi.org/10.1016/j.giq.2015.08.004.

Merton, R. 1967. *On Theoretical Sociology: Five Essays, Old and New*. New York: The Free Press.

Miles, M. B. and A. M. Huberman. 1994. *Qualitative Data Analysis: An Expanded Sourcebook*. Thousand Oaks: Sage.

Morén, S. and B. Blom. 2003. "Explaining Human Change: On Generative Mechanisms in Social Work Practice." *Journal of Critical Realism* 2 (1): 37–60. doi:10.1558/jocr.v2i1.37.

Næss, P. 2019. "'Demi-regs', Probabilism and Partly Closed Systems." *Journal of Critical Realism* 18 (5): 475–486. doi:10.1080/14767430.2019.1644951.

Parton, N. 1994. "The Nature of Social Work under Conditions of (Post) Modernity." *Social Work and Social Sciences Review* 52 (2): 93–112.

Patton, M. Q. 2008. *Utilization-Focused Evaluation*. Thousand Oaks: Sage.

Pawson, R. 2006. *Evidence-Based Policy: A Realist Perspective*. Thousand Oaks: Sage.

Pawson, R. 2013. *The Science of Evaluation: A Realist Manifesto*. Thousand Oaks: Sage.

Pawson, R. and N. Tilley. 1997. *Realistic Evaluation*. Thousand Oaks: Sage.

Powell, J. 2002. "The Changing Conditions of Social Work Research." *British Journal of Social Work* 32 (1): 17–33. doi:10.1093/bjsw/32.1.17.

Rogers, P. J. 2008. "Using Programme Theory to Evaluate Complicated and Complex Aspects of Interventions." *Evaluation* 14 (1): 29–48. doi:10.1177/1356389007084674.

Scott, D. 2013. *Education, Epistemology and Critical Realism*. Abingdon: Routledge.

Van Belle, S., R. van de Pas and B. Marchal. 2017. "Towards an Agenda for Implementation Science in Global Health: There Is Nothing More Practical than Good (Social Science) Theories." *BMJ Global Health* 2 (2). doi:10.1136/bmjgh-2016-000181.

Van Berkel, R. and E. Knies. 2016. "Performance Management, Caseloads and the Frontline Provision of Social Services." *Social Policy & Administration* 50 (1): 59–78. doi:10.1111/spol.12150.

Vandekinderen, C., R. Roose, P. Raeymaeckers and K. Hermans. 2020. "The DNA of Social Work as a Human Rights Practice from a Frontline Social Workers' Perspective in Flanders." *European Journal of Social Work* 23 (5): 876–888. doi:10.1080/13691457.2019.1663408.

3
BRIDGING THE GAP BETWEEN PHILOSOPHY AND EMPIRICAL RESEARCH

A Critical Realist Methodology Using Quantitative Methods

Catherine Hastings

Introduction

Before I enrolled in my PhD in 2015, I worked for over a decade as an applied social research and evaluation consultant for social enterprise, government, and community (not-for-profit) legal centres. In retrospect, I operated within a relatively pragmatic research paradigm. I was sceptical of empirical data's capacity to represent the entirety of a complex reality and frustrated by the assumptions of quantitative methods in the way they were taught to me. Importantly, I was aware of a disconnect between the 'answers' to so-called 'wicked' social problems provided in research literature and the types of answers or knowledge needed by policymakers, activists, and programme practitioners seeking societal change. After discovering critical realism, my doctoral research rapidly became grounded in an explicitly critical realist approach to causal explanation. My PhD was motivated by the impacts of homelessness and extreme poverty on families, asking how disadvantage and other factors increase housing insecurity and explaining why some impoverished Australian families experience homelessness and others do not (Hastings 2020).

In this chapter, I first introduce key problems in the literature seeking to explain the causes of homelessness. Second, I describe my experiences of critical realism and highlight some of the potential I saw that motivated and justified my initial investment. Third, I outline my methodology: what I did, in what order, and why. Finally, I highlight aspects of the philosophy that provided my project with practical analytical frameworks.

Problems Explaining Homelessness

Extreme disadvantage and social exclusion, with associated experiences of loss, fear, and trauma, are implicated in long-term effects on the life outcomes of children. Homeless families may experience challenging, even traumatic, experiences linked to sustained poverty and insecurity (Hulse and Sharam 2013). There is abundant evidence of the potential of adverse childhood events associated with homelessness and extreme disadvantage to negatively influence the trajectories of young people later in life (Keane, Magee, and Kelly 2016). Therefore, housing and housing security matter in the context of intergenerational inequality and the (re)production of disadvantage.

However, as I started to work with the homelessness literature, particularly with that part most concerned with establishing the causes of homelessness, I realised it is difficult to articulate a consistent and comprehensive account of why some families become homeless, and others do not. The problem starts within the broader homelessness literature and its attempts to explain the causes of homelessness more generally. Despite the importance of the problem, international homelessness research is characterised by a diversity of causality findings owing to a variety of homelessness definitions (Chamberlain and Mackenzie 1992; Smith 2013), ideological and welfare state contexts (Fitzpatrick and Stephens 2014; Minnery and Greenhalgh 2007), and research approaches (Fitzpatrick and Christian 2006). Additionally, the homeless population is heterogeneous. People experiencing homelessness can be, for example, young, old, male, female, single, a family, homeless once or many times. There is a difference within groups and over time in how homelessness develops and is experienced. Complexity, contingency, and context are inherent to homelessness causality.

There is also, what I consider to be, an ontological problem in homelessness causality literature, particularly in how it deals with conceptualising social structure and human agency (Hastings 2021b). Johnson and Jacobs (2014) outline two types of causal explanations: those that focus on how the actions of individuals (agency) are the primary driver of homelessness and those that understand social and economic structures as having the principal role. Each approach embodies assumptions about the ontology of the social world. Individual explanations give primacy to the active role of people as agents to make decisions that have consequences for their lives and their individual characteristics. Conversely, structural explanations give prominence to factors such as poverty, housing, and labour market conditions in their accounts. Both approaches reflect opposite sides of an ontological debate about a dualist structure/agency dichotomy: whether it is structure (holism) or agency (individualism) that has primacy in generating the structures of the social world (Little 1991). There are also causal explanations that seek to integrate human agency and social factors; however, they struggle with how structure and agency relate ontologically as an inter-dependent duality.

The Promise and Challenge of Critical Realism

Working with the literature, I identified that causal explanation of homelessness needed to move beyond descriptive and atheoretical accounts; engage with causal complexity; and better integrate structural and individual explanations. I was influenced by Fitzpatrick's (2005) call for a greater role for social theory in explaining homelessness. At the same time, that paper makes a compelling argument for critical realism as a meta-theoretical framework for homelessness research, with a particular focus on critical realism's thinking about causality.

Inspired by Fitzpatrick's paper, I explored critical realism further. Although the thesis' primary research objective was to explain family homelessness in Australia, I became convinced that my best hope of achieving this was through engagement with critical realism. I began to see how thinking through a critical realist lens enabled me to diagnose with greater clarity the incapacity of the homelessness causality literature to offer serious explanations. I also became convinced that critical realism's ontological, epistemological, and axiomatic presuppositions offered a powerful toolkit for thinking about causality and the other themes I wanted to explore in the thesis. Therefore, a secondary focus of the project became one of operationalising the critical realist philosophy in quantitative empirical research.

Before my encounters with critical realism began, I had determined some goals for the project, which impacted my later choices. First, I wanted to use the PhD as an opportunity to develop my quantitative methods toolkit. Second, I wanted to take advantage of three existing, large, and underutilised quantitative data sources that researchers had thus far not employed to investigate family homelessness. Through engagement with authors such as Porpora (2010), Olsen and Morgan (2005), Bramley and Fitzpatrick (2018), and Næss (2004), I developed the position that all methods are potentially possible *as long as they are used appropriately* – that is, reflected the ontological and epistemological assumptions of critical realism. Qualitative, quantitative, and mixed method research methods are simply tools or techniques. What is important is the basis upon which a researcher incorporates methods into a methodology, that is, the specific "combination of techniques, the practices we conform to when we apply them, and our interpretation of what we are doing when we do so" (Olsen and Morgan 2005, 257).

Considering the ramifications of the ontology of the social world on social research practice, Bhaskar (2016) explains:

> We are then equally and irreducibly embodied and part of nature, and emergent, conceptualising, reflexive and self-conscious beings. It is the fact that social life has an interior, at least partially conceptualised and reflexively accessible, that makes the rich, thick descriptions of qualitative research. Many of these hermeneutical features can, however, be seen to be complexly interwoven with the extensive materially embodied features of social life, amenable to quantitative research. Social research involves a constant toing and froing, moving back and forth between the inner and outer, the internal and extensional, the intensive and the extensive.
>
> (82)

In other words, different research methods offer distinct lenses to the 'emergent, concept- and activity-dependent, value drenched and politically contested part of the natural world' (that is, the social world) and are legitimate activities of explanatory investigation and critique (Bhaskar 2016, 82). I agreed that knowledge derived from quantitative methods was only going to do part of the job. Due to the time and other constraints of the doctoral process, I was unable to collect other forms of data. Instead, I relied extensively on the resource of existing interdisciplinary literature, particularly research based on qualitative data that sought to understand the experience of people at risk of and experiencing homelessness.

Developing a Methodology

The methodology I developed for approaching quantitative empirical research in my doctorate was explicitly critical realist in its orientation (Hastings 2021a). Fundamentally, my approach needed to be consistent with the critical realist position that reality consists of the domains of the real, actual, and empirical; is stratified and emergent; and causal mechanisms are discovered through conceptual abstraction and theorising (Bhaskar 2016). In practice, this meant that my data were simply a form of evidence of events at the *empirical* (or observed) level of reality. However, causal mechanisms producing these events are embedded in the nature of objects (including social structures) at the level of the *real*, that we cannot directly see or experience. Consequently, I knew I would need to theorise structures and mechanisms when developing causal explanations.

Theorising is then an integral part of developing explanations through critical realist social research. As a result, at each stage of the process, I was asking questions. I asked questions of the data as I made decisions about coding, which descriptive and multivariate techniques to employ and what to include and exclude from the analysis. I asked interpretive questions of myself – involving imagination and logic – in response to the data. I argue that asking questions and suggesting possible answers is a process of theorising. We seek answers to our questions about *why*, for *whom*, and in what *context* things emerge. We start with the incomplete empirical information we obtain about the world through observation. Then, our abstractions, interpretations, generalisations, concepts, and models are how we find, develop, and use patterns to see explanatory shapes in the causal complexity that is the reality of our social world.

Instead of conceptualising events and their regularities or patterns as the fundamental unit of analysis (as is typical in the more positivist-orientated quantitative methodologies I had been taught), realism required me to focus on exposing the underlying structures of the world to uncover causal processes. My work with data was a path of exploration (rather than confirmation) with the goal of explanation (rather than prediction) and theoretical (rather than empirical) generalisations (Bhaskar 2016). According to critical realism, knowledge about our world develops when we see things happen and try to understand *why* they could have happened (Danermark et al. 2002). Therefore, for example, I needed to go beyond identifying and describing the characteristics of disadvantage associated with homelessness; to theorise how the powers or mechanisms of disadvantage are developed and may impact a person's housing security. I needed to be attentive to stratification and emergent powers and sensitive to contexts' constraining and enabling effects (Gorski 2004; Sayer 2000).

Critical realism's depth ontology motivated the two key stages in my methodology – *empirical* and *theoretical* analysis – and defined the research design of the thesis. Although described separately here, I found the edges of these stages blurred in practice. Progress towards a deeper and richer explanation, or causal model, involved an iterative and circular process of engagement with literature, data, and theory, 'underlaboured' by the ideas and conceptual frameworks of critical realist thinking.

Empirical Analysis

The first stage, *empirical analysis*, is concerned only with exploring the data: what can we observe about the world at the empirical level of events. It is a *descriptive* phase. In my thesis, quantitative methods, even panel regression modelling, were used purely descriptively. The usual questions of understanding or defining causality in quantitative approaches – identifying differences between correlation and the potential to detect or prove causation in various methods – are not relevant. What is observable in the empirical domain is not direct evidence of causality. Therefore, I started from the standpoint that observations are simply events, regardless of the data structure or the data analysis method used.

In the statistical analyses, I was looking for patterns suggesting the presence of structures, mechanisms, and contexts relevant to answering the core research question of this thesis: What are the causal mechanisms of contemporary 'cultural' homelessness for disadvantaged Australian families with children? I asked questions of my datasets to identify consistent and inconsistent patterns in the data. Depending on the data's structure, I asked questions along the lines of:

- What are the characteristics of those most often homeless?
- What types of homelessness are associated with different externally related groups of people experiencing homelessness?
- Are there differences in housing insecurity outcomes between groups, distinguished by their demographic characteristics, individual background, recent events, and environmental contexts?
- What are the reasons homeless families understand as the source of their housing insecurity?

The nature of these questions and literature evidence guided my choice of statistical methods and modelling strategy. I was further inspired by what each preceding analysis suggested regarding the presence or absence of associations, the relative magnitude of associations, and how combinations of variables seemed to cluster, 'work' together, or in opposition.

Theoretical Analysis

Causal explanation is the product of *theoretical analysis* to describe the real domain – underlying structures and causal mechanisms – based on the indications, hints, patterns, and signals observable in the empirical domain of observed events. Therefore, the second analysis stage of my project required *structural analysis* (to theoretically establish the relational and structural nature of the phenomenon of family homelessness through abstraction) and *causal analysis* (to theoretically establish the mechanisms, powers, and conditions by which the phenomenon is generated).

Structural analysis

Causality is embedded in the inherent nature of a phenomenon. Therefore, my first step towards theorising causality was to move from concrete description to conceptual abstraction through *structural analysis*, that is, focusing on the nature of family homelessness (as well as those objects related to it) and separating which attributes of the objects are characteristic – or determine their nature – and which are contingent. As the objects of social science are relational, I needed to also distinguish between necessary and contingent relations that are substantial (real connections between objects) and formal relations (common characteristics of groups). Danermark et al. (2002, 46) suggest that 'whether a relation is necessary or contingent for a certain research object is thus not a logical question but one that can only be answered through concrete study'. The initial stages of exploring relations *within* and *between* the social objects of my study occurred as I looked for patterns in the data as part of the empirical analysis. Then, there was a shift to interpretation, theorising, and judgement as I abstracted from the data to define the internal and external relations of the object and its fundamental nature.

Bhaskar challenges us to understand the nature of objects in terms of how stratification, causal powers, and generative mechanisms make the phenomenon what it fundamentally *is* (rather than something else). This includes by identifying what is absent, or what has been absented (or excluded) for the phenomenon to be what it has become (Norrie 2010). It is a cognitive process through which what I knew about homelessness was reinterpreted to give an improved understanding of observable events, the connections, relations, and properties of the social object (Hastings 2021a). At this stage of analysis, I asked the kinds of questions suggested by Sayer (1992, 91), including: 'What does the existence of this object (in this form) presuppose? Can it exist on its own as such? If not, what else must be present [or absent]? What is it about the object that causes it to do such and such?'. And the key question suggested by Danermark et al. (2002, 47) of

'What cannot be removed without making the object cease to exist in its present form?'. My questions concerned structures at the social world's normative, social, and individual levels, each relevant to generating a model of the interrelated objects implicated in causing (and protecting) families from homelessness.

Causal analysis

Abstract concepts about the structure of social objects operated as a prompt for the next stage of my theoretical analysis – developing explanations of the mechanisms behind an object's existence through *causal analysis*. Research claims about causality in critical realism require a move from the empirical to the transfactual (theoretical) and from the abstract to 'concrete universality'. They also incorporate a specific 'holistic' conception of conjunctive and relational causality (Bhaskar 2016, 92). Therefore, to develop a critical realist explanation I needed to redescribe or recontextualise what I saw in the data in theoretical language (abduction), in order to evoke mechanisms (Porpora 2011). The related and very similar logic of retroduction – a mode of inference – I used to ask how the nature of the phenomenon can be explained by identifying causal powers and their generative mechanisms. Through retroductive inference I aimed to answer the question: what makes the phenomenon possible? (Danermark et al. 2002). I was inspired by Bhaskar, who describes the process of causal analysis as 'imagining a model of a mechanism that, if it were real, would account for the phenomenon in question' given a particular set of circumstances and when combined with other mechanisms in specific combinations (2016, 79). Therefore, I also engaged in retrodictive thinking to ask "what mix of causal powers interacted in what way to produce any particular event" (Elder-Vass 2015, 81). At the same time, to settle on the explanation developed by my research, I explored, evaluated, and eliminated competing potential explanations (Bhaskar 2016, 80–82).

I experienced abstraction, abduction, retroduction and retrodiction as interrelated, iterative, and recursive processes. Therefore, to develop a model to explain family homelessness, I asked myself questions such as:

- What does the existence of family homelessness in this form presuppose and what are its preconditions?
- What is constitutive necessity versus an accidental contingency?
- Can family homelessness exist without this? Is the condition, or set of conditions, necessary or sufficient?
- What else must be present?
- What is it about this factor (structure) that allows it to generate the outcomes, characteristics, and functions of being homeless for a family?
- What conditions or contexts trigger this mechanism?
- Are there other ways of framing the phenomenon and providing alternative interpretations?

My earlier empirical data analysis stage and ongoing engagement with existing literature and theory suggested the answers to these questions. I relied on analysis frameworks developed from the writings of Bhaskar and Archer (such as those profiled in the next section) to scaffold and support my thinking whilst developing questions and speculating about their answers. I also used mid-range social theory to facilitate and inspire theoretical explanation.

Finding Inspiration in Ontology

There are many practical examples in my thesis of how the abstract philosophical ideas of critical realism 'underlaboured' my research practice by influencing my research design and the development of a quantitative empirical research methodology. I want to profile two important areas of critical realist thinking – relating to stratification – that impacted my approach to the project and the development of analytical frameworks.

Stratification

Reality is a stratified phenomenon, with hierarchically organised levels of causal powers working through generative mechanisms. An essential feature of stratification is that properties and causal powers emerge at each level, with the properties of emergent phenomena irreducible to those of their constituents (Sayer 2000). Recognising the stratified nature of social reality had two major ramifications for my study. First, the mechanisms bringing about homelessness could be operating within cultural, normative, and other structures or at the level of individual experiences, agency, and people's psychological processes. This suggested an interdisciplinary approach was required, using empirical and theoretical knowledge from the areas of knowledge relevant to each stratum (Danermark 2019). Second, critical realist conceptions of the relationship between structure and agency provided frameworks for thinking about their interactions. These offered approaches for bridging the analytical and conceptual divide between structural and individual 'risk factors' in homelessness literature.

Interdisciplinarity

Critical realism reveals why it is impossible to develop knowledge about a stratified social world within a single discipline or order of knowledge. Instead, it justifies and encourages engagement in interdisciplinary or inter-level emergent knowledge creation (Danermark 2019). Critical realist thinking about interdisciplinarity, including advice on applying it, provided a framework for me to evaluate and incorporate methods, findings, and theory from different fields of research (Bhaskar, Danermark, and Price 2018; Bhaskar and Danermark 2006; Danermark 2019). Although a sociologist, I also engaged with research developed within, for example, psychology, social work, economics, political economy, health, and social policy disciplines. Critical realism provided a 'common ground' or a meta-theoretical framework for interdisciplinarity (Porpora 2010), as the philosophy's ontological and epistemological assumptions provided a basis upon which I could interpret and synthesise the insights of each field. I could incorporate findings from research reflecting multiple 'lenses' on the problem. Instead of being confused and frustrated by a fragmented literature, I became excited by the potential to develop an emergent *transdisciplinary* account when supported by critical realism.

Structure and agency

To understand what shapes social life, it is necessary to grasp the natures of, and the dynamic relation between, social structure and agency. From a critical realist vantage point, people are agents because of their capacity to conceive, set, and work to achieve goals. Structures emerge from human agency but have properties of their own, different from those of people's properties (Danermark et al. 2002). I needed to examine the relationship between agents and structures to understand family homelessness. Critical realism's stratified ontology provided a basis from which I could understand better these complex interactions (Archer 2011) and a framework through which I could integrate the structural and individual factors into one explanatory model for family homelessness.

Bhaskar's *Transformational Model of Social Activity* (TMSA) provides an important conceptual resource for understanding social structures and agency as two distinct (but interdependent) kinds of things by virtue of the different powers and properties they possess (Bhaskar 2016). The model depicts society and social forms as pre-existing but reproduced (or transformed) by human agency over time. This inspired me to play with tense and the order in which I framed questions about the interaction of, for example, features of the housing market; housing events that may happen to impoverished families; and a family's decision-making given the resources they have to meet challenges to their housing security. Whilst framing and answering these questions, I would attempt to hold the duality of social structure and human agency in mind – situating each within a stratified, emergent conception of social reality. Further, using Bhaskar's *Four Planar Social Being*, every social event for social beings can be analysed in terms of stratification occurring simultaneously across four dimensions of: material transactions with nature; social interaction between people; social structures 'proper'; and in the 'stratification of the embodied personality' (for example our consciousness, psychology and intentionality or agency) (Bhaskar 2016, 12). I used these conceptions of stratification in the social world to inspire further questions and direct my literature searches.

Archer's work was also important as it further assisted me to analytically decouple structure and agency. Her *morphogenetic sequence* provided me a framework for practical analysis of how social structures are changed through human agency, and how their existence can be explained in particular times and places

(Archer 2011). I used the questions suggested by Archer when she outlines the phases of structural conditioning, social interaction, and structural elaboration (or change) as analytical prompts: What are the components of the thing I am studying? How have they changed? Who was responsible? What interactions brought it about? What was wanted or not wanted because of what is there? Who did what, with or against whom, and with what outcome? Who had the resources? (2011, 62–66). In this way, I was prompted to ask questions about how structure was constraining and enabling agency and how agency was shaping structural relations and their causal powers over time.

As an emergent property of being human, the *internal conversation* has relational properties enabling interactions between the mind and the world, thereby describing the process through which structure is mediated by agency at the interface of the two (Archer 2003). Whilst social structure conditions actors, this conditioning is always mediated by the reflexive deliberation of the agent on the course of action to be followed (Bhaskar 2016). "People's relation to the world is one of concern" (Sayer 2011, 1), meaning, how we act is influenced by our values, ethical judgements, normative evaluations, and relationships with others. Archer's work encouraged me to think about the interaction of personal 'concerns' and social identities – that is, the reflexive processes through which structure is mediated by agency. Her distinction of the differences between persons, actors, and agents also provided a helpful way to conceptualise how the roles people play as actors express their concerns; and how structures, such as disadvantage, *work* to limit the capacity of agents to resist homelessness via a person's "position on society's distributions of scarce resources" (Archer 2003, 118).

Conclusion

In addition to impacting my project design and suggesting the two-stage methodological approach to empirical research I describe above, critical realism provided various philosophical concepts which I used as analytical tools. These tools helped me at the empirical stage of the project, when looking for patterns in the data, and in the second stage when theorising the nature and relations of structures and the interactions of causal mechanisms across strata, particularly those incorporating social structures and human agency. Asking analytical questions as part of this process does not mean that I always found 'an answer', the only answer, or even asked the right or sufficient questions. However, critical realism's conceptual frameworks provided prompts that deepened and extended – or 'underlaboured' – my critical and analytical thinking in response to data and existing literature and strengthened the causal explanation my thesis developed.

Engagement with critical realism required me to make a significant intellectual commitment. Initially, there was a steep learning curve, and I experienced feelings of trepidation and insecurity about my capacity to 'get' the philosophy and work out how to operationalise it in my project. However, what I found in the philosophy, and the community of critical realists with whom I connected (Hastings, Davenport, and Sheppard 2021), enriched my doctoral project and continues to support my academic work. I also feel that I have only scratched the surface of what the philosophy can offer, which motivates me to keep exploring its potential in the future.

References

Archer, M. 2003. *Structure, Agency and the Internal Conversation*. Cambridge: Cambridge University Press.
Archer, M. 2011. "Morphogenesis: Realism's Explanatory Framework." In *Sociological Realism*, edited by Andrea Maccarini, Emmanuele Morandi, and Riccardo Prandini, 59–94. Oxon: Routledge.
Bhaskar, R. 2016. *Enlightened Common Sense: The Philosophy of Critical Realism*. Abingdon: Routledge.
Bhaskar, R. and B. Danermark. 2006. "Meta-theory, Interdisciplinarity and Disability Research: A Critical Realist Perspective." *Scandinavian Journal of Disability Research* 8 (4): 278–297. https://doi.org/10.1080/15017410600914329.
Bhaskar, R. B. Danermark, and L. Price. 2018. *Interdisciplinarity and Wellbeing: A Critical Realist General Theory of Interdisciplinarity.*. London: Routledge.
Bramley, G. and S. Fitzpatrick. 2018. "Homelessness in the UK: Who Is Most at Risk?" *Housing Studies* 33 (1): 96–116. https://doi.org/10.1080/02673037.2017.1344957.
Chamberlain, C. and D. Mackenzie. 1992. "Understanding Contemporary Homelessness: Issues of Definition and Meaning." *The Australian Journal of Social Issues* 27 (4): 274–297.
Danermark, B. 2019. "Applied Interdisciplinary Research: A Critical Realist Perspective." *Journal of Critical Realism* 18 (4): 368–82. https://doi.org/10.1080/14767430.2019.1644983.
Danermark, B., M. Ekstrom, L. Jakobsen, and J. Karlsson. 2002. *Explaining Society: Critical Realism in the Social Sciences*. 2nd ed. London: Routledge.
Elder-Vass, D. 2015. "Developing Social Theory Using Critical Realism." *Journal of Critical Realism* 14 (1): 80–92. https://doi.org/10.1179/1476743014Z.00000000047.
Fitzpatrick, S. 2005. "Explaining Homelessness: A Critical Realist Perspective." *Housing Theory and Society* 22 (1): 1–17. https://doi.org/10.1080/14036090510034563.
Fitzpatrick, S. and J. Christian. 2006. "Comparing Homelessness Research in the US and Britain." *European Journal of Housing Policy* 6 (3): 313–333. https://doi.org/10.1080/14616710600973151.
Fitzpatrick, S. and M. Stephens. 2014. "Welfare Regimes, Social Values and Homelessness: Comparing Responses to Marginalised Groups in Six European Countries." *Housing Studies* 29 (2): 215–234. https://doi.org/10.1080/02673037.2014.848265.
Gorski, P. 2004. "The Poverty of Deductivism: A Constructive Realist Model of Sociological Explanation." *Sociological Methodology* 34 (1): 1–34.
Hastings, C. 2020. *Family Homelessness in Australia: A Quantitative Critical Realist Study*. Sydney: Macquarie University.
Hastings, C. 2021a. "A Critical Realist Methodology in Empirical Research: Foundations, Process, and Payoffs." *Journal of Critical Realism* 20 (5): 458–473. https://doi.org/10.1080/14767430.2021.1958440.
Hastings, C. 2021b. "Homelessness and Critical Realism: A Search for Richer Explanations." *Housing Studies* 36 (5): 737–57. https://doi.org/10.1080/02673037.2020.1729960.

Hastings, C., A. Davenport, and K. Sheppard. 2021. "The Loneliness of a Long-Distance Critical Realist Student: The Story of a Doctoral Writing Group." *Journal of Critical Realism* 21 (1): 65–82. https://doi.org/10.1080/14767430.2021.1992740.

Hulse, K. and A. Sharam. 2013. *Fighting for My Family: A Longitudinal Study of Families Experiencing Homelessness.* Melbourne: Swinbourne Institute for Social Research. http://apo.org.au/research/fighting-my-family-longitudinal-study-families-experiencing-homelessness.

Johnson, G. and K. Jacobs. 2014. "Theorising Cause." In *Homelessness in Australia: An Introduction*, edited by Chris Chamberlain, Guy Johnson, and Catherine Robinson, 30–47. Randwick: UNSW Press.

Keane, C. A., C. A. Magee, and P. J. Kelly. 2016. "Is There a Complex Trauma Experience Typology for Australians Experiencing Extreme Social Disadvantage and Low Housing Stability?" *Child Abuse & Neglect* 61: 43–54. https://doi.org/10.1016/j.chiabu.2016.10.001.

Little, D. 1991. *Varieties of Social Explanation: An Introduction to the Philosophy of Social Science.* Oxford: Westview Press.

Minnery, J. and E. Greenhalgh. 2007. "Approaches to Homelessness Policy in Europe, the United States, and Australia." *Journal of Social Issues* 63 (3): 641–655. https://doi.org/10.1111/j.1540-4560.2007.00528.x.

Næss, P. 2004. "Prediction, Regressions and Critical Realism." *Journal of Critical Realism* 3 (1): 133–164. https://doi.org/10.1163/1572513041172713.

Norrie, A. 2010. *Dialectic and Difference.* Oxon: Routledge.

Olsen, W. and J. Morgan. 2005. "A Critical Epistemology of Analytical Statistics: Addressing the Sceptical Realist." *Journal for the Theory of Social Behaviour* 35 (3): 255–284. https://doi.org/10.1111/j.1468-5914.2005.00279.x.

Porpora, D. 2011. "Recovering Causality: Realist Methods in Sociology." In *Sociological Realism*, edited by Andrea Maccarini, Emmanuele Morandi, and Riccardo Prandini, 149–167. Oxon: Routledge.

Porpora, D. 2010. "Do Realsits Run Regressions?" In *After Postmodernism – An Introduction to Critical Realism*, edited by Jose Lopez and Potter Gary, 260–266. London: The Athlone Press.

Sayer, A. 1992. *Method in Social Science: A Realist Approach.* 2nd ed. London: Routledge.

Sayer, A. 2000. *Realism and Social Science.* Thousand Oaks: Sage.

Sayer, A. 2011. *Why Things Matter to People: Social Science, Values and Ethical Life.* Cambridge: Cambridge University Press.

Smith, J. 2013. "Methodological Problems of Sampling Young Homeless People in Four European Societies with Different Levels of Service Provision and Definitions of Homelessness." *Housing, Care and Support* 16 (2): 64–75. https://doi.org/10.1108/HCS-03-2013-0005.

4
PARENT ENGAGEMENT IN STUDENT LEARNING

Using Critical Realism to Uncover the Generative Mechanisms Needed for Teachers to Embrace Parent Engagement in Their Teaching Practice

Catherine Mary Quinn

On reflection of my research experience, my early pathway meanderings were due to a lack of a solid understanding of the different philosophical positions. This lack of understanding resulted in not only three changes in the philosophical framing of my work but also changes in the focus of the research and a change in university. As a practicing educator in secondary schools for over 28 years, the only exposure to philosophy was as student at Teacher's College at the start of my career and the completion of a Masters in Educational Administration in mid-1990s. Despite some introductory units at the beginning of the Doctorial work, it was assumed that I would have the philosophical understanding that was necessary at this level. This was not the case for me. I was very much guided by the philosophical area of interest of my supervisors. While this is not necessarily a bad thing, it does carry consequences if the student experiences a change in supervision. Which is what happened to me. With a change in supervisor came a change in philosophical underlabouring of the research. This fact is important in understanding my journey to critical realism.

A person's view of reality, and how knowledge is constructed within that reality (their epistemology), impacts on more than just the methodology chosen for their research. It also informs the values and beliefs they choose to live by and apply to their work, in my case, education. It is hoped that the following paragraphs, outlining the different philosophies chosen and their relationship with critical realism, might not only give more credence to critical realism but also provide impetus to explore what was missing in the other philosophies. For this researcher, it was a convoluted journey to locate a suitable philosophical position, despite all the reading and processing that had already taken place. Here I argue that the importance of having a sound underlabouring philosophical position to research is not fully understood by all researcher students when they begin.

DOI: 10.4324/9781003193784-4

This was true for me. As part-time researcher and full-time teacher, I was influenced by the philosophical stance of my research supervisors.

In this chapter, I will first outline the focus of my doctoral research, why it is important to me and, in doing so, discuss important related methodological matters it raised. My attention will then turn to describing my journey through the different philosophical positions that eventually led me to critical realism. I make the point that this journey – from constructivism to Bourdieu and ultimately to critical realism – was not a waste of time. Instead, the journey was one of an awakening. Just as humans are individuals, so too are their views of the world. Realist research of the human world required understanding how people make (ontological and epistemological) sense of the world: what is truth (knowledge) and what is reality.

Focus of the Research

The area of interest for my research is parents' engagement in their children's learning. This interest is founded on the knowledge that parent engagement is increasingly seen by governments and researchers in Australia and elsewhere as a lever to enhance student academic achievement. *Parent engagement* implies that parents ought to be an integral part of the process of their child's learning. On a personal level as a parent with three adult children all of whom had learning difficulties, I feel that the education of the child starts long before formal education and, for parents, is never ending in some ways. I came to my research with the understanding that parents have a place alongside educators in the education of their children. My review of the research literature (Goodall and Vorhaus 2011; Pushor 2015) and the recent experience nationally and internationally of COVID lockdowns and the role parents were asked to play in home-schooling, confirmed this. However, the research has identified that, despite over 50 years of research by experts establishing that parent engagement in their children's learning has benefits for students (Hattie 2009; Jeynes 2012), there has not been widespread uptake of it in teachers' practice (Pushor and Amendt 2018) and the culture of schools. As a result, parents, who have the potential to contribute to their children's learning, are often undervalued and positioned as less important in the children's education.

I provide a brief overview of the research, so that the reader can understand my journey. My research was about teachers and the practice of engaging parents for enhancing student learning. More specifically the research has sought to understand if enhancing teachers' understanding of parent engagement mediates self-stated changes in teaching practice and has explored the enabling and constraining factors of those processes. Hence, it sought to uncover what conditions were needed for teachers to embrace parent engagement in their teaching practice.

Data collection for this research took place in two Catholic schools, one secondary and one primary both in southern Queensland, Australia. Prior to data collection, I mentored a team of three to five teachers in both schools over a

12-month period. I was the 'knowledgeable other' working towards enhancing the teachers' understanding of *parent engagement*. The team of teachers in both schools was purposefully selected by the Principals.

The research design was qualitative, and data were collected from interviews and surveys with the primary and secondary schoolteachers. It was considered appropriate for the interviews to include both participants and non-participant teachers so that a comparison could be made between those who had participated in the 12 months of mentoring and a similar number of teachers who did not participate in the mentoring. These teachers again were purposefully selected by the principal mainly for convenience for school timetabling. Data were enriched by open-ended survey questions given to the whole teaching staff of both the primary and secondary school. This allowed insight into how the team that had been mentored perceived *parent engagement* in comparison to the other teaching staff within that school context. Thematic analysis of the data took place using the NVivo. Discussion centred on teachers' perceptions of the role of *parent engagement* in the stratified activity of educating their students, firstly between members of the individual schools and then between the teachers at the different school types, that of primary and secondary school.

Before elaborating on the journey, I feel I need to explain some of the key aspects of critical realism that particularly relate to my research and that led me to my current position. I do this not only for the reader who may be new to critical realism but also to set the context for why it appealed to me. Next, I overview other philosophical positions I explored before finally settling on critical realism as the philosophical underlabouring of the research. A researcher new to the philosophical position of critical realism may find that it is not always written in a way that is easy to understand. Bear with me as I outline these theoretical terms which I will later relate more practically to my research.

Key Aspects of Critical Realism

For me it was brought home strongly in the paper *What Is Critical Realism?* (Archer et al. 2016, 2) that it is not an empirical programme, nor a methodology and not even truly a theory because it explains nothing. While there are now many researchers across the globe employing critical realism, Archer et al. (2016, 1) notes that there is no one set of beliefs, methodology, or framework that epitomises critical realism. They suggest instead it is a 'heterogeneous assemblage of elements drawn from a relatively common genetic pool' which unites scholars and brings critical realism together as a meta-theory. All scholars are committed "to formulating a properly post-positive philosophy" (Archer et al. 2016, 2) but they agree that there is a commitment to four main aspects: *ontological realism; epistemic relativism; judgemental rationality; and a cautious ethical naturalism.* I will return to these critical realist commitments at relevant points in the chapter to not only explain them but also outline their importance to my research journey.

It is not the intention of this chapter to provide definition of these commitments, but it is important to highlight that at its foundation, critical realism holds to *ontological realism*, i.e., things can exist without human knowledge of them. Distinguishing between the world and our experiences of it has been important to my understanding of critical realism and the research that I embarked on. Bhaskar, the originator of critical realism, distinguishes between the *Intransitive Dimension* (ID), i.e., knowledge not produced by humans at all, such as knowledge about the universe, and *Transitive Dimension* (TD), e.g., the theories that humans have about the universe that change with time. Another aspect of this ontology states that reality is not simple and so is stratified into three domains of *The Real Domain, The Actual Domain, and The Empirical Domain*, and these have become crucial for my research as will be showcased. The *Real Domain* is whatever exists whether humans have knowledge of it or not (Sayer 2000). The *Real Domain* of reality can include physical items like coal or social like bureaucracies (Sayer 2000) and these possess structures and causal powers (passive or activated) called 'mechanisms' (Shipway 2011). The *Actual Domain* of reality is about the events which occur in the world as a result of activating the structures and mechanisms of the *Real Domain*. The *Empirical Domain* of reality relates to the individual experiences each person has with what happens in the world. This *Empirical Domain* was the focus of one of my first choices of philosophical view for my research. It was chosen to underlabour my research on the phenomenon of *parent engagement* because ultimately the participants were experiencing a reality about which I sought information. I will explain how it falls short of a comprehensive view of reality and why critical realism became more suited to underlabour my research.

The Journey to Critical Realism as the Philosophical Underlabouring of the Research

Interpretivism was the earlier choice of paradigm which is associated with the ontological position of constructivism. Constructivism holds that there are multiple realities that are "constructed in and out of interaction between human beings and their world and developed and transmitted within an essentially social context" (Crotty 1998, 42) and as such different human beings can have a different understanding of the same phenomenon. This resonated because the participants in my study would express their interpretations of their experiences with parent engagement. Interpretivism was thought to be a good fit for an earlier focus on implementing a professional development programme developing *parent engagement* in a primary school. Since the purpose of the research was exploring the experiences of the participants in a professional development programme, *Parents in Partnership*, the constructivist approach that honoured the individual perspectives of the teachers, parents, and students of that cohort was chosen.

However, the problem with the constructivist paradigm for this research is that too much emphasis is put on the realities experienced by the individual participants in the *Empirical Domain* and the *Actual Domain*, and I have since recognised that each person has a different recollection and perception of events and see it from their perspective and experience it through their unique life circumstance. Using the interpretivist paradigm, findings are interpreted, and this interpretation is an inductive process. In attempting to understand the meaning the phenomenon *parent engagement* has for those involved, the researcher builds towards theory from observations and intuitive understandings gleaned from working with the teachers, parents, and students of the cohort (Merriam 2002). Although the description of stakeholders' experiences allows for deeper understandings of the phenomenon of *parent engagement* and the development of home school partnerships from each of their perspectives, the researcher cannot go beyond simply conveying the position and perspectives of the participants. I felt hindered by this. My 'missionary zeal', as one of my supervisors labelled the need to have a positive effect on the world and share my new-found knowledge of the benefits of *parent engagement* with others, is important for me. Education has an emancipatory mission which critical realism allows researchers to explore beyond what is experienced and observed. From my experience, the transferability of research using the constructivist/interpretivist ontological view to other situations, in this case other school contexts, is the responsibility of the reader who believes what the researcher has found and recognises that it (or any part of it) to be transferable, rather than the responsibility of the original researcher to make it transferable (Lincoln and Guba 1985).

On the other hand, although, critical realists have the concept of multiple perceptions in common with constructivists, they differ in their belief that these perceptions are about a single, mind-independent reality. Bhaskar's stratified reality allowed this research to explore not only the *Empirical Domain* of teachers' perceptions of the role of *parent engagement* in the stratified activity of educating their students but also to acknowledge that part of that stratified reality of educating students happens outside of school, especially in the home. According to Goodall (2021), teachers can be unaware of, or discount, the effect of *parent engagement,* such as a parent reading to the child in the home or the soccer coach teaching how to co-operate as a team, because this happens in the *Actual Domain*. The *Real Domain* holds "the mechanisms that can produce events in the world" (Blom and Moren 2011, 62).

According to Blom and Moren (2011, 63) critical realism "changes the focus from events that can be empirically observed to generative mechanisms" ... "that actually exist in the world but are to be regarded as potential or tendential". As the aim of the research was to explore what conditions were needed for teachers to embrace parent engagement in their teaching practice, the concept of critical realism of generative mechanisms allows for the exploration of what encourages and constrains in all three domains. In other words, what generative mechanisms are needed to trigger this reality. Hence, the *Real Domain* holds the potential of all parents to engage with their child's learning as well as the potential for teachers to embrace *parent engagement* in their teaching practice and the ability of education systems to develop the culture and practices to enhance the potential of all students to flourish in life by embracing parent engagement.

Using the explanatory power of critical realism, and connecting fact and value, allowed me to hypothesise about the generative mechanisms based partly on empirical observations but also using analytical means (Blom and Moren 2011, 63). Explanatory power is what critical realists describe as *judgemental rationality* which allows researchers to "assert that there are criteria for judging which accounts about the world are better or worse" (Archer et al. 2016, n.p.). The researcher has the ability to use this explanatory power to compare the alternative theories of the multiple possible explanations in the *Transitive Dimension* (TD). A judgement can be made in the TD because this dimension holds the theories that humans have about the universe which change with time as opposed to the *Intransitive Dimension* (ID) which holds truths about reality that humans may not be aware of (yet). This judgement for my research was about which of the possible explanations has a set of mechanisms which will interact to generate teachers embracing *parent engagement* in their teaching practice (Wynn and Williams 2012, 795). However, the epistemological position of critical realism acknowledges that these judgements, and the theory developed about reality, are relative to the historical, social, and cultural context of the time in which the events took place, which means it is also fallible and emergent (Archer et al. 2016, n.p.). *Epistemic Relativism* is the term used by critical realists to describe theories that are pertinent to a particular context and time and can change as context and time changes and a new awareness of knowledge emerges. My research explored the *epistemic relativism* of teachers as they became more aware of the benefits of parent engagement in their teaching practice. Teachers uninformed approach to the theory of teaching and learning in relation to parent engagement became infallible and a new theory emerged.

As a researcher, I was now armed with a broader perspective of reality which allowed more analysis from the experiences of the individual participants. Critical realism permitted these more detailed causal explanations in terms of both the individual participants' interpretations as well as the structures and mechanisms that interacted to enable or constrain teachers embracing *parent engagement* in their teaching practice. However, before I reached this stage in the journey there was one more philosophical underlabouring of this research. Another change in supervisor and with this came a change in philosophical view, this time that of Pierre Bourdieu. Again, I was very much guided by the particular philosophical area of interest of the supervisor. I will outline below what drew me to the work of the French sociologist.

The Journey Takes Another Twist

Working in a school environment for many years one comes to realise that it is more than just the individual actors that create reality. There are many influences: the seen and unseen; from areas of government to education system requirements;

through to public expectations. The constructivist's ontological view is that reality is constructed from the engagement of each person with their own reality (Feast and Melles 2010). This subjective construction of knowledge had relevance to this research because individuals in schools are exposed to the same objective rules and systems but each, in their own individual way, navigates through these, yet I was aware that there could be more to an analysis than this. Bourdieu's concepts of *habitus, field and capital* (Bourdieu 1977) suggest a different way of knowing – a 'transcendence' of the two traditional forms of knowing: *subjectivist* usually associated with constructivism and qualitative methods of research; and *objectivist* usually associated positivism and quantitative methods of research. This he called 'praxeological knowledge' (Bourdieu 1977). Praxeological knowledge, or practical reason, is Bourdieu's own version of knowledge and has emphasis on "being inherently reflexive since it turns back the epistemology of analysis onto the analysis and those who analyse" (Grenfell 2007, 210).

When relating Bourdieu's theory of knowledge to the field of education, Lingard and Christie (2003) suggest it:

> deals with what has been a central theoretical conundrum for sociology; that is, how one gives recognition to the impact of structures and social facts upon individual practices, while simultaneously recognizing the recursive nature of the impact of individual practices on such structures. This is the structure/agency dilemma of modernist social theory. It suggests that what we do is framed by the institutional structures in which we are located, but that those structures are in turn the sedimented effects of previous acts of human agency and power relations.
> (Lingard and Christie 2003, 60)

Bourdieu (1990, 122) saw himself as a 'constructivist structuralist' or 'structuralist constructivist' as he saw strengths and weakness in both approaches to knowledge. According to Webb et al. (2002, 32), Bourdieu accepted that subjectivism was useful in that it draws attention to the ways in which agents, at a practical, everyday level, negotiate various attempts by for example, governments, bureaucracies, institutions, capitalism, to tell them what to do, behave, and how to think:

> but it [subjectivism] fails to take into account the close connection between the objective structures of a culture, which include the values, ideas, desires and narratives produced by, and characteristic of, cultural institutions such as the family, religious groups, education systems and government bodies, on the one hand, and the specific tendencies, activities, values and dispositions of individuals, on the other,
> (Webb et al. 2002, 32)

Structuralist constructivism is not unlike the position held by critical realism. Critical realism holds a realist view of ontology that there is a mind-independent reality. In doing so it also has points in common with the 'objective' ontological view of positivism but differs in that instead of proposing that there is a single concrete reality, realism suggests there are multiple perceptions and multiple possible explanations about a single mind-independent reality (Wynn and Williams 2012). Hence, critical realism steers a 'middle path' between positivism and constructivism yet "leverages elements of both to provide new approaches to developing knowledge" (Wynn and Williams 2012, 787). As such critical realists acknowledge the role of the subjective knowledge of the social actors, as does constructivism, as well as "the existence of independent structures that constrain and enable these actors to pursue certain actions in a particular setting" (Wynn and Williams 2012, 788).

So why the change to critical realism. You guessed it another change in research supervision. Along came Brad Shipway (2011) author in this area and now my passionate supervisor. That was one reason, but the more I read not only his work and that of other writers in this area the more it made sense, even though it is not always written in language easy to understand. The strong ontological position on reality that things can exist without human knowledge resonated with my religious upbringing. Together with the ability to use explanatory nature of critical realism to go further than just explore the empirical experiences of humans and develop theory on the generative mechanisms that need to be present for teachers to embrace parent engagement are two of its aspects that were of interest to me.

However, on a personal level, as an educator and now researcher, I want to have an impact on the students with whom I work, and the readers of my work. The constructivist/interpretivist view falls short in allowing me as a researcher 'to make things better' and move towards the emancipation of teachers and parents and in doing so enhance students' learning. In some ways, Bourdieu's work has been used to show how schools contributed to social reproduction and continuing inequality in society (Lareau 1987). On the other hand, Bhaskar's concept of the *primacy of absence* leading to the idea of emancipation as 'absenting constraints on absenting absences' has allowed me to explore the absenting of the constraining factors such as the absence of training, the absence of understanding of parent engagement and its effects on student achievement which were identified in the review of literature. The emancipatory impetus in critical realism allowed me to explore different *modes of power relations* that were used by teachers depending on their positioning of parent knowledge (engagement). Parents were positioned by different teachers along a continuum of 'less knowing' (Pushor 2015) to one of 'partnership', where parental knowledge of their children is dialectically transposed and seen as complementary by teachers and schools to their professional pedagogical knowledge (Pushor 2015). The connecting of fact to value by some critical realists allowed me to make some claims about the conditions under which teachers and families can work together to enhance student learning. *Cautious Ethical Naturalism* as described by Archer et al. (2016, n.p.) below suggests that:

values are open to *empirical* investigation and critique. As a result, in theory at least, insofar as values are concerned with a degree of both empirical and ontological investigation, the social sciences may be able to tell us something about the "good" life or the "good" society and the conditions under which human beings can "flourish".

Conclusion

The importance of an underlabouring meta-theory to research was not fully understood by me or for that matter many of my students who I have just finished marking their mini thesis work for the culmination of their Master of Teaching degree. A person's view of reality, ontology, and how knowledge is constructed within that reality, i.e., their epistemology, affects more than just the methodology chosen for their research but the values and beliefs they choose to live by and apply to their work, in my case, education. The journey I have taken from constructivism to Bourdieu and ultimately to critical realism has been an awakening that just as humans are individuals, so too is their view of the world. By keeping in mind, the different ontological and epistemological perspectives humans hold help to make sense of the world of others, particularly why we might conflict with others.

The benefit of critical realism for me was ultimately the ability to make judgements between differing explanations and develop theories about what could make the world a better place for those requiring emancipation from absences in their lives. The absence in this thesis was that of teachers' embracing parent engagement in their children's learning. The generating mechanisms needed to 'absent this absence' are outlined in the research. Now the goal is to use this knowledge to transform the positioning of parents as less important in their child's education to one of partnership with teachers. A world where parental knowledge of their children is dialectically transposed and seen as complementary by teachers and schools to their professional pedagogical knowledge.

References

Archer, M., C. Decoteau, P. Gorski, D. Little, D. Porpora, T. Rutzou, C. Smith et al. 2016. "What is critical realism?" *Perspectives: A Newsletter of the ASA Theory Section*, Fall 2017 http://www.asatheory.org/current-newsletter-online/what-is-critical-realism.
Blom, B. and S. Moren. 2011. "Analysis of generative mechanisms." *Journal of Critical Realism* 10 (1): 60–79. doi:10.1558/jcr.v10i1.60
Bourdieu, P. 1977. *Outline of a Theory of Practice*, Melbourne: Cambridge University Press.
Bourdieu, P. 1990. *The Logic of Practice*, Cambridge: Polity Press.
Crotty, M. 1998. *The Foundations of Social Science Research: Meaning and Perspective in the Research Process*, Sydney: Allen and Unwin.
Feast, L. and G. Melles. 2010. "Epistemological Positions in Design Research: A Brief Review of the Literature." Paper presented at Connected 2010 2nd International Conference on Design Education, University of New South Wales, 28 June–1 July 2010.

Goodall, J. 2021. "Parental engagement and deficit discourses: absolving the system and solving parents." *Educational Review* 73 (1): 98–110. doi:10.1080/00131911.2018.1559801

Goodall, J. and J. Vorhaus. 2011. *Review of best practice in parental engagement.* Ref: DFE-RR156. Retrieved from UK Department of Education: Institute of Education https://www.gov.uk/government/uploads/system/.../DFE-RR156.pdf

Grenfell, M. J. 2007. *Pierre Bourdieu Education and Training,* New York: Continuum Books.

Hattie, J. 2009. *Visible Learning: A Synthesis of over 800 Meta-analyses Relating to Achievement,* New York: Routledge.

Jeynes, W. 2012. "A meta-analysis of the efficacy of different types of parental involvement programs for urban students." *Urban Education* 47 (4): 706–742. doi:10.1177/0042085912445643.

Lareau, A. 1987. "Social class difference in family–school relationships: The importance of cultural capital." *Sociology of Education* 60: 73–85.

Lincoln, Y. S. and E. G. Guba. 1985. *Naturalistic Inquiry.* London: Sage Publications.

Lingard, B. and P. Christie. 2003. "Leading theory: Bourdieu and the field of educational leadership—an introduction and overview of this special issue." *International Journal of Leadership in Education* 6 (4): 317–333.

Merriam, S. B. 2002. *Qualitative Research in Practice: Examples for Discussion and Analysis.* San Francisco: Jossey-Bass.

Pushor, D. 2015. "Walking alongside: A pedagogy of working with parents and family." In *International Teacher Education: Promising Pedagogies, Part B,* edited by C. Craig and L. Orland-Barak, 233–253. Bingley, UK: Emerald Group Publishing Ltd.

Pushor, D. and T. Amendt. 2018. "Leading an examination of beliefs and assumptions about parents." *School Leadership & Management* 38 (2): 202–221. doi:10.1080/13632434.2018.1439466.

Sayer, A. 2000. *Realism and Social Science.* London: Sage.

Shipway, B. 2011. *A Critical Realist Perspective of Education.* London: Routledge.

Webb, J., T. Schirato, and G. Danaher. 2002. *Understanding Bourdieu.* London: SAGE.

Wynn, D. J. and C. K. Williams. 2012. "Principles for conducting critical realist case study research in information systems." *MIS Quarterly* 36 (3): 787–810.

5
ON THE ANTI-IMPERIALIST POSSIBILITIES OF CRITICAL REALISM

Omar Kaissi

Introduction: Request to Dissent

A colleague involved in Master's dissertation supervision recently shared his regret that he had emphasised the teaching of technical matters related to methodology and methods over what he referred to as the 'fundamentals' of doing research. These fundamentals included the capacity for critical thinking and argumentation as well as the ability to adequately articulate the focus, aims, and contributions of research. I share his regret. If anything, at least from the 1970s onward, the history of research in my field, education, has been marked by a peculiar overemphasis on methodology (see Ball 1997) for a critique of the methodologisation of social theory in the sociology of education. The result has not only been the subordination of ontology to epistemology, but, perhaps more detrimentally, the reduction of the 'sociological imagination' (Mills 1959) to a technicist rendering of methodology.

Indeed, I have encountered such reductivity in my own career as a doctoral researcher. Increasingly disenchanted by the deafening screams of epistemic righteousness from both the positivist and interpretivist diehards of educational research, I began to search for a fresh perspective: a new paradigm, a daring redirection of thought, that could serve as a viable alternative to what were presented to me as *the* settled but competing conventions framing research theory and practice. It is in this context that I found critical realism. As a philosophy of science developed by Roy Bhaskar (1979, 2011) and inscribed into sociology by Margaret Archer (1995, 2000), critical realism stood out to me for three reasons: its emphasis on ontology, its epistemological (and, by extension, methodological) openness, and its subscription to post-positivist notions of truth and rationality.

The aim of this chapter is to expand and build on these reasons to possibilities of using critical realism as an anti-imperialist analytical underlabourer for the social sciences in general and, more specifically, in the field of education. Firstly, I begin by explicating the meaning of anti-imperialism in the context of research methodology. I maintain that, in virtue of its revindication of ontology, critical realism enables modes of theorising and investigating social reality that transcends the imperialist (absolutist) tendencies towards ontic closure in both positivism and interpretivism. Secondly, I present a detailed account of how critical realism was operationalised in my own PhD project – a study of knowledge production in gender and education (G&E) research on boys and masculinities in western contexts. Here, my aim is to demonstrate, in a grounded way, the anti-imperialist capacities of a critical realism-informed methodology. Thirdly and finally, I conclude with some thoughts on critical realism-informed research as a type of high-risk, albeit educative, research whose methodological enhancement entails, beyond research practice, engagement with forms of research activism.

Packing for the Journey: The Anti-Imperialist Possibilities of Critical Realism

There are three reasons as to why critical realism appeals to me. The first is *ontological underlabouring* (Bhaskar 1978), whereby ontology precedes epistemology. Practically speaking, this implies that the researcher treats their research as concerned first and foremost with understanding what constitutes, mediates, and/or governs the relationship between the continuities and contingencies of the event or phenomenon under investigation (DeLanda 2006; Reed 2009; Sayer 2000). In essence, underlabouring is about consciously adopting and working towards realising the presupposition that reality is as much constructed by social agents as it is announced to them. This demands that adequate sociological theorising provides accounts of how, as Archer (1982, 455) has put it, "men [sic] constitut[e] society" while giving explanatory weight to "the social formation of human agents".

The second reason is the *epistemological open-endedness* of critical realism, which is a powerful enabler of methodological versatility. Given that society, as Bhaskar (2011) argues, is an open system, there can be no definitive answers to the question of how to know and/or investigate social reality. Unless and until the researcher is able to present a defensible explanation of the ontological composition of the event or phenomenon that is the subject of their interest, they should not entertain epistemological and methodological claims. In other words, the continuous ontologisation of the social is a must because, as Khun (1962) argues, paradigms are not sacred. What is more, particularly in educational research practice, the continued prevalence of the quantitative-qualitative-pragmatic 'holy trinity' seems to me to betray a certain end-of-ontology doctrine which is incompatible with the ontic-centredness of critical realism.

My third reason is that critical realism is not only at ease with rationality (Moore and Muller 1999) but also holds that a form of truth-laden, *judgmental rationality*, that is, 'mak[ing] rational judgments between competing claims' (Jessop 2005, 43, emphasis added), may be necessary to maximise explanatory power. Indeed, particularly in the field of education, where policy-research relations are abiding (Shain and Ozga 2001) and ethico-normative considerations are crucial, the license for judgmental rationality is indispensable. The example of teaching the Nazi Holocaust is prime here. According to Bhaskar (1979), several claims can be made: (1) that Jews in Europe 'lost their lives', (2) that they were 'killed', and (3) that they were 'systematically murdered'. All three are empirically accurate, but it is the third claim only which can be argued to be the most capable of providing an adequate explanation of what happened.

Collectively, these reasons – ontological underlabouring, epistemological open-endedness and judgmental rationality – constituted my entry point into critical realism. Through them, I have come to view critical realism as a mode of theorising about and/or investigating social reality that is anti-imperialist. My use of this term is inspired by Archer's (2007, 39) critique of positivism and interpretivism as forms of 'sociological imperialism' which constitute two sides of one coin: a problematic relationship with naturalism. Her argument is that, rather than reclaiming the social subject, what interpretivism ended up doing, paradoxically, is reproducing them in exactly the same manner as positivism, that is, 'exclusively as society's gift' (39). In other words, if, in the latter paradigm, the subject is nothing but an object of the 'social physics' of the world (see Lenzer [1975]), in the former paradigm, they are rendered an emergent construction, always *sous rature* (i.e., under erasure) (Derrida 1976), for they contain multitudes of contexts, discourses, meaning-making systems, and mediated connectivities and relationalities which require reiterative deconstruction and historicisation. Hence, for me, both the hyper-naturalist (structuralist-oriented) transcendentalism of positivism and the hypo-naturalist (agentic-oriented) transcendentalism of interpretivism stood guilty of harbouring a certain deep-rooted imperialist tendency to foreclose the possibility of knowing reality *as it is*. To be more precise, it is the possibility of a naturalist knowledge that is capable of explaining reality without falling to those debilitating dualisms (e.g., mind and body; structure and agency) which conflate ontic and epistemic and, in effect, make it difficult to imagine social change.

In short, it is this promise of revindicating ontology in ways which may assist in redressing (and going beyond) the positivist-interpretivist deadlock of imperialisms in the field of education which made critical realism unique in my eyes. And it is with not only a deep appreciation, but also a careful understanding, of this uniqueness that I endeavoured to self-identify as a critical realist, positioning the entirety of my research practice within the territory of critical realism.

The Journey: Operationalising Critical Realism to Investigate Knowledge Production

This section presents a detailed account of the methodological operationalisation of critical realism in my PhD project, "Research corporeality in education: An investigation of knowledge production in gender and education research on boys and masculinities" (Kaissi 2019). The focus of the project was corporeal knowing[1] in G&E research on boys and masculinities in schools in four contexts – UK, US, Canada, and Australia. Through an in-depth examination of both existing literature and the life and career histories of prominent G&E scholars, the project aimed to construct a collective story (Richardson 1997) of scholarship that reveals predominant theoretical, ideological, and political challenges to corporeal knowing in the field of education in general and knowing about boys in particular. Figure 5.1 describes my project's critical realist research design. Using it, I will discuss, step by step, my methodological journey with critical realism. This discussion will then be followed by a set of critical reflections through which the argument for the anti-imperialist analytical capacities or possibilities of critical realism will be made.

The first step of my journey comprised adopting dualistic ontological assumptions regarding the relationship of agency and structure in the field of education. This relationship was conceived as threefold. Firstly, the relationship was taken as *naturalistic*, in the sense that the agency of the G&E scholar and the social structures which inform modes of institutionalised knowledge production in the field cannot be reduced to each other (Bhaskar 1979, 2011). Human agency and social structures were fundamentally different kinds of things. Secondly, the relationship was understood as *morphogenetic*, meaning that social change is possible because structures are "open-ended and not 'finalistic'" (Archer 2007, 37). And thirdly, it was seen as a *strategic*, in the sense that change in modes of knowledge production does not self-emerge, but rather involves complex agentic negotiations of the 'strategic selectivities' of structures that function to "privilege some actors, some identities … some spatial and temporal horizons, some actions over others" (Jessop 2005, 48).

The second step comprised an attempt to extrapolate epistemologically from this view of agency and structure in order to construct a viable model of inquiry about corporeal knowing in G&E research on boys. Building on Bhaskar's (1979) conception of a stratified ontology, I determined that corporeal knowing as a mode of knowledge production can be investigated on the basis of it occurring

Dualistic ontological assumptions → A stratified model of inquiry → Extensive and/or intensive methods and methodologies

FIGURE 5.1 Doing Critical Realist Research: From Assumptions to Methods in Three Steps

on three distinct but interrelated levels: the empirical, the actual, and the real. Then, following Pawson and Tilley (1997), I used the concepts of context, regularity, and causal mechanism as a methodological toolkit to examine knowing across these levels. Each concept, as shown below, was assigned an accurate definition relevant to the aim of investigation:

- *Context*: On the empirical level, there are two contexts in which corporeal knowing occurs: the G&E research literature on boys and masculinities and the life and career histories of G&E scholars in the field of education.
- *Regularity*: On the actual level, there are field structures (e.g., governmental, institutional, and professional) which have the effect either of enabling or constraining the collective agency of G&E scholars in the field. These structures yield ways of and potential limitations to corporeal knowing which are formalised and reified through practice, thus constituting identifiable regularities (patterns or associations).
- *Causal mechanism*: On the real level, ways of and potential limitations to knowing can be explained by positing hypothetical models of generative mechanisms. These models are capable of revealing "what things must go together, and what could happen, given the nature of the objects" (Sayer 2000, 11).

The interrelationship between these concepts – "Regularity = Mechanism + Context" (Pawson and Tilley 1997, xv) – was understood as carrying two fundamental implications for the effective implementation of a critical realism-informed methodology. The first is that any given event, phenomenon or mode of production, such as corporeal knowing, can be explained retroductively, that is, through positing "the causal powers and mechanisms that can produce [it, or, for that matter, produce the regularities through which it materialises on the empirical level]" (Hu 2018, as quoted in Price and Martin 2018, 90). The second is that the causal workings of hypothetical models of generative mechanisms are not fixed, but rather impacted by the conditions of change or permanence that agents produce and reproduce in their daily interactive relationships within social fields (Collier 1994).

Finally, having made these ontological, epistemological, and methodological choices, the third step comprised selecting appropriate research methods and processes. Critical realism gives equal recognition to the value and explanatory potentialities of both quantitative and qualitative approaches (Sayer 1992), and so opting exclusively for qualitative methods was not taken to be incompatible with the critical realist underpinnings of research design. Moreover, it is the context of investigation at every stage of my project which predetermined the choice of methods. To illustrate, I provide below a brief account of each context, showing how data generation, analysis, and interpretation were conducted concurrently with my critical realist methodological toolkit to uncover mechanisms.

For the G&E research literature, the first context of investigation, I used the integrative literature review (Torraco 2005) as a data generation and analysis method to construct a representative sample of documents in the form of journal articles. This sample was analysed inductively to generate conceptual themes (e.g., masculinities and social class) and, from these themes, infer regularities that reflect predominant ways of knowing (e.g., individual agency) and limitations to knowing (e.g., childhood sexuality) about boys. Analysis, then, was followed by a "creative process [of interpretation]" (Torraco 2005, 362) using both the extant literature and the theories capable of explaining inferred regularities. Two hypothetical models of generative mechanisms – the shift from sociological to social theory in the sociology of education (a theoretical mechanism) and the sociocultural construction of childhood in western societies (an ideological mechanism) – were posited as a result of this process. The potentially causal (enabling and/or constraining) workings of these mechanisms on corporeal knowing in the field were subsequently mapped and examined.

As for the life and career histories of G&E scholars, the second context of investigation, I conducted semi-structured interviews with eight scholars from the UK, US, Canada, and Australia. To make sense of the interview data, I borrowed from Holland and Lave (2001, 11) their conceptualisation of social agents' oral histories as dialogical constructs that bring the 'intimate I' to the 'collective We'. The 'I' was understood as reflecting personalised engagement in knowledge production (i.e., scholars as individual knowers); the 'We' was understood as reflecting structured engagement (i.e., scholars as a community of knowers). For each mode of engagement, I used thematic analysis (Braun and Clarke 2006) and social theory (e.g., Bourdieu's [1990] theory of practice to examine structured engagement) to generate themes and infer additional regularities (e.g., the predisposition towards intellectuality) which may pose limitations to knowing about boys. Then, in a way similar to my treatment of the document data, I subjected the interview data to a process of interpretation which enabled me to posit two more, here political, not theoretical or ideological, causal mechanisms – body alienation in academia and state-led hysteresis (i.e., the field-habitus mismatch which, according to Bourdieu [2000], results from structural change).

Upon close examination, what these data-analytic and data-interpretive processes reveal is the complementarity of extensiveness and intensiveness in the methodological operationalisation of critical realism in my project. For, following Sayer (2000, 27), it can be argued that the extensiveness of analysis evident in the 'formal associations or regularities' inferred from G&E scholars' research practice, lives, and careers was (as should be in critical realist inquiry) conveniently succeeded by an intensiveness in interpretation. What I mean by 'intensiveness' here is a theoretical deepening of analysed data intended not only to "seek substantial connections between phenomena" (27), or the observed regularities, but also to posit the causal mechanisms, and the relations between mechanisms, which can provide *real* explanations of why phenomena persist.

Finally, to meet the aim of investigation, I constructed a collective story of scholarship that makes visible the most pressing theoretical, ideological, and political challenges confronting corporeal knowing in G&E research on boys today. Crafted through synthesising between my four hypothetical models of generative mechanisms, the story makes two main conceptual contributions to the field of education: firstly, it offers an account of the inversely proportional relationship between G&E scholars' epistemic labour, on the one hand, and the de-corporealising labour of positioning in an academic field, on the other; and secondly, it offers a new framework for reflexive research practice. The framework comprises a set of courses of action which call upon G&E scholars to 'own their narrative', to revitalise, continue to practise, and defend their corporeal knowing against policy-driven attempts to redefine what counts as knowledge and who count as knowers in the field of education.

Reflections on Design, Contextuality, and Causality

I now turn to a critical reflection on the research design described above. My aim is to reveal what precisely has led me to think about critical realism as infused with anti-imperialist possibilities for enhancing the theoretical and empirical study of realities, both in education and the wider society.

My findings, the four hypothetical models of generative mechanisms, are neither objective generalisations nor interpretations constructed arbitrarily from the mind of the researcher. Rather, because I have undertaken research as an under-labourer, not a positivist "seafaring explorer" or a constructivist "bricklayer" (Bauman and May 2001, 171), I have come to view them as "empirical possibilities" (Moore and Muller 2002, 634) whose explanatory power depends on the initial conditions of their positing (e.g., the focus of investigation, the research settings, and the theoretical frameworks deployed) remaining intact. That is to say, if they were to be de-contextualised, they would lose their power to yield "a good approximation of the truth" (Popper 1994, 181) at a specific time, in specific places, with specific people and on the basis of specific research choices. For the sake of conceptual clarity, this preconditioning of explanatory power on contextual boundaries and specificities has been referred to in my project as *causal-contextual inter-dependency*; in other words, it is because, not in spite, of the contextual that the causal is possible, and efficacious.

To defend this notion of inter-dependency, I had to show how each of my hypothetical models of generative mechanisms complied with it. For example, regarding the shift from sociological to social theory, I argued that the fact that social theory is predominant in the social sciences today does not mean that it, the shift, can be considered to be (equally) causally efficacious everywhere, outside the specific field of study where it was initially posited. To be sure, inter-field synergies are undeniable, but to entertain them, I contended, would necessitate an alteration of initial conditions (here, scope of inquiry) which risks destabilising the mechanism in question in such a way that it may end up mis-firing, mis-explaining, within both the 'guest context', whatever that may be, and the 'host context', the field of education. It is through this reasoning that I have come to realise that the causal and contextual are inextricably linked. To use a metaphor, contextuality is a necessary straitjacket for causality; the more qualified the understanding of contextualities, the more plausible, better informed, and defensible the causal mechanisms and relations purported to explain the real nature of things.

Thus, it is in thinking about ontological underlabouring in critical realist research as an invitation to rewrite, not write off, the interrelationship of the causal and contextual that the argument for the anti-imperialist possibilities of critical realism started to take shape in my mind. As I see it, critical realism-informed methodology is neither context-exclusionary (positivist imperialism) nor context-revolutionary (interpretivist imperialism). Nor is it context-transcendent (post-qualitative imperialism) or context-diffusionary (new-materialist imperialism). Rather, as simple as it may sound, it must be *context-respecting*. In other words, because critical realism acknowledges the contributions of contextualist social science to illuminating the world "as a text, as discursively constructed" (Apple 1993, 307), it respects deeply the notion of the contextual and seeks to articulate its intrinsic causativeness. Indeed, for me, this is precisely why critical realism should be at the forefront of the methodological advancement of social science: it is needed to make possible a philosophy of naturalism that grounds causation within the situated, emergent, and open-ended nature of things.

Particularly in the field of education, if such alarming developments as positivistic methodologism (Lather 2016) are to be properly tackled, the question of the possibility of naturalistic reconciliation between contextuality and causality should be seen as imperative. And, perhaps, the first challenging step in this regard is to look for ways in which the causal can be used to liberate the contextual from the imperialist epistemological tendencies of both positivist and interpretivist schools of thought. These tendencies, contrary to what the post-structuralists and post-modernists of the paradigm wars had envisaged (see Bryman [2008]), culminated in the over-theorisation and, thus, reduction of the contextual to a state of disposability, to being nothing but that which Bhaskar (2011, viii), citing Locke, describes as "rubbish ... [laying] in the way to knowledge". This is unfortunate, for just as the causal need not be a relic, something to historicise rather than continuously seek, the contextual need not be rubbish.

What Next? Towards Progress *for* Methodology

Rutzou (2016) argues that there is antagonism towards critical realism in the social sciences. I concur. However, I contend that it is not so much antagonism informed by objections to critical realism's ontological presuppositions or epistemological frailty (see Pratt [2013]) but one that stems from serious *ontological fear*, that is, the fear of accepting that 'what is', by dint of 'that is' being complex, requires constant examination. Or, if not fear, it could be what Banfield (2016, 3) describes as 'ontological shyness' rooted in a deep suspicion of naturalism, one which can lead to "block[ing] our [i.e., scholars'] vision of the 'sociological imagination'" (Wexler 2000, 11). In any case, be it fear, shyness or – why not? – sheer indifference, it seems to me that it is "the seriousness with which critical realism takes ontology" (Banfield 2016, 3) that raises eyebrows about its foundations, aims, and the value of its contributions to social science research.

Admittedly, I have no wider empirical evidence to support this claim about anti-critical realism antagonism. Instead, what I have is my own personal experience as an academic researcher whose choice to work with critical realism had at times felt like a punishment, a deviance from the order of the day which, to quote Delamont (2005, 95), "deserves to be hit with a thunderbolt for presumption". (It is tempting here to add that, had it not been for my preoccupation with defending critical realism, I would have had enough time to muse over my PhD project and put forth such arguments as the one presented in this chapter regarding the anti-imperialist analytical possibilities of critical realism. Hence why I am ever grateful to the editors of this book!) In conclusion, then, what I shall do is share and reflect on a mini anecdote to present what I think is the most pressing challenge confronting us, critical realist scholars and researchers, in the field of education and beyond.

In 2019, I participated in the Fifth Annual Conference of the *Centre for the Study of Global Ethics* at The University of Birmingham, UK. The theme for that year was 'Bodies and embodiments', and the aim of my presentation was to examine the personal and professional implications of one of the four hypothetical models of generative mechanisms posited in my project: body alienation in academia. Sadly, it did not go well. In Q&A, one audience member objected: "What is new about all this? Okay, scholars are tired, but people will always complain anyway". I have to confess, I went speechless. I couldn't argue back. In retrospect, however, I think I should have replied by emphasising that critical realism-informed research is not interested in unknowns ('What is new about all this?'), but rather in explanations which may, only may, point us to the causal workings of things – to what lurks beneath empirical reality, on the real level. That is to say, I should have clarified that my research was not so much about working conditions in academia (empirical reality) as about the attempt to find a causal link between the declining status of corporeal knowing, on the one hand, and the endangerment of academics' bodies, on the other (see Barcan 2013) for a compelling account of the effects of output-oriented accountabilities on academics' physical and mental health. In philosophical terms, what I was trying to do is explain whether and how *corpus* partakes of the conditioning of *logos* and vice versa.

According to Biesta et al. (2019, 3), "research that operates in a problem-posing rather than a problem-solving mode is ... not just research on or about or for education, but is, in a sense, itself *a form of education* as it tries to change mindsets and common perceptions" (emphasis added). For me, critical realism-informed research is exactly that type of research. In addition to offering itself as a meta-theoretical framework of understanding (Archer et al. 2016), its educative functions include the centralisation of ontology, ontological underlabouring, and, as I have argued throughout this chapter, the possibility of an analytical anti-imperialism vis-à-vis questions of contextuality and causality. The problem, however, is that more needs to be done to present and promote critical realism as a form of education in and of itself, for, judging by my conference experience, there is not only antagonism towards it but also a great amount of ignorance about it.

This brings me to my final point. On its own, progress *through* methodology, by which I mean the technical concern with enhancing the robustness of research designs, won't suffice to make the case for critical realism-informed research. What we need, too, is progress *for* methodology, by which I mean forms of activism aimed at better presenting critical realism – what it is, what it does, and why others should listen and engage with it more seriously. This is precisely the direction in which I intend to steer the next chapter of my methodological journey. As I continue to do critical realist research in the field of education, I will aim to build alliances with other critical realist scholars and researchers to educate colleagues, including students, about critical realism. There is also the need, more broadly, to educate our fellow citizens, but I will leave this subject for another opportunity.

Note

1 Corporeal knowing is my own compound conceptual term. In my PhD project, it denotes a mode of knowledge production in the social sciences that is anti-naturalist in three main respects: (1) its naïve ontological transcendentalism, evident in claims to the possibility of knowing through the collapsing of dualistic distinctions (e.g., structure and agency) and de-valuing of dualism itself, even on the analytical level; (2) its predominantly interpretivist episteme, evident in philosophical and methodological claims to the possibility (and superiority) of knowing which places emphasis, sometimes exclusively, on the bodily modalities of knowledge (e.g., identity, embodiment, voice, and experience); and (3) its axiological liberationism, evident in claims that knowing must be tied not to the nature of things (what *is*), but rather to the possibility of becoming-ness of things (what *ought*).

References

Apple, M. W. 1993. "What Post-modernists Forget: Cultural Capital and Official Knowledge." *Curriculum Studies* 1 (3): 301–316. doi: 10.1080/0965975930010301

Archer, M. S. 1982. "Morphogenesis Versus Structuration: On Combining Structure and Action." *The British Journal of Sociology* 33 (4): 455–483. doi: 10.2307/589357

Archer, M. S. 1995. *Realist Social Theory: The Morphogenetic Approach.* Cambridge: Cambridge University Press.

Archer, M. S. 2000. *Being Human: The Problem of Agency.* Cambridge: Cambridge University Press.

Archer, M. S. 2007. "The Trajectory of the Morphogenetic Approach: An Account in the First-Person." *Sociologia, Problemas e Práticas* 54: 35–47. https://sociologiapp.iscte-iul.pt/pdfs/54/550.pdf

Archer, M. S., C. Decoteau, P. Gorski, D. Little, D. Porpora, and H. R. Bernard. 2016. "What Is Critical Realism?" *Perspectives*. Advance online publication. http://www.asatheory.org/current-newsletter-online/what-is-critical-realism

Ball, S. J. 1997. "Policy Sociology and Critical Social Research: A Personal Review of Recent Education Policy and Policy Research." *British Educational Research Journal* 23 (3): 257–274. doi: 10.1080/0141192970230302

Banfield, G. 2016. *Critical Realism for Marxist Sociology of Education*. Oxon: Routledge.

Barcan, R. 2013. *Academic Life and Labour in the New University: Hope and Other Choices*. London: Routledge.

Bauman, Z., and T. May. 2001. *Thinking Sociologically*. Malden: Blackwell.

Bhaskar, R. 1978. *A Realist Theory of Science*. Hassocks: Harvester Press.

Bhaskar, R. 1979. *The Possibility of Naturalism: A Philosophical Critique of the Contemporary Human Sciences*. Atlantic Highlands: Humanities Press.

Bhaskar, R. 2011. *Reclaiming Reality: A Critical Introduction to Contemporary Philosophy*. London: Routledge.

Biesta, G., O. Filippakou, E. Wainwright, and D. Aldridge. 2019. "Why Educational Research Should Not Just Solve Problems, But Should Cause Them As Well." *British Educational Research Journal* 45 (1): 1–4. doi: 10.1002/berj.3509

Bourdieu, P. 1990. *The Logic of Practice*. Translated and edited by Richard Nice. Stanford: Stanford University Press.

Bourdieu, P. 2000. *Pascalian Meditations*. Cambridge: Polity.

Braun, V., and V. Clarke. 2006. "Using Thematic Analysis in Psychology." *Qualitative Research in Psychology* 3 (2): 77–101. doi: 10.1191/1478088706qp063oa

Bryman, A. 2008. "The End of the Paradigm Wars?" In *The SAGE Handbook of Social Research Methods*, edited by Pertti Alasuutari, Leonard Bickman and Julia Brannen, 12–25. London: Sage.

Collier, A. 1994. *Critical Realism: An Introduction to Roy Bhaskar's Philosophy*. London: Verso.

Delamont, S. 2005. "Four Great Gates: Dilemmas, Directions and Distractions in Educational Research." *Research Papers in Education* 20 (1): 85–100. doi: 10.1080/0267152052000341345

DeLanda, M. 2006. *A New Philosophy of Society: Assemblage Theory and Social Complexity*. London: Continuum.

Derrida, J. 1976. *Of Grammatology*. Translated and edited by Gayatri C. Spivak. Baltimore: Johns Hopkins University Press.

Holland, D., and J. Lave. 2001. "History in Person: An Introduction." In *History in Person: Enduring Struggles, Contentious Practice, Intimate Identities*, edited by Dorothy Holland and Jean Lave, 3–37. Santa Fe: School of American Research Press.

Hu, X. 2018. "Methodological Implications of Critical Realism for Entrepreneurship Research." *Journal of Critical Realism* 17 (2): 118–139. doi: 10.1080/14767430.2018.1454705

Jessop, B. 2005. "Critical Realism and the Strategic-Relational Approach." *New Formations: A Journal of Culture, Theory and Politics* 56: 40–53. https://www.researchgate.net/publication/263691122_Critical_Realism_and_the_Strategic-Relational_Approach

Kaissi, O. 2019. "Research corporeality in education: An investigation of knowledge production in gender and education research on boys and masculinities." PhD diss., The University of Manchester.

Khun, T. S. 1962. *The Structure of Scientific Revolutions*. Chicago: Chicago University Press.

Lather, P. 2016. "Post-face: Cultural Studies of Numeracy." *Cultural Studies ↔ Critical Methodologies* 16 (5): 502–505. doi: 10.1177/1532708616655771

Lenzer, G., ed. 1975. *Auguste Comte and Positivism: The Essential Writings*. New York: Harper & Row.
Mills, C. W. 1959. *The Sociological Imagination*. Oxford: Oxford University Press.
Moore, R., and J. Muller. 1999. "The Discourse of 'Voice' and the Problem of Knowledge and Identity in the Sociology of Education." *British Journal of Sociology of Education* 20 (2): 189–206. doi: 10.1080/01425699995407
Moore, R., and J. Muller. 2002. "The Growth of Knowledge and the Discursive Gap." *British Journal of Sociology of Education* 23 (4): 627–637. doi: 10.1080/0142569022000038477
Pawson, R., and N. Tilley. 1997. *Realistic Evaluation*. London: Sage.
Popper, K. 1994. *The Myth of the Framework: In Defense of Science and Rationality*. London: Routledge.
Pratt, A. C. 2013. "'… The Point Is to Change It': Critical Realism and Human Geography." *Dialogues in Human Geography* 3 (1): 26–29. doi: 10.1177/2043820613485048
Price, L., and L. Martin. 2018. "Introduction to the Special Issue: Applied Critical Realism in the Social Sciences." *Journal of Critical Realism* 17 (2): 89–96. doi: 10.1080/14767430.2018.1468148
Reed, M. 2009. "Critical Realism: Philosophy, Method or Philosophy in Search of a Method." In *The Sage Handbook of Organizational Research Methods*, edited by David Buchanan and Alan Bryman, 430–448. London: Sage.
Richardson, L. 1997. *Fields of Play: Constructing an Academic Life*. New Brunswick: Rutgers University Press.
Rutzou, T. 2016. "Putting Critical Realism into Practice." *Critical Realism Network*. Advance online publication. http://criticalrealismnetwork.org/2016/01/11/putting-critical-realism-into-practice/
Sayer, A. 1992. *Method in Social Science: A Realist Approach*. London: Routledge.
Sayer, A. 2000. *Realism and Social Science*. London: Sage.
Shain, F., and J. Ozga. 2001. "Problems and Issues in the Sociology of Education." *British Journal of Sociology of Education* 22 (1): 109–120. doi: 10.1080/01425690020030819
Torraco, R. J. 2005. "Writing Integrative Literature Reviews: Guidelines and Examples." *Human Resource Development Review* 4 (3): 356–367. doi: 10.1177/1534484305278283
Wexler, P. 2000. *Mystical Society: An Emerging Social Vision*. Boulder: Westview Press

6
COBBLING TOGETHER METHODS FOR A COHERENT CRITICAL REALIST METHODOLOGY

Searching for Mechanisms

Bree Weizenegger

Introduction

I discovered critical realism by happy accident. At the time, I was just beginning my PhD journey and grappling with how to conduct research into the causes of change for victim/survivors engaging in feminist-informed, sexual assault counselling. While I wanted to adopt a qualitative feminist research approach, I was struggling with aligning its traditionally postmodernist and social constructionist methodologies with an area of human experience that undeniably impacts the material reality of its victims. It felt like there was a fundamental incompatibility between the philosophy of these methodological approaches and the lived experience of victims of sexual violence.

For me, these incompatibilities were twofold. Firstly, sexual violence has real material consequences beyond the ways in which it is linguistically constructed. I did not want to use methodologies that could reduce victims' experience of violence to the language that constitutes it. I resonated with statements within the critical realist literature such as the following: "While it is true that social life is linguistic, we cannot then conclude that social life exists only in language… Therefore, while we have a concept of *hunger*, this concept is not the end of the story; the physical lack of food is also important" (Bhaskar, Danermark, and Price 2018, 80).

Secondly, I did not want to use methodologies that promoted a view of reality as subjectively constructed and, thus, that there are no truth-like discoveries we can make about the common experience of sexual violence or its recovery. We must be realists to commit to emancipatory knowledge and practice; it is a matter of necessity that we do say something about the common experience of sexual violence beyond an individual subjective reality if we are to discover ways of collectively preventing and addressing its impacts. Material feminist academic Susan

Hekman highlights the importance of this commitment to realism for political endeavours when she writes: "Feminists want to be able to make statements about reality – that women are oppressed; that their social, economic, and political status is inferior to that of men; that they suffer sexual abuse at the hands of men. If everything is a linguistic construction, then these claims lose their meaning. They become only one more interpretation of an infinitely malleable reality" (2010, 3).

After centuries of the reality of sexual violence being denied, and the experience of sexual violence being so individualised that victims believed they might be uniquely alone, I thought it an important political commitment that my research did not unwittingly replicate these injustices by adopting a relativist approach. I therefore investigated alternative feminist philosophy and theory – namely material feminism – and it was via this circuitous route that I stumbled upon critical realism.

What attracted me most to critical realism were its depth ontology and the possibility of researching those things which occupy many feminist counsellors' minds: structures of oppression, their internalisation, and a non-reductive understanding of their impact on the experience of being human. Better yet, critical realism offers a philosophy that acknowledges the structures of both our social world – and minds – as *real* (Bhaskar, Danermark, and Price 2018; Collier 1994; Danermark, Ekström, and Karlsson 2019). The structures of oppression may not be real in the same way as the bones in my hand or the dirt beneath my feet, however they are real in the sense that they are *causally efficacious*; their existence in the world *causes things to happen* and – regardless of whether we can directly observe them or not – because they cause observable effects, they are real and thus researchable (Porpora 2015).

When I discovered critical realism, I felt like I had found the philosophy that was capable of 'underlabouring' my research (Bhaskar and Danermark 2006, 282). Bhaskar, along with his collaborators and successors, has provided us with a meta-theory capable of conceiving the world as common sense[1] imagines it to be (i.e., the world is obviously not just constant conjunctions, nor just subjective experiences), and in the process has provided us with the conceptual tools to research those things which are hidden – but causally efficacious – to establish a critical explanatory social science.

Of course, for those of us who become interested in utilising critical realism in our research, the question quickly arises: 'But how?' As I was descending further and further into the writings of critical realism to try and answer this methodological question, my primary supervisor, Professor Louise Harms, gently asked me during a supervision session: 'How do you want to use critical realism within your research? As an umbrella, or as a raincoat?' I think she was tactfully giving me the option to not get too deeply lost in philosophy. I somewhat defiantly replied, 'A raincoat!' but, I knew I was not entirely telling the truth: by this stage, critical realism had already gotten under my skin.

Resultantly, the only answer to the question 'But how?' became 'Somehow', and this chapter represents a partial account of the ways in which I stumbled about as a non-philosophically trained social worker, trying to work out the 'how' of doing critical realist research. I offer here my confusion and subsequent decision-making as a transparent account of my experience working with critical realism in the hope that it may offer some useful reflections or guidance or, maybe, reassurance in other researchers' struggles. I describe below the critical realist research stages of 'abduction' and 'retroduction', using examples from my own data, to introduce the different methods I cobbled together to create a critical realist-aligned methodology. I also discuss the significant difficulties I experienced in trying to understand the difference between retrodiction and retroduction, and my attempts to complete these inferential steps. The account below is partial, but so may be the logic and deployment of methods; all errors are humbly my own.

Choosing Coherent Methods

Even though there is no pre-packaged, ready-to-use 'critical realist methodology',[2] critical realism's unique ontological and epistemological configuration has methodological *implications* for method selection. Foremost among these is the inclusion of methods that can accommodate the depth analysis required to search for mechanisms operating at levels deeper than the empirical (Bhaskar, Danermark, and Price 2018). This therefore excludes methodological designs that rest solely on inductive or deductive approaches. Rather, designs must instead include methods that can accommodate the use of abduction and retroduction (Bhaskar 2016; Danermark, Ekström, and Karlsson 2019). Another way to state this is: coherent methods for critical realism must accommodate the use of pre-existing theory. This is because it is not within the empirical data that we search for mechanisms but, rather, within the ontological depths of the Real. It is a move of retroductive abstraction requiring the use of theory to discover something about causation. I thus cobbled together my methodology utilising:

- Bhaskar's model of scientific activity, offering the steps of analysis to guide my research process: this is the RRRIREI(C)[3] model (Bhaskar 2016, 79–82; Bhaskar, Danermark, and Price 2018, 46);
- a version of thematic analysis known as 'template analysis' to conduct data analysis (Brooks et al. 2015; King 2004); and
- an adapted version of the 'context, mechanism, outcome' (CMO) heuristic popularised by realist evaluation (Blom and Morén 2010; Pawson and Tilley 1997) to support the conceptualisation of mechanisms.

A Note on RRRIREI(C)

In developing a new philosophy of science, Bhaskar outlined the steps required for the social sciences to conduct explanatory research; this is how those of us new to critical realist research know to use abduction, retroduction, or retrodiction (e.g., Bhaskar 2008, 125; 2014, 305). These models of scientific activity appear briefly in Bhaskar's writings as the acronyms 'RRREI(C)' (utilising the logic of retrodiction) and 'DREI(C)' (utilising the logic of retroduction),[4] but how to conduct this kind of scientific activity is not fully explained. In later publications Bhaskar combined both these models to form a unified general model, the 'RRRIREI(C)' model of scientific activity (e.g., Bhaskar 2016, 80–81). I chose this model as it was helpfully suggested to me by Dr Leigh Price when I presented my initial research plan at the 2018 International Association of Critical Realism's (IACR) PhD course in Lillehammer, Norway.

Into the methodological gap of Bhaskar's earlier writing stepped Danermark and colleagues (Danermark, Ekström, and Karlsson 2019; Danermark et al. 2002), providing a resource in the form of their book *Explaining Society: Critical Realism in the Social Sciences*. In it, they explicate and extend Bhaskar's previous writings on the conduct of social science research and offer methodological guidelines for those wishing to engage in explanatory social science research. Judging by the frequency with which it is referenced in critical realist research, their book has become indispensable in providing researchers the tools to understand critical realism's methodological requirements. It took me some time to work out that the steps outlined in Bhaskar's RRRIREI(C) were comparable to those of Danermark and colleagues – as Table 6.1 shows.[5]

The model similarities meant that at those times when there was not enough information in Bhaskar's writing about RRRIREI(C), I could draw on the work of Danermark and colleagues (Danermark, Ekström, and Karlsson 2019; Danermark et al. 2002) and those who had used this reference in their own research (e.g., Craig and Bigby 2015; Eastwood, Jalaludin, and Kemp 2014; Raduescu and Vassey 2008, 2009). Below I discuss how I tackled the second and third steps in Bhaskar's RRRIREI(C) model – abductive re-description and retroduction.

Abductive Re-description

I began abductive re-description when I engaged with my empirical data and commenced coding interview transcripts. In the abductive re-description stage of the scientific process, we are beginning to see and redescribe the empirical

TABLE 6.1 Stages of Explanatory Critical Realist Research: Model Comparison

Danermark and colleagues	*Bhaskar's RRRIREI(C)*
1. Description	1. Resolution
2. Analytic resolution	2. Abductive re-description
3. Abduction and theoretical re-description	3. Retroduction
4. Retroduction	4. Inference to the best explanation
5. Retrodiction and contextualisation	5. Retrodiction
	6. Elimination
	7. Identification of antecedents
	8. Correction

data as *something else*. This 'something else' is often a reframing or re-conceptualisation of the empirical data that allows for new connections to be made and new ideas regarding causation to emerge (Lennox and Jurdi-Hage 2017). An example from within my research might help to illustrate this stage: a victim/survivor participant stated that before she commenced feminist counselling, she felt to blame for the numerous acts of sexual violence committed against her. With reference to a man masturbating in front of her on the train, she states:

> I remember the other counsellor saying to me 'And why do you think that happened?' And she wanted me to say, 'Because that was a bad person sitting opposite me on the train.' And instead of seeing that all I could see was, I don't know, I should have found a carriage where there were more people. It's like I had to find the answers myself. But all I've got is these twenty years of self-blame. I couldn't dig my way through that to see the situation for what it was.

If I were to code this data inductively, I might choose codes such as 'self-blame' or 'finding own answers for causes of sexual violence'. To abductively redescribe this data, utilising theories from within my discipline of sexual assault and feminist counselling, I redescribed this section of data as 'internalisation of rape myths'.[6] However, if I were a psychologist-researcher using discipline specific knowledge to redescribe this data, I might code it as 'cognitive distortion'. Neither abduction is wrong – remember the purpose of abductive re-description is to re-conceptualise data so that it might tell us something about causation. However, while the psychologist-researcher is drawing on a micro-regress to theories of cognition and neurophysiology to explain this participant's self-blame, I – as a feminist-researcher – am using a 'macro-regress' (Sayer 1992, 119) to social structures to explain causes of victim self-blame (i.e., the reproduction of patriarchy through rape myths).[7]

Being able to complete a macro-regress is a gift of critical realist ontology – social structures themselves may not be visible in an empirical sense, however they are real in the sense that they are causally efficacious. This participant's self-blame is evidence of such social structures. However, the psychologist-researcher's own professional ontology and epistemology prevent her from conceptualising or investigating it and, thus, may offer an incomplete picture of causation regarding emotional and mental distress. Abductive re-description therefore begins the process of conceptualising empirical data in different ways to reveal the possible mechanisms responsible.

Coding

I want to speak briefly here about my coding of the data, as I completed it across stages one and two of RRRIREI(C). I used a form of thematic coding known as 'template analysis' (Brooks et al. 2015; King 2004). Template analysis is not bound by any one epistemology and, like general thematic analysis, can be applied across a wide range of theoretical and epistemological approaches (Braun and Clarke 2006; Brooks et al. 2015). What distinguishes template analysis from other forms of thematic analysis is its use of *a priori* codes. Coding is therefore not inductive. Rather, it is guided instead by pre-defined codes decided by the researcher and drawn from knowledge and theories within their field (Brooks et al. 2015). These *a priori* codes are formalised into a list of codes – a 'template' – and used to categorise the data. Realist social work researcher, Mansoor A. F. Kazi, has also referred to the template codes as 'bins' (2003, 45) to sort data.

The list of codes initially included in the template is not intended to be exhaustive but rather to provide 'higher-order' codes to guide analysis (King 2004). Further codes are added to the template during analysis, usually as 'lower-order' codes underneath the original ones. This hierarchical coding allows for an analysis of the data at increasing levels of specificity (King 2004), as the original codes will almost inevitably be too imprecise or inaccurate for any meaningful qualitative data analysis. I constructed the initial higher-order codes for the template from my research aims (e.g., impacts of sexual violence, theories used by counsellor/advocates), my interview questions (e.g., what changes have you noticed? Why do you think these occurred?), and possible indicators of the use and effects of different clinical interventions (e.g., feminist, trauma, common factors, etc.).

It is this use of *a priori* codes that drew me to template analysis as a method for critical realist research. The stages of explanatory social science research require the use of pre-existing theory through which to contextualise and redescribe the research data (Bhaskar, Danermark, and Price 2018; Danermark, Ekström, and Karlsson 2019). Employing a method of data coding that restricts analysis of the data to only that which is contained within the data – in other words, induction – is ontologically shallow as it remains at the level of the empirical.[8]

CMOs in Data Analysis

Once I completed data coding, I confronted the task of trying to arrange the coded data such that I could begin to map mechanisms more precisely. To do this, I used an adapted version of the 'CMO' heuristic (Pawson and Tilley 1997), known as 'CAIMeR' (Blom and Morén 2010). Swedish social workers Björn Blom and Stefan Morén adapted the original CMO concept to develop a more sensitive and relevant model for use in complex human services interventions. CAIMeR is an acronym for: context, actors, interventions, mechanisms, and results.

Using the CAIMeR conceptual framework to support the discovery of mechanisms involved a multi-step process. First, I unpacked my data into an Excel spreadsheet. I did this so as to more completely abduct each piece of data; while I had coded my interview transcripts in NVivo by assigning them abducted codes, the data in each code was still in the participants' original words. I therefore

Methods for a Coherent Critical Realist Methodology   69

TABLE 6.2 Data Abduction and Coding

Abducted code	Original data	Abducted data
Increase in self-worth	She's giving an acknowledgement to me, and I'm like 'Oh, she's helping me and wanting to extend the sessions, maybe I'm not a bad person, maybe I'm not so bad as I think I am.' Which is really giving me that validation of, someone I really respect is helping me so therefore I must be okay. So that's been a huge thing as well	When my counsellor advocated for me, I felt an increase in self-worth
Being seen as worthy by the counsellor	(As above)	My counsellor valuing me, allowed me to value myself

'opened up' (i.e., unpacked) those codes which I believed were relevant to the categories of CAIMeR, by summarising and rewriting the data *as if* it were being restated through the lens of the abducted code. I provide a detailed example to illustrate this below and in Table 6.2.

A victim participant within my own research described how her perception of herself as a bad person changed during counselling; she believed this change was in part due to her counsellor advocating for her to receive additional sessions from the agency. I had previously abducted this empirical data during coding using clinical theories regarding the impact of complex post-traumatic stress disorder: the two codes are 'Increase in self-worth' and 'being seen as worthy by the counsellor' (first column in Table 6.2). When I unpacked these two codes into the Excel spreadsheet, I restated each of the original data excerpts (second column) into a summarised version using the frame of the abducted code (third column).

The second step in contextualising my data using the CAIMeR framework involved printing out the entire third column which contained the relevant now-abducted data excerpts and, after cutting out each of the individual excerpts, I arranged them under the CAIMeR headings on (many) sheets of A1 paper. The two examples above were slotted under 'result' (i.e., an increase in self-worth) and 'mechanism' (i.e., being seen as worthy by the counsellor). I continued this with all the now-abducted data excerpts, placing each under the CAIMeR heading I believed it to be relevant to. As per suggestions within realist evaluation (e.g., Pawson 2013, 21–23), I did not 'generalise' the data, but rather attempted to maintain the individual context, actor, intervention, and result sequence for each participant.

From the CAIMeR configurations, I began to see repeated patterns emerge in relation to the changes participants experienced during counselling (R), interventions that evoked these (I), and mediating contextual factors (C). At this stage, I had included participant ideas of mechanisms (M) in the CAIMeR configuration (answers to my interview question 'What do you think caused that change?'), however participant accounts of reality may be partial and, therefore, fallible (Bhaskar 2016, 60). Staying at this level of analysis would not result in the discovery of causative mechanisms; this level of analysis is more akin to constructionist and postmodernist research that uses induction to highlight the multiple perspectives of its participants. For identification of mechanisms, further steps of analysis are required.

Searching for Mechanisms
Attempt #1: Leading with retrodiction

Retroduction and retrodiction are both included in Bhaskar's RRRIREI(C) model and, while I had read everything I could find on retrodiction,[9] trying to synthesise various disjointed accounts left me with confusion regarding their use during analysis. Retrodiction is a method of analysis to be used when the researcher already knows the mechanisms likely to be in operation, and the aim of the research is to identify *which combination* of these known mechanisms have been activated in this *context* to create the results we empirically observe (Bhaskar, Danermark, and Price 2018; Elder-Vass 2015). Because the researcher is drawing on knowledge of the tendencies of *known mechanisms* in a retrodictive analysis, there is likely to be a comprehensive body of knowledge already available within the researcher's field of study to draw upon (Danermark, Ekström, and Karlsson 2019). For my research – because there is already established clinical literature in the fields of sexual assault, feminist counselling, and trauma counselling – I believed that the mechanisms would already be well known and thus retrodiction was the correct analysis to use. However, while this may be true to a certain extent, when I began attempting to identify mechanisms, I did not know how to begin using the existing literature with my data to do so.[10] I will describe my first attempt at doing so, before outlining my corrections.

I began my retrodictive analysis by focusing in on the mechanisms (M) within my CAIMeR configurations. One of the common results (R) I had identified using the CAIMeR heuristic was a reduction in self-blame for victim/survivors. And this reduction seemed to be regularly preceded by discussion in counselling (interventions (I)) about gender roles and rape myths. So, a pattern had emerged between intervention (I) and result (R), and I began to search for the intervening mechanisms (M) that might explain this connection.

I began searching for mechanisms within the existing clinical literature by asking myself, 'What in this literature could articulate the mechanisms that are creating these results?' However, identification of the mechanisms eluded me. I found I could easily identify the general theories that contained the possible mechanisms – literature around consciousness raising, rape myths, gender roles – but when I came to identify the *actual* mechanisms in a precise way, I could not. I tried variations on the general theories – exposing rape myths, undoing rape myths, a shift in consciousness, awareness of gender roles, etc. – however none of these seemed to be precise enough. How would I know when I had identified the correct mechanism, I wondered? I really wasn't sure.

I sought the advice of an academic at my university who I knew to utilise a realist approach in research – Dr Brad Astbury.[11] After describing my difficulty in identifying more precise mechanisms, Dr Astbury gave the advice that attempting to identify mechanisms solely out of the data (i.e., inductively) may not illuminate as much as hoped, and it is often necessary and fruitful to also look to established critical social theory for mechanisms (personal communication, June 7, 2019). I was initially confused, as I believed that I *was* looking at theory to attempt to identify my mechanisms and *not* identifying them out of the data. However, in trying to understand these issues, I slowly began to realise my errors. I had believed I was using a retrodictive analysis but, rather than first articulating the known mechanisms from the literature and then turning to the data to *identify* which of these mechanisms were operating in this context, I was focusing instead on trying to *search* for mechanisms essentially from within the data. I was trying to complete a flawed version of retroduction instead of retroduction, and doing it all inductively, by trying to find correlations between my abducted data and the literature. What became apparent to me was that I needed to *begin* with retroduction in order to penetrate the domain of the real – my attempt at what I thought was retroduction had left me hopelessly inductive.

Attempt #2: Leading with retroduction

In a retroductive analysis, we are trying to identify mechanisms that may explain the event under study (Bhaskar 2016). To begin this, we ask: 'What must be true for X to be the case?', where X is the phenomenon we are witnessing (Danermark, Ekström, and Karlsson 2019). However, what makes retroduction a scientific inference rather than a pure act of creativity is *understanding the fundamental nature of mechanisms*. We are asking our retroductive question within the context of how the world works which, within a critical realist ontology, is in part explained by the structure and action of mechanisms.

Mechanisms consist of structures, which are those things which make it what it is and act the way it does (i.e., constitute its powers and liabilities [Danermark, Ekström, and Karlsson 2019]). When completing a retroductive analysis, we are therefore not generally asking 'what must be true?', but more specifically 'what must be true of the structures which might produce these effects?' (Sayer 1992). So, with the *structure* of mechanisms in mind, I asked myself the question: What structures must be in existence, what basic conditions must exist, for participants to experience a shift in their emotional and psychological processes (self-blame) once they are introduced to ideas regarding social power (gender roles) and false beliefs (rape myths)?

I began free association writing about this. For what I was seeing to have occurred, it must be true that there are structures in society that promulgate ideas about what it entails to behave like a man and a woman, and who is responsible when sexual violence occurs. It also must be true that humans have their own internal structures which mean they have the liability to be shaped by society, to internalise ideas that may not reflect the reality of social relations. It must also be true that humans have their own structures that prevent this process of socialisation from being known to them.

With these thoughts about structures in mind, I started investigating critical social theory regarding dominant ideology and false ideology. I rediscovered the Marxian concept of 'false consciousness' (Augoustinos 1999), a concept describing the way in which individuals within society are prevented from seeing the dynamics of social power that cause and perpetuate systems and relationships of oppression (Mullaly 2002). Instead, dominant ideology positions members of the oppressed groups as either causing, or being deserving of, their oppression (Jost 1995). A false consciousness is therefore held when an individual or group of individuals have a 'false' understanding regarding the causes of their experience of disadvantage, suffering, or oppression.

In locating this theory, I believe I had discovered a more precise way of describing a mechanism whose actualisation I was seeing in my empirical data – *a change to false consciousness*, which allowed victims to see previously obscured social dynamics and resulted in a new understanding of the causes of sexual violence (i.e., 'it wasn't my fault').[12] Of course, there are further important steps in the RRRIREI(C) research process to test and refine the presence and activation of this mechanism. But, at this point, I felt quite thrilled that I had used the steps of retroduction and 'discovered' something in my data that I hadn't quite seen before.

Concluding Remarks

As you may have concluded by now, I found using critical realism within my research *hard*. This is not an uncommon proclamation from many of my fellow students and realist researchers I have variously met at conferences and study groups. Our many tortured complaints include the density of philosophical concepts, the lack of readily available methodology, and the general mental labour of having to re-imagine our research through different ontological levels and domains. You can see from my account above how each of these difficulties tripped me up, at different times, on my research journey. But I didn't consider choosing a different philosophical or methodological path. Why? Because at the risk of sounding trite, or twee, there can be no other option in the social and psychological sciences when we are pursuing emancipatory changes to knowledge and practice. We require a meta-theory that can be maximally inclusive as to causally relevant levels of reality (Bhaskar and Danermark 2006). In a complex open system, answers to the causes – and cures – of human suffering require this maximal inclusiveness. I therefore firmly believe that the difficulties involved in working through the methodological requirements of a critical realist study are well worth the final causal explanations – and I enthusiastically encourage you to discover this yourself.

Notes

1 Common sense realism is a basic assumption of critical realism, that is, objects exist and endure independently of their being perceived (see Psillos [2007, 399]).
2 And, more importantly, nor should there be – methods must be adapted to suit the particular object/s and levels under study, and thus decided upon individually for each research study (Danermark, Ekström, and Karlsson 2019).
3 RRRIREI(C) stands for: resolution, abductive re-description, retroduction, inference to the best explanation, retrodiction, elimination, identification of antecedents and, correction. Also see Table 6.1.
4 RRREI(C) is an acronym for: resolution, abductive re-description, retroduction, elimination, identification of causal antecedents, and correction. DREI(C) is an acronym for: description, retroduction, elimination, identification of causal antecedents, and correction. For further information, see Bhaskar (2010, 2016) and Bhaskar, Danermark, and Price (2018).
5 This is now more so the case, as retroduction has been explicitly named and included in the second edition of *Explaining Society* (Danermark, Ekstrom, and Karlsson 2019, 129–130).
6 Rape myths is a term from within the sexual assault research field which describes false beliefs that are widely held by members of society that serve to either minimise the nature of sexual violence, blame the victim, or excuse the perpetrator (Lonsway and Fitzgerald 1994). Examples are: she was dressed provocatively so she must have wanted it; she kissed him so she was sending mixed signals; real rape is committed by strangers; only depraved men rape, etc.
7 Any discussion of critical realist ontology or research is incomplete without an understanding of 'level stratification' (Elder-Vass 2007, 160). We must know the level, or lamination of levels, that we are using within our research to appropriately abduct and retroduct the data. For further information on the level stratification of reality, see Danermark, Ekström, and Karlsson (2019, 50–52); Elder-Vass (2007); Collier (1994).
8 I am familiar with arguments stating the inclusion of abduction in second-generation constructivist grounded theory (CGT) (Charmaz 2016; Reichertz 2007) transforms CGT into a usable methodology for critical realist studies. I have several objections to this integration – too great to detail here – which pertain to the following: abduction and retroduction are not the same thing (e.g. Chiasson 2005; Danermark, Ekström, and Karlsson 2019) and retroduction *must* be included in critical realist research; there is a lack of ontology within CGT and thus an impossibility of discovering mechanisms and their powers, relations, and tendencies; and, there is a lack of clear steps in CGT regarding how to choose between competing theories (e.g., judgemental rationality). Attempts at integration of CGT and critical realism in a theoretical (e.g., Oliver 2012) and applied (e.g., Kempster and Parry 2014) vein have not specifically addressed these issues, although this has not stopped the increasing appearance of critical realist research using 'GT' as its entire methodology. More work is needed to integrate grounded theory and critical realism to produce a coherent 'critical realist grounded theory' methodology.
9 I couldn't find a comprehensive account of retroduction in a single source. I had to synthesise brief descriptions from multiple sources to more fully understand it. Apart from Bhaskar, Danermark, and Price (2018, 51 and 111) and Danermark, Ekström, and Karlsson (2019, 129), I suggest Pratten (2007, 196), Lawson (1997, 243–244), McAvoy and Butler (2017, 2018), Wynn and Williams (2012), and Isaksen (2016).
10 I now believe that the realist evaluation process of first defining programme theories is a very good model of retrodictive analysis. In my first attempt described above, I was essentially using my data to search for my programme theories – a backwards and incorrect analysis.

11 Dr Astbury has himself published on the phenomenon of mechanisms and identifying them in research analysis. See Astbury and Leeuw (2010) and Astbury (2018).
12 Although embraced by early feminist theorists, the idea of a 'false consciousness' has fallen into disrepute due to the inherent inference that "some women [are] simply deluded while… other women [have] the ability to see the truth" (MacKinnon 1983, 637). False consciousness therefore fell victim to the relativist approach to research and theorising that popularised the idea that no one truth exists, and all subjectivities are correct. As a realist researcher, I believe that there does exist false or inaccurate knowledge about the world – this is a fundamental tenet of distinguishing ontology from epistemology. Bhaskar himself discussed the idea of false consciousness as a "disjuncture, mismatch or lack of correspondence… between belief and object" (2009, 120). Although the task of *determining whose perspective* is false, and how to determine such things, involves moral complexity, I do not believe we should shy away from (i.e., become irrealist about) the idea that false ideas exist and have the potential to harm humans, non-humans, and our wider social and ecological systems.

References

Astbury, B. 2018. "Making Claims Using Realist Methods." In *Doing Realist Research*, edited by N. Emmel, J. Greenhalgh, A. Manzano, M. Monaghan, and S. Dalkin, 60–78. London: Sage Publications.
Astbury, B. and F.L. Leeuw. 2010. "Unpacking Black Boxes: Mechanisms and Theory Building in Evaluation." *American Journal of Evaluation* 31(3): 363–381. https://doi.org/10.1177/1098214010371972.
Augoustinos, M. 1999. "Ideology, False Consciousness and Psychology." *Theory & Psychology* 9(3): 295–312. https://doi.org/doi.org/10.1177/0959354399093002.
Bhaskar, R. 2008. *A Realist Theory of Science*. 2nd ed. London: Routledge.
Bhaskar, R. 2009. *Scientific Realism and Human Emancipation*. Routledge. https://doi.org/10.4324/9780203879849.
Bhaskar, R. 2014. *The Possibility of Naturalism: A Philosophical Critique of the Contemporary Human Sciences*. 4th ed. London: Routledge.
Bhaskar, R. 2016. *Enlightened Common Sense: The Philosophy of Critical Realism*. London: Routledge.
Bhaskar, R. and B. Danermark. 2006. "Meta-theory, Interdisciplinarity and Disability Research: A Critical Realist Perspective." *Scandinavian Journal of Disability Research* 8(4): 278–297. https://doi.org/10.1080/15017410600914329.
Bhaskar, R., B. Danermark, and L. Price. 2018. *Interdisciplinarity and Wellbeing: A Critical Realist Theory of Interdisciplinarity*. London: Routledge.
Blom, B. and S. Morén. 2010. "Explaining Social Work Practice—The CAIMeR Theory." *Journal of Social Work* 10(1): 98–119. https://doi.org/10.1177/1468017309350661.
Braun, V. and V. Clarke. 2006. "Using Thematic Analysis in Psychology." *Qualitative Research in Psychology* 3(2): 77–101. https://doi.org/10.1191/1478088706qp063oa.
Brooks, J., S. McCluskey, E. Turley, and N. King. 2015. "The Utility of Template Analysis in Qualitative Psychology Research." *Qualitative Research in Psychology* 12(2): 202–222. https://doi.org/10.1080/14780887.2014.955224.
Charmaz, K. 2016. "Shifting the Grounds: Constructivist Grounded Theory Methods." In *Developing Grounded Theory: The Second Generation*, edited by B.B.J.M. Morse, K. Charmaz, A.E. Clarke, J. Corbin, and P.N. Stern, 94–112. London: Routledge.
Chiasson, P. 2005. "Abduction as an Aspect of Retroduction." *Semiotica* (153): 223–242. https://doi.org/10.1515/semi.2005.2005.153-1-4.223.

Collier, A. 1994. *Critical Realism: An Introduction to Roy Bhaskar's Philosophy*. London: Verso.
Craig, D. and C. Bigby. 2015. "Critical Realism in Social Work Research: Examining Participation of People with Intellectual Disability." *Australian Social Work* 68(3): 309–323. https://doi.org/10.1080/0312407X.2015.1024268.
Danermark, B., M. Ekström, L. Jacobsen, and J.C. Karlsson. 2002. *Explaining Society: Critical Realism in the Social Sciences*. 1st ed. London: Routledge.
Danermark, B., M. Ekström, and J.C. Karlsson. 2019. *Explaining Society: Critical Realism in the Social Sciences*. 2nd ed. London: Routledge.
Eastwood, J.G., B.B. Jalaludin, and L.A. Kemp. 2014. "Realist Explanatory Theory Building Method for Social Epidemiology: A Protocol for a Mixed Method Multilevel Study of Neighbourhood Context and Postnatal Depression." *SpringerPlus* 3(12): 1–12. https://doi.org/10.1186/2193-1801-3-12.
Elder-Vass, D. 2007. "Re-examining Bhaskar's Three Ontological Domains: The Lessons from Emergence." In *Contributions to Social Ontology*, edited by C. Lawson, J.S. Latsis, and N. Martins, 160–177. London: Routledge.
Elder-Vass, D. 2015. "Developing Social Theory Using Critical Realism." *Journal of Critical Realism* 14(1): 80–92. https://doi.org/10.1179/1476743014Z.00000000047.
Hekman, S.J. 2010. *The Material of Knowledge: Feminist Disclosures*. Bloomington: Indiana University Press.
Isaksen, K.R. 2016. "Reclaiming Rational Theory Choice as Central: A Critique of Methodological Applications of Critical Realism." *Journal of Critical Realism* 15(3): 245–262. https://doi.org/10.1080/14767430.2016.1169369.
Jost, J. 1995. "Negative Illusions: Conceptual Clarification and Psychological Evidence Concerning False Consciousness." *Political Psychology* 16(2): 397–424. https://doi.org/10.2307/3791837.
Kazi, M. 2003. *Realist Evaluation in Practice*. London: SAGE Publications.
Kempster, S. and K. Parry. 2014. "Critical Realism and Grounded Theory." In *Studying Organizations Using Critical Realism: A Practical Guide*, edited by P.K. Edwards, J. O'Mahoney, and S. Vincent, 86–108. Oxford: Oxford University Press.
King, N. 2004. "Using Templates in the Thematic Analysis of Text." In *Essential Guide to Qualitative Methods in Organisational Research*, edited by C. Cassell and G. Symon, 256–270. London: SAGE Publications.
Lawson, T. 1997. *Economics and Reality*. London: Routledge Press.
Lennox, R. and R. Jurdi-Hage. 2017. "Beyond the Empirical and the Discursive: The Methodological Implications of Critical Realism for Street Harassment Research." *Women's Studies International Forum* 60: 28–38. https://doi.org/10.1016/j.wsif.2016.11.010.
Lonsway, K.A. and L.F. Fitzgerald. 1994. "Rape Myths." *Psychology of Women Quarterly* 18(2): 133–164. https://doi.org/10.1111/j.1471-6402.1994.tb00448.x.
MacKinnon, C. 1983. "Feminism, Marxism, Method, and the State: Toward Feminist Jurisprudence." *Signs* 8(4): 635–658. https://www.jstor.org/stable/3173687.
McAvoy, J. and T. Butler. 2017. "Causal Framework through Retroduction and Retrodiction." Paper presented at the 25th European Conference on Information Systems (ECIS), Guimarães, Portugal, June 5–10. https://www.researchgate.net/publication/318493985_Causal_Framework_Through_Retroduction_And_Retrodictionrg/10.1080/14767430.2018.1455477.
Mullaly, R.P. 2002. *Challenging Oppression: A Critical Social Work Approach*. Oxford: Oxford University Press.

Oliver, C. 2012. "Critical Realist Grounded Theory: A New Approach for Social Work Research." *British Journal of Social Work* 42(2): 371–387. https://doi.org/10.1093/bjsw/bcr064.

Pawson, R. 2013. *The Science of Evaluation: A Realist Manifesto*. London: SAGE publications.

Pawson, R. and N. Tilley. 1997. *Realistic Evaluation*. London: SAGE Publications.

Porpora, D. 2015. *Reconstructing Sociology: The Critical Realist Approach*. Cambridge: Cambridge University Press.

Pratten, D.P. 2007. "Explanation." In *Dictionary of Critical Realism*, edited by M. Hartwig, 193–196. London: Routledge.

Psillos, S. 2007. "Realism." In *Dictionary of Critical Realism*, edited by M. Hartwig, 397–400. London: Routledge.

Raduescu, C. and I. Vessey. 2008. "Causality in Critical Realist Research: An Analysis of Three Explanatory Frameworks." Paper presented at the 11th International Association for Critical Realism Annual Conference (IACR), London, UK, July 11–13. https://www.researchgate.net/publication/43528895_Causality_in_Critical_Realist_Research_An_Analysis_of_Three_Explanatory_Frameworks.

Raduescu, C. and I. Vessey. 2009. "Methodology in Critical Realist Research: The Mediating Role of Domain Specific Theory." Paper presented at the 15th Americas Conference on Information Systems (AMCIS), San Francisco, United States, August 6–9. https://aisel.aisnet.org/amcis2009/433.

Reichertz, J. 2007. "Abduction: The Logic of Discovery of Grounded Theory." In *The SAGE Handbook of Grounded Theory*, edited by A. Bryant and K. Charmaz, 214–228. London: SAGE Publications.

Sayer, A. 1992. *Method in Social Science: A Realist Approach*. 2nd ed. London: Routledge.

Wynn, D., and C. Williams. 2012. "Principles for Conducting Critical Realist Case Study Research in Information Systems." *MIS Quarterly* 36(3): 787–810. https://doi.org/10.2307/41703481.

7
A CRITICAL REALIST PERSPECTIVE ON THE 'QUALITY AND REFORM DANCE' IN THE AUSTRALIAN VOCATIONAL EDUCATION AND TRAINING (VET) SECTOR

The Road Less Travelled

Deborah Johnson

My journey into critical realism began when I researched the Vocational Education and Training (VET) sector in Australia. This chapter explains my choice of critical realism for this enquiry. Critical realism offered a depth ontology which brought explanatory power to my research. It provided conceptual and methodological strategies to expose the often-hidden dynamics in the Australian VET sector. This chapter establishes why no other research paradigm offered the same opportunities to understand the sector. It also shares my reflective insights when engaging with critical realism as a beginner researcher and the challenges and key learnings experienced.

Critical realism is not a widely applied philosophical perspective in VET research, and as such, this chapter has been entitled 'a road less travelled'. The VET sector in Australia exists in a perpetual state of review and reform, with quality improvement often a stated driver. Critical realism offered a fresh, more nuanced understanding of what is driving the 'quality and reform dance' in Australia's VET sector. My research suggests that this partnership, which I metaphorically refer to as a *dance*, of quality and reform begs appraisal. Applying critical realism to discussion around quality in the VET sector tests the fecundity of critical realism as a depth ontology through which new insights can be revealed. This chapter offers my reflective insights into a critical realism journey. The chapter begins by considering my research context: the Australian VET sector where this journey began. Next, it discusses the ontological and epistemological maze that I experienced as novice researcher and offers critical realism as the way forward, yet the road less travelled. A few key critical realism concepts are then discussed which offer some insights into my approach. Finally, challenges and key learnings are addressed as I negotiated the critical realism journey.

DOI: 10.4324/9781003193784-7

Where My Journey Began

All research enacts an ontological and epistemological position: research is written from somewhere, and *where* matters. Collins reminds us that ontological paradigms provide the lens through which we view the world: "Different lenses necessitate different assumptions about the nature of the world" (2010, 47). Research draws on a pool of ontological lenses. These different lenses are central to competing views of the world and should inform properly conceived research. For Wight, this is grounded in:

> competing visions of how the world is and how it should be ... consider Every ontology is political ... As such, understanding the ontological differences that lie at the heart of competing visions of the world should be the aim of any properly conceived critical discipline.
>
> (Wight 2006, 2)

The researchers' challenge is to recognise and then reflect on the ontological lens that is guiding their research. Examining my ontological positioning was an essential starting point for this research and where my journey with critical realism began. First, we need to consider the research context.

This research was conducted in the Australian VET sector. Decades of research and reform have been conducted into VET (Goozee 2001) to address issues of quality, yet discussions continue to rage and are said to have reached a fever pitch in recent years (Griffin 2017, 7). Why ongoing reform fails to achieve quality remains unanswered. It would seem that quality remains an elusive imperative for the VET sector, with reform its perpetual partner. My research conducted critical discourse analysis into recent review documents to investigate the inherent conceptions of quality driving reform. This research was curious about this 'quality and reform dance'. It sought to bring a deeper understanding of quality to the discourse by exposing underlying mechanisms and causal powers perpetuating this dance. To do so, this research needed a different ontological lens than the discourse it was reviewing. It needed an ontological lens capable of identifying mechanisms operating beneath the surface. An ontology capable of depth analysis and explanatory critique. An ontology capable of identifying mechanisms that may operate at their smoothest when unnoticed or taken for granted. An ontology that asks *why phenomena occur and what mechanisms are driving them?* This research began by searching for such an ontology.

The Road Less Travelled

As a meta-theory, critical realism calls us to engage in self-reflexive research. In steering a mid-way between constructivism and positivism, it calls the researcher to a renewed emphasis on ontology. It encourages the researcher to question the nature of reality. Having engaged in undergraduate and postgraduate study, research was not new to me. In my early research years, the research choice was between constructivist and positivist philosophies. Pereira summarises the distinctions between constructivist and positivist ontologies, stating: "Idealists regard the object of knowledge as human constructs imposed upon the phenomenon and positivists rely on a sequence of events in accounting for the world" (2012, 9). Constructivists see knowledge as mainly context-dependent and constructed by the knower, whilst positivists see knowledge (especially truth-claims) as trans-contextual and something that the knower apprehends, not constructs. Critical realism was only emerging when I was engaged in undergraduate study and was outside of my frame of reference. Given the choices available, my research applied a constructivist lens with qualitative methodologies.

More recently, on commencing my doctoral research in the field of Education, the same choice seemed almost pre-determined. For the beginner researcher, an internet search is likely to generate similar outcomes, with the same preference evident in many key research texts. Consider, for example, Leavy (2017), the prescribed text for my doctoral research studies. As a relatively newer text, it seemed comprehensive – *Research Design: Quantitative, Qualitative, Mixed Methods, Arts-Based, and Community-Based Participatory Research Approaches* – yet *critical realism* was only mentioned superficially when labelled postpositivist. Leavy is not alone. It was not uncommon for me to find critical realism absent in research texts. Perhaps this is because critical realism can be bewildering and even overwhelming to newcomers, especially to those unfamiliar with critical realist language and not grounded in the philosophy (like me at the time). Critical realism is not intuitive. Archer et al. (2016) acknowledge that defining critical realism is not an easy task. Instead, critical realism adopts a meta-theoretical position providing a philosophically informed account of the sciences to support research. Critical realism advocates for a renewed emphasis on ontology. It calls the researcher to engage in a self-reflexive inquiry into our ontology, distinguishing between ontology and epistemology. Perhaps the complexity of the philosophy accounts for its underrepresentation in many mainstream research texts.

However, as the ontological orientation intrinsically informs research, whether acknowledged or not, intentionally considering the research lens is essential. My research was concerned not to describe VET reviews but to *deconstruct* them. It sought to uncover and explain the *mechanisms* that triggered the events. Failure to do so would compromise this research's rigour by allowing its findings to be just another description of the Australian VET sector and, in so doing, perpetuate the very practice that this research was seeking to arrest. To achieve this depth analysis, the ontological lens needed to enable this. At this formative point in my journey, I was introduced to Roy Bhaskar's (1975) philosophy of critical realism by Brad Shipway, one of my doctoral supervisors.

Shipway, an academic and author, introduced critical realism as an approach that positions itself as "an alternative to positivist and interpretivist paradigms and leverages the elements of both to provide new approaches to developing knowledge" (Wynn and Williams 2012, 787). For research seeking to navigate the positivist-constructionism divide, critical realism provides an alternative path between the naïve realism of positivism and constructionism (Fairclough 2005). Although leaving hypothesis testing behind (Olsen 2007), critical realism manages to offer a scientifically grounded way to conduct social science research "in the same way as the concrete or applied natural sciences do" (Collier 1994, 162). It provides an alternate path for researchers. So, my journey with critical realism began as did my exposure to the key tenets of the philosophy. In reality, many critical realism concepts informed my research. However, for this context, only three are offered for discussion. They are the concept of depth ontology, retroduction, and *fact to value* argument.

A Critical Realist Illumination of the Road Less Travelled

As my study aimed to interrogate why the Australian VET sector was engaged in a perpetual 'quality and reform dance', an ontology capable of examining this pattern was essential. Recent national discourse had declared that the Australian VET sector was in crisis, concluding that "there are underlying problems that previous government reviews have not been able to correct or fix" (Mosely, Wrigley and Key 2020, 2). Furthermore, Guthrie and Clayton report that "the number and frequency of policy and implementation failures ... create an image of the sector which suggests that it is unusually susceptible to poor policy decisions. Actual or perceived policy failure conveys a widely held sense of crisis in ... the sector itself" (2018, 7). Given this context, my research needed an ontological and epistemological lens capable of critiquing and interpreting the world and our knowledge of the world (Guba and Lincoln 1994). It needed to interrogate existing facts operating in the sector. Critical realism offered this depth analysis.

Depth ontology

Critical realism is premised on a conception of ontological depth or depth analysis, calling the researcher to a renewed emphasis on ontology. It encourages the researcher to question the nature of reality. It proposes: "When a stratum of reality has been described, the next step should be to examine what mechanisms underlie or intersect" (Joseph 1998, 79). Critical realism questions existing facts and events, using them as a springboard to uncover the "complex, layered and contingent processes or structures which cause those regularities, facts and events" (Archer et al. 2016, 8). For my research, as a depth ontology, critical realism rendered explicit what was implicit and made sense of and explained the world behind *appearances*. Analysis with critical realism provided detailed causal explanations of events and uncovered and described the mechanisms that produced these events. This involved moving beyond facts and events to uncovering the generative mechanisms which created them. For my research to bring a more profound, nuanced understanding to the VET sector, critical realism provided an ontology capable of investigating the structures and processes that produced the facts that were driving reform.

Retroduction

Critical realism achieves depth analysis by a process termed retroduction. Retroduction is a "... mode of inference in which events are explained by postulating [and identifying] mechanisms which are capable of producing them ..." (Sayer 1992a, 107). Retroduction supports reasoning about why things happen, including why data appears the way it does (Olsen 2007, 1). It involves "moving from a conception of some phenomenon of interest to a conception of a different kind of thing (power, mechanism) that could have generated the given phenomenon" (Lawson 1997, 236). In effect, retroduction is a process of moving backwards. It asks, "what must be true in order to make this event possible?" (Easton 2010, 123). As an epistemological process, retroduction identifies mechanisms capable of explaining what caused particular events to occur. Retroduction guided my research to identify generative mechanisms driving the 'quality and reform dance'.

However, at this point in my research, the application of retroduction became daunting. Critical realism is not intuitive. Olsen suggests that while "retroduction is a way of naming the process of getting-to-know, ... there is no recipe for how to do it – just a lot of creative exploration and ethical inquiry" (Olsen 2007, 4). For a new critical realism researcher, my need for direction and structure far outweighed my need for choice. Where to begin? I turned to Bhaskar as founder and seminal author.

Bhaskar proposed a process to support retroductive research. Abbreviated to RRRE (Resolution, Re-description, Retroduction, and Elimination), these four phases were offered as a guide for the critical realism researcher. According to Bhaskar:

- Phase 1 involves the "resolution of a complex event into its components [causal analysis]".
- Phase 2 is the "re-description of component causes".
- Phase 3 is the "retroduction to possible [antecedent] causes of components via independently validated normic statements".
- Phase 4 involves the "elimination of alternative possible causes of components" (Bhaskar 1998, 129).

Initially, Bhaskar's phases and explanations were confounding. However, other authors helped to bring clarity. To engage in retroduction, realist questions need to be asked. They might include "Why do we have data that suggest X exists?" (Olsen 2007, 2) "What must be true for (X) ... to be possible?" (Belfrage and Hauf 2017, 10). The aim is to move from observable phenomena back to possible explanations for those phenomena. Hence the *retro* in retroduction. Examining the historical, political, and social context allows the examination of the claim that X does exist. The arguments that arise allow the realist researcher to move "from a description of some phenomenon to a description of something which produces it or is a condition for it" (Bhaskar 1986, 11). The researcher is then able to propose explanations for X, which are informed by existing theories. They may be "either everyday theories making sense of people's experiences or scientific theories" (Belfrage and Hauf 2017, 10). In practice, retroductive research is an iterative process (Dubois and Gadde 2002) which calls the researcher to move between "observable phenomena and possible explanations in an endeavour to gain deeper knowledge of complex reality making" (Belfrage and Hauf 2017, 10). Over time, the researcher is able to offer alternative theories to explain phenomena to offer an argument that moves from social phenomena to a theory that is able to account for those phenomena, at all times being reflective about the role of the researcher in producing knowledge (Sayer 1992b).

For my research, this retroductive process was indeed iterative. A literature review had established that existing reviews into the Australian VET sector, and their subsequent reforms, failed to achieve quality gains. The literature also established that quality in VET reviews is rarely defined. Given the contested nature of the term *quality*, my research was interested in the paradigms of quality operating. Further, it was interested in the mechanisms driving these paradigms. Easton suggests that the research questions must be of the form "What caused the events associated with the phenomenon to occur?" (2010, 123). For my study, research questions focused on whether the paradigms of quality driving VET reform generated the 'quality and reform dance'. It questioned if there was a misfit between the conceptions of quality operating and the quality gains sought. Engaging critical discourse analysis, this research sought to identify the quality paradigms and to uncover undisclosed philosophies and generative mechanisms driving the reform agenda. In doing this, it aimed to move from observable phenomena to possible explanations for those phenomena. It sought to move from a description of phenomena to a description of what may have produced the phenomena.

Engaging in a process of retroduction, neoliberalism was identified as one generative mechanism operating in VET reviews and driving reform agendas. The research was able to propose explanations for this phenomenon informed by existing theories. In this case, a neoliberal economic theory of rationalisation and privatisation explained the priorities and direction of the reform. Quality was defined as efficiency and productivity, making quality gains an economic venture. At this point in realist research, the researcher offers alternative theories to explain the phenomena. The aim is to offer an argument that moves from social phenomena to a theory that could account for those phenomena (Sayer 1992b). To provide analytical depth, a fact to value argument was developed.

Fact to Value Argument

In research, there is often an assumed divide between *facts* and *values*. Data and statistics generate beliefs to the status of 'fact'. In contrast, critical realism suggests that the value/fact dichotomy is 'leaky' (Gorski 2017, 423). Values seep into our 'facts' and shape them. This is inevitable. Even *what/which* data is deemed as important is itself a *value* decision (Shipway 2011). Rather than denying the impact of values on our research, critical realism argues that research is never situated in a value-free zone. Values influence all research. There is no neutral position from which to view the world or assess theory.

Critical realism contends that humans have beliefs about beliefs and ideas about ideas (Shipway 2011). To challenge these beliefs and ideas, two criteria must be met. Beliefs or ideas can be established as false if a superior explanation exists for the phenomenon. But first, it must be established why these illusory, inadequate, or misleading beliefs were held in the first place. Why there was a mismatch in reality about the belief and what it was about? When analysis addresses these two criteria, it is possible to offer a fact to value argument.

For this research, neoliberalism was proposed as a generative mechanism driving reform in the Australian VET sector. To question its efficacy, a fact to value argument was needed to challenge these existing facts and beliefs. This argument sought to interrogate if a neoliberal philosophy provided a suitable fit to achieve quality gains in the VET sector. This analysis commenced with unpacking the key principles of neoliberalism and why it was considered suitable by its proponents. To establish the contrary, neoliberalism's track record for achieving quality gains in VET then needed review. In developing these arguments, it was possible to establish that there is little evidence that neoliberal principles provide an appropriate fit for VET in Australia. Critics of neoliberalism argue that educators are de-professionalised and delegitimised through education reform (de Saxe, Bucknovitz and Mahoney-Mosedale 2020). Wheelahan adds that the Australian government's neoliberal ideology undermines vocational education institutions (2013). In summary, this fact to value argument established a mismatch between the paradigms of quality driving the VET reform agenda in Australia and the stated priority of quality educational gains. It established a misalignment between the paradigms of quality operating and the outcomes sought.

It has been established that critical realism provided the lens that this research needed to conduct depth analysis into the Australian VET sector. A process of retroduction and the development of a fact to value argument supported this analysis. The following section offers reflective insights on this journey. Included are the challenges for a researcher grappling with critical realism and several key learnings.

Negotiating the Critical Realism Journey

For those interested in research with a socially progressive purpose, critical realism is your choice. For my research, there was an apparent mismatch between the rhetoric in the discourse and what I was observing. The reviews failed to offer adequate explanation to explain the 'quality and review dance'. Something was missing. The research needed to dig deeper. Critical realism offered the capacity to do this. To take that different path, critical realism offered me tools to move from surface level analysis to identifying causal mechanisms generating the patterns that I was observing.

However, commencing the journey with critical realism was challenging. The concepts are complex, and their meanings entwined. Below are my reflective insights into critical realism based on the road I travelled. I gather them under four themes: understanding critical realist language, learning critical realism in its application, clarity of purpose, and accessibility of critical realism research.

Understanding Critical Realist Language

A colleague wanting to understand critical realism purchased Hartwig's (2007) *Dictionary of Critical Realism* as an introductory text. They quickly became disillusioned with the complexity and density of the concepts explained. My experience was the same as I began reading Bhaskar's seminal writings. It was daunting. Critical realism is not for the faint-hearted. Critical realism demands rigorous engagement. It is not possible to 'dip your toe in the water' with this philosophy. The density of the philosophy makes this improbable. To understand one concept, many need to be understood. Yet, to understand many, you need to understand the one. As a beginner researcher, this intellectual rigour created waves of uncertainty that left me questioning my ability to negotiate this philosophy. Yet, at the same time, as new concepts were discovered, their fit and relevance motivated me to keep moving forward.

In hindsight, I reflect that whilst the writing of Roy Bhaskar must be tackled as the seminal author, more accessible texts and sources proved a more fitting starting place. Of particular benefit for me was the critical realism network website. The critical realism network charter is to 'create a community of scholars and educators with the aim of fostering a dialogue about the direction of contemporary social theory and the potential impact of critical realism'.[1] Its forums, webinars, and videos provided an accessible entry point into critical realism concepts, introducing language and notions for the beginner. The critical realism network is championed by the 'Human Flourishing and Critical Realism in the Social Sciences' project, led by Professor Philip Gorski (Sociology, Yale University). The project's goal is to generate broader awareness and understanding of critical realism, and it does so well.

Learning Critical Realism through Its Application

Whilst each of us have preferred ways to negotiate tasks – some read instructions whilst others just 'do it' – my experience of critical realism is that the concepts gained clarity in philosophical application. Progressively reading theory and applying it provided a helpful rhythm. It allowed me to proceed, aware that I did not understand all nuances of the philosophy and yet permitting myself to learn progressively. I have found writing to be a rigorous form of thinking. Tussling with realist concepts whilst writing helped and continues to help consolidate my understanding of the critical realism philosophy. This organic process allowed concepts to be explored as their relevance came into focus. Consequently, I would write and then rewrite, adjusting my work as my understanding deepened. Critical discourse analysis provided a methodology that supported this well. I acknowledge though, that alternative methodologies might not support this fluid process.

Clarity of Purpose

One complexity of researching with critical realism is knowing how to effectively embed the concepts into writing. Initially, I found myself tangled in sentences as I tried to capture and reference all relevant realist concepts. If I wrote of generative mechanisms, should I also refer to stratified domains and intransitive dimensions? Should the role of demi-regularities, practical adequacy, or judgemental rationality be acknowledged? This was partially my need to give legitimacy to my writing by demonstrating an understanding of realist concepts and that my research was rigorous and had intellectual merit. However, it was also in response to critique that critical realism's application is often "simply alluded to without any distinction being made between critical realism as a methodology and its particular application" (Joseph 1998, 73).

As I grappled with writing realist research, I realised that the purpose of my writing would determine how critical realism should be referenced. If the paper's purpose was to demonstrate the merit of critical realism for research, then modelling and explaining the application of specific concepts was vital. There are many examples of this in the literature. Fletcher, for example, elucidates the application of abduction and retroduction in critical realism research. She states: "Abduction and retroduction – the analytical tools available to us as critical scholars – help us move beyond individual explanations or experiences, to draw connections and build explanations through the integration of theory. Sometimes, retroduction may also challenge researchers' own initial theories and expectations" (Fletcher 2020, 184). Fletcher's application of these analytical tools elucidates how to apply them in research. When critical realism is described in this way, showcasing key concepts allows the writing to take form and direction. Likewise, Decoteau (2016) used abduction, abstraction, and retroduction to explore the relationship between structure and agency in ethnographic research.

In contrast, Archer et al.'s (2013) *Critical Realism – Essential Readings*, Hartwig's (2007) *Dictionary of Critical Realism,* and Shipway's (2011) *A Critical Realist Perspective on Education* are examples of writing with a broader purpose. As reference books or tools for the researcher, these sources elucidate realist concepts and unpack the philosophy. For the researcher, being clear about the purpose of each paper will guide the way that critical realism is referenced.

Accessibility of Critical Realist Research

One enduring concern I held was that the complexity of critical realism would interfere with the accessibility of my research for a wider audience. Applying realist language in writing risks confusing or alienating an unfamiliar audience. Critical realism, as a philosophy, has been criticised as being too opaque and deploying too much jargon (Hartwig 2007), with its founder, Bhaskar, having a reputation for 'impossible difficulty, if not downright obscurity' in his writing (Hartwig 2007, xvii). In his *Dictionary of Critical Realism*, Hartwig justifies the complexity of critical realism. He states: "Just as the tools of the various skilled trades need to be precision-engineered for specific, interrelated functions, so meta-theory requires concepts honed for specific interrelated tasks: it is impossible to think creatively at that level without them" (2007, xviii). However, regardless of how this complexity is justified, it risks impacting on the accessibility of realist research, making it exclusive and only available to 'those in the know'. You cannot intuit with critical realism. The complexity of the philosophy does not allow it. My purpose in investigating the VET sector was to draw attention to dynamics operating to inform future discourse on quality and reform in the Australian VET sector. If my philosophical choice interfered with this message, discussions about the VET sector would remain lost in jargon, silencing the research findings.

To address these concerns about accessibility, I developed a novice's glossary of critical realism to supplement my research. This glossary of critical realist terms was intentionally brief. It aimed to orient the reader to the concepts which I referred to without addressing nuances. It sought to provide enough meaning to offer a glimpse into the world of critical realism without endeavouring to fully elucidate the meaning of the terms employed. Writing this glossary for my readers also consolidated my understanding of the concepts being discussed. It is hoped that this glossary ensures that my message about the VET sector was not silenced by the language used.

This journey touched on a few realist concepts in the hope of demonstrating the philosophy's capacity to support depth analysis in research. Critical realism offers a distinctive approach to research by including analytical processes such as retroduction and fact to value analysis. For those interested in rigorous intellectual work with a socially progressive purpose, critical realism enables this.

Conclusion

This chapter presented an emerging researcher's experience of applying critical realism to discourse in the Australian VET sector. The application of critical realism sought to interrogate the 'quality and reform dance' and enabled a more nuanced analysis of the data and its context. Critical realism as a depth ontology offers tools to inform and guide research.

To suggest that this chapter was cursory would be generous. Dictionaries of critical realism have over 500 entries. However, the intention here was to offer a roadmap or guide into realist research to arouse curiosity about the possibilities that this meta-theory can offer. In doing so, this chapter hoped to demonstrate the robust and rigorous nature of critical realism. Critical realism offers a toolkit to equip the researcher to engage in depth and rigorous enquiry. It supports analysis at every step of the research journey. Critical realism has indeed positioned itself in the research world as a properly conceived post-positivist social science philosophy.

Acknowledgements

My journey in critical realism and my doctoral studies has been both enabled and capably supported by the support of three skilled academics who have earned my respect and acknowledgement: Brad Shipway, Chris Zehtner, and Jenny Johnston.

Note

1 https://www.youtube.com/c/CriticalRealismNetwork/featured.

References

Archer, M., R. Bhaskar, A. Collier, T. Lawson, and A. Norrie. 2013. *Critical Realism – Essential Readings*. London: Routledge.
Archer, M., C. Decoteau, P. Gorski, D. Little, D Porpora, T. Rutzou, C. Smith, G. Steinmetx, and F. Vandenberghe. 2016. "What Is Critical Realism?" *Perspectives* 38 (2):4–9.
Belfrage, C., and F. Hauf. 2017. "The Gentle Art of Retroduction: Critical Realism, Cultural Political Economy and Critical Grounded Theory." *Organization Studies* 38 (2):251–271. doi: 10.1177/0170840616663239.
Bhaskar, R. 1975. *A Realist Theory of Science*. Leeds: Leeds Books.
Bhaskar, R. 1986. *Scientific Realism and Human Emancipation*. London: Verso.
Bhaskar, R. 1998. *The Possibility of Naturalism. A Philosophical Critique of the Contemporary Human Sciences*. 4th ed. Hemel Hempstead: Harvester Wheatsheaf.
Collier, A. 1994. *Critical Realism: An Introduction to Roy Bhaskar's Philosophy*. London: Verso.
Collins, H. 2010. *Creative Research: The Theory and Practice of Research for the Creative Industries*. 2nd ed. New York: Bloomsbury Visual Arts.
Decoteau, C. 2016. "The AART of Ethnography: A Critical Realist Explanatory Research Model." *Journal for the Theory of Social Behaviour* 47 (1): doi: 10.1111/jtsb.12107.
deSaxe, J. G., S. Bucknovitz, and F. Mahoney-Mosedale. 2020. "The Deprofessionalization of Educators: An Intersectional Analysis of Neoliberalism and Education "Reform"." *Education and Urban Society* 52 (1):51–69. doi: org/10.1177%2F0013124518786398.
Dubois, A., and L. Gadde. 2002. "Systematic Combining: An Abductive Approach to Case Research." *Journal of Business Research* 55 (7):553–560. doi: 10.1016/S0148-2963(00)00195-8.
Easton, G. 2010. "Critical Realism in Case Study Research." *Industrial Marketing Management* 39 (1):118–128. doi: 10.1016/j.indmarman.2008.06.004.

Fairclough, N. 2005. "Peripheral Vision: Discourse Analysis in Organization Studies: The Case for Critical Realism." *Organizational Studies* 26 (6):915–939. doi: 10.1177/017084060505461.

Fletcher, A. J. 2020. "Critical Realism: Philosophical and Methodological Considerations." In *Qualitative Analysis: Eight Approaches for the Social Sciences*, edited by M. Jarvinen and N. Mik-Meyer, 173–194. London: Sage.

Goozee, G. 2001. *The Development of TAFE in Australia*. 3rd ed. Leabrook: National Centre for Vocational Education Research.

Gorski, P. S. 2017. "From Sinks to Webs: Critical Social Science after the Fact-Value Distinction." *Canadian Review of Sociology* 54 (4):423–444. doi: 10.1111/cars.12169.

Griffin, T. 2017. *Are We All Speaking the Same Language? – Understanding "Quality" in the VET Sector*. Adelaide: National Centre for Vocational Education Research.

Guba, E., and Y. Lincoln. 1994. "Competing Paradigms in Qualitative Research." In *Handbook of Qualitative Research*, edited by N. Denzin and Y. Lincoln, 105–117. Thousand Oaks: Sage.

Guthrie, H., and B. Clayton. 2018. *VET Policy: Processes, Stakeholders and Issues*. Melbourne: Institute University of Melbourne.

Hartwig, M., ed. 2007. *Dictionary of Critical Realism*. London: Routledge.

Joseph, J. 1998. "In Defence of Critical Realism." *Capital and Class* 22 (2):73–106. doi: 10.1177/030981689806500107.

Lawson, T. 1997. *Economics and Reality*. London: Routledge.

Leavy, P. 2017. *Research Design: Quantitative, Qualitative, Mixed Methods, Arts-Based, and Community-Based Participatory Research Approaches*. 1st ed. New York: Guilford.

Mosely, G., C. Wrigley, and T. Key. 2020. "White Spaces for Innovation in Tertiary Education: Australian Public Provider Perspectives." *International Journal of Training Research* 18 (3): 191–210. doi: 10.1080/14480220.2020.1860303.

Olsen, W. 2007. "Critical Realist Explorations in Methodology." *Methodological Innovations Online* 2 (2):1–5. doi: 10.4256/mio.2007.0007.

Pereira, L. 2012. "A Critical Realist Exploration of the Implementation of a New Curriculum in Swaziland." Doctor of Philosophy thesis, Rhodes University.

Sayer, A. 1992a. "Problems of Explanation and the Aims of Social Science." In *Method in Social Science*, edited by A. Sayer, 232–257. London: Routledge.

Sayer, A. 1992b. *Realism and Social Science*. London: Sage.

Shipway, B. 2011. *A Critical Realist Perspective on Education* London: Routledge.

Wheelahan, L. 2013 *The race to the bottom in the VET market & why TAFE cannot win*: IPART Review – Pricing VET under Smart and Skilled. https://www.ipart.nsw.gov.au/sites/default/files/documents/online_submission_-_individual_-_l_wheelahan_-_3_may_2013.pdf

Wight, C. 2006. *Agents, Structures and International Relations: Politics as Ontology*. Cambridge: Cambridge University Press.

Wynn, D., and C. Williams. 2012. "Principles for Conducting Critical Realist Case Study Research in Information Systems." *MIS Quarterly* 36 (3): 787–810. doi: 10.2307/41703481.

8
THE UTILITY OF CRITICAL REALISM IN INDIGENOUS RESEARCH

Cassandra Diamond

This is the story of how I came to discover critical realism, how I've used it to underpin my research, and how I see it complementing Indigenous research methods. In what follows, I explore those critical realist concepts that have had the most utility in my work and have best served to support approaches to Indigenous research.

My introduction to critical realism was courtesy of Ian Mackie and Gary MacLennan in 2018. Dr Gary MacLennan has applied critical realism in his writings ranging from film and poetry to education and Dr Ian Mackie has similarly authored articles featuring critical realist approaches to Indigenous education. I asked them to help me improve some of the resources in a programme I had taken over management of in late 2017. The suggestions they made to the programme contained critical realist content intermingled with other work from writers and philosophers that I had never heard of. In fact, at that stage I wasn't interested in any of it – unless I could see it had a direct practical application to the work I was doing. I'll admit I didn't see any place for philosophy in my work. Practical theory and evidence-based practice was different. My past encounters with philosophy were confined to a university course I took as a student in 1994. It centred on Foucault and I barely passed. Philosophy was like maths to me – another language that I wasn't all that keen to learn.

I stayed in touch with Ian and Gary after our project was completed. Over time they intensified their campaign to get me to pursue a postgraduate research degree. I resisted. But they were persistent. They had an annoying habit of continually introducing me to researchers using critical realism. On one particular occasion, Ian arranged for me to meet Dr Brad Shipway – under the guise of 'just hearing what an honours degree would be like'. By the end of the meeting, I'd decided to enrol in a Bachelor of Education (Honours) with Brad as my

DOI: 10.4324/9781003193784-8

supervisor. At the age of 43, I decided to go back to university – 24 years after my experience with Foucault.

At the same time, I had applied for a new job and decided to wait on the outcome of the recruitment process before working on a research proposal. I won the role and tailored my research to match my job description which tasked me with leading Australia's first national STEM[1] Academy for Aboriginal and Torres Strait Islander females aged 13–25 years. In working on the initial project plan for the Academy, I found very little research or evidence that would help me build an evidence-based programme to drive success for young Indigenous women. I was also wrestling with how to support these students to experience success in mainstream schooling and tertiary education systems that are inherently hostile and racist (Bodkin-Andrews and Carlson 2014). Furthermore, sending them out into workplaces and other institutions that were and continue to be dominated largely by non-Indigenous men (Office of the Chief Scientist 2016) was also problematic.

When I say 'racist' with reference to schools, universities, workplaces, and other institutions, I refer to the institutional racism (grounded in the structures and mechanisms of Australian society) that underpins them. These institutions have been built by and for the people in this country who are of Anglo-Saxon descent and describe their culture and society as 'Western', and for most of this country's history has sought to exclude Aboriginal and Torres Strait Islander people (Bodkin-Andrews and Carlson 2014). They are dominated by false narratives of the 'settlement' of this country, the effects of that 'settlement' and the policies that come with that world view, and they continue to perpetuate institutional racism through inaction. These are the environments where young Aboriginal and Torres Strait Islander women, who are seen as 'other' are expected to succeed (Sarra 2011).

How could I engage young Aboriginal and Torres Strait Islander women in spaces and places that might not be safe for them? How to encourage and support them to succeed when the cards are already stacked against them? How do we show them the long history Aboriginal and Torres Strait Islander people have as scientists and researchers when there are still articles being published that insist that 'western science' is the dominant form of credible knowledge (Pearson 2018)? And more to the point – how do I manage my own anger and frustration and pain to get figure this all out?

Critical realism makes its grand entrance at this stage of my story. I'll admit right now, I'm a novice in terms of my level of insight and understanding into what is an incredible lens through which to view the world. The very first thing I learned about critical realism is that while it is described as a philosophy, it appeared to me as a scaffold that I could use to support the intellectual and emotional challenges of doing my research. I also figured out that critical realism relates well to Indigenous research methods and supports and complements what I wanted to do with my Honours research. I wanted to make very sure that the work I did would be totally focused on building an approach to Indigenous

STEM education that would not only be based on evidence but would work for the young women I was seeking to support.

In choosing critical realism as the underlying philosophy for my research I thought about how well it would support the use of Indigenous research methods. There were a number of elements of critical realism that appealed to me, the first being critical realism's insistence that ontology cannot be reduced to epistemology – that human understanding captures only a tiny part of a larger reality (Fletcher 2017). This stance complements the ontology described by Foley (2003) when discussing the work of Professor West, which points out that Aboriginal and Torres Strait Islander people are very aware of their ontology and understand its nature and origins.

Another aspect of critical realism that appealed to me is the idea of emancipation and goal of human flourishing. As described by Rigney (2006) and Foley (2019), Indigenous research methods and approaches focus on a number of important factors that resonate strongly with the theme of human emancipation in critical realism:

Resistance as the emancipatory imperative – the research is undertaken as part of the struggle by Indigenous people for self-determination.

Political integrity – in order for Indigenous research to further the cause of self-determination and emancipation the research must be undertaken by an Indigenous researcher – this ensures accountability to the Indigenous community who will be impacted by or benefit from the research.

Privilege Indigenous voices – particularly when it comes to research about the lived experience of Indigenous people.

Foley (2019, 27) argued that: "Indigenous methodology is the holistic process of knowledge in its recognition – application, search and at times discovery. I reiterate, it is undertaken for and primarily by Indigenous people for their betterment be this in the metaphysical or physical worlds of the Indigenous academic realm".

Of course, the most useful thing about critical realism for my purposes is the concept of stratified reality or layered ontology (see Table 8.1). The empirical, actual, and real are the layers that form our world (Bhaskar 2008). The idea of layering reality allowed me to think about some of the things I had been wrestling with in a different way.

TABLE 8.1 Layered Ontology (Bhaskar 2008)

Empirical: Events observed or experienced
Actual: Events that may or may not be observed
Real: Causal structures, powers and mechanisms

Thinking about the problems I was wrestling with (institutional racism, the challenge of engaging Aboriginal and Torres Strait Islander women with STEM, and my own personal frustrations at the limitations of the bureaucratic system in which I had to work), I was able to use layered ontology to better understand the issues, and what the way forward might be.

Young Aboriginal and Torres Strait Islander women have a specific set of challenges or experiences in traditional structures such as schools. This is a mind-independent reality. The education they receive and the collective experience of being educated is an event which is both observed and not observed. Finally, the young women have their own experiences and outcomes of being educated, which is the event they personally experience.

Being able to think about this in a way that was almost compartmentalised, helped me analyse the yarns[2] I had collected. What were the experiences? What was being education like for the women I spoke to? What went unseen or was untapped in that process? These kinds of questions allowed me to pick out more from the yarns I collected that I had thought possible and provided me with a rich and deep source of data to work with.

I was also able to make a link between layered ontology and a description of Indigenous Philosophy offered by Foley (2003) shown in Figure 8.1. There are

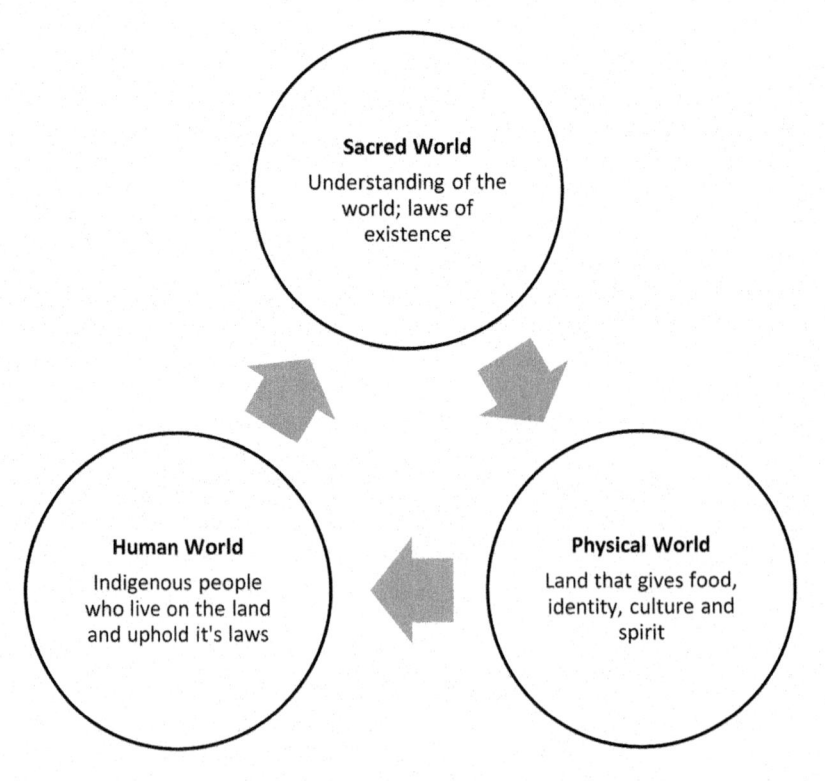

Sacred World
Understanding of the world; laws of existence

Human World
Indigenous people who live on the land and uphold it's laws

Physical World
Land that gives food, identity, culture and spirit

FIGURE 8.1 Indigenous Philosophy

three concepts that exist for Aboriginal and Torres Strait Islander people and their ways of being, knowing, and doing. The sacred world represents our understanding of the world and laws of existence that are crucial for survival. The physical world is the land which gives us our food, culture, spirit, and identity. Finally, the human world is made up of the Aboriginal peoples and Torres Strait Islander peoples who live on the land and uphold it (Figure 8.1).

When I looked at these concepts further, I realised something. The sacred world could also be described as the real world; the empirical layer can also be seen as the human world, and finally the physical world aligns to the actual strata in critical realism. This understanding was helpful for me, it was a contextualised view of two new concepts that made sense to me, and helped me to better understand them both by understanding them together.

To further add to this understanding, the idea human flourishing – and that of the post-modern morphogenetic society (Archer 1995) also wandered in. This idea of a society being one that is in a permanent state of change, with few opportunities to stabilise social norms (Gorski 2017) at first seemed like no big deal to me. I grew up in a time when contemporary information technology was just beginning to develop apace. The internet was still mostly something governments used, and social media wasn't developed to the degree it is today. I remember mobile phones so big they came with their own carry bag. From a personal perspective, I also came from a large family who all lived close by, and all of my understanding of societal norms came from that experience.

Once I started reading and thinking though, particularly about Aboriginal and Torres Strait Islander people on this continent I realised that for us, post-modernity kicked in 242 years ago. We still have access to many of the pre-modern morphostatic ways of being (Archer 1995). These are ways we solidly ground ourselves: a world outlook based on 80,000 years of what I would call, 'good practice'. Of course, I am referring here to human flourishing which I simply take to mean humans living their best lives. Gorski (2017) points out a range of requirements for human flourishing, including having access resources and/or infrastructure that will help them develop skills to engage in the activities that will contribute to their best lives. Add to this the idea that society and people have some latent or untapped potential whose development has been suppressed, and the absence of this manifests in ill-being (Gorski 2017) – what do you get? A description of Aboriginal and Torres Strait Islander people's ongoing struggle to flourish on this continent since invasion.

So, what does this have to do with me and what I was researching? Stepping further along the road to emancipation, I realised that I could provide solid footing for myself and the young women in the work I do by connecting to the knowledge, custom, and lore that had been built and handed down for generations. The students and I had solid, unchanging, unmoving ground that we could stand on when we were uncertain, or worried, or frightened. I do not want to encourage the thinking that Aboriginal and Torres Strait Islander knowledge and practice (traditional) is all pre-modern and 'in the past', that is far from the case. No other civilisation on earth has survived as long as we have, and that is a testament to our adaptability. What I do think is unchanged is our relationships – to one another, to the land and sea, and to our ancestors. It is this that is the 'solid ground' I talk about, the morphostatic ways of being. These ways of being provide us with an anchor in the sea of uncertainty that is our society and postmodern world.

I am an Indigenous woman, a Torres Strait Islander woman to be more precise, who is still impacted by past government policies, specifically, the removal of children. I am unable to identify myself more precisely as my family's access to government records that would allow us to track and find my grandmother's family has been fraught with delays and refusals. I suspect that as my uncles age and tire, I may never get the answers I seek about my own family's history. This means at times I struggle with feelings of anger, frustration, and alienation. My own identity as a black woman is one that has been hard-won and that I am proud of. It does however mean that I am often subject to the stereotype of 'angry black woman' broadly across both my professional and personal life. And I am angry – the words I read and the actions I witness both anger and traumatise me as I continue to research and work in this space.

These ways of being able to think were a revelation to me – I was able to separate out the areas that were bothering me, and then focus my thinking on each without feeling overwhelmed or angry. This way of thinking gave me the ability to do the work without taking on too much in terms of my research questions, and in a conversation, I recall having with my supervisor 'I want to be a slightly annoyed black woman instead of an angry black woman'.

The layered ontology helped me map what the benefit of my research would be – quite simply, I was able to clearly articulate how STEM education would not only do all things the government, schools, and our society expect – increase the chances of these young women to finish high school, go to university, and get jobs. But it would also do the things I wanted it to do – build a generation of young women with skills that would transform their own education and in the long run, their communities.

The approach to 'anchoring' both myself in doing the research and the young women my programme works with has also been something of an 'aha' moment for me. Culture provides safety, it provides connection to family and country. When I conducted my research, I heard in the yarning process a diversity of stories that supported this, and I was able to pick up on concepts that I had not previously considered in my analysis. It also pointed me at ways of doing this for the programme, how to give cultural connection and safety a place or primacy in all the work that we do.

An additional aspect that I find personally exhilarating is epistemic relativism (Sarra 2011). The very idea that what I figure out can be built on and improved by someone coming after me is at the very core of what I want to do. If the creation of knowledge is about digging through layers of reality – you can only dig so far before you run out of time, capacity, money, or will. It's always possible to dig further and figure out more, so the knowledge that we create in our lifetime, or in our research, will absolutely be surpassed. For me, this is so important as a Torres Strait Islander woman, as the goal of my research and work is to create knowledge that will benefit my people. Acknowledging that what I have done isn't 'all there is' allows for me to pass on what I've learnt to others, just as the ancestors who have come before me have passed their knowledge to us, which we have built on, and adapted.

This is where another concept in critical realism that resonates with me, socialisation, a process that allows the 'stocks of skills, competences and habits appropriate to given social contexts' to be passed on (Bhaskar 1998, 36). By researching ways to support young Aboriginal and Torres Strait Islander women to succeed in STEM I was able to also build my knowledge base on what I wanted to pass on to these young women that was different and would ultimately allow them to challenge and transform their education, work, communities, and lives.

By being led through this process by Indigenous research methods and using critical realism to help frame my thinking, I was able to complete a research degree and learn a great deal. I have come away from the experience with ways to further engage in research work in a way that will not hurt me, but I've also been able to translate a lot of my thinking into practice. The programme I manage is using the framework I developed as part of my research degree, the team have developed a cultural safety framework which not only addresses the need for culturally safe service delivery but also to help the young women in the programme build their own personal sense of identity and connection in a safe way. We are supporting the young women in our programme to learn in ways that work for them, we give them access to infrastructure and resources to build skills and we will support them to ultimately succeed and change the worlds in which they live and work.

Notes

1 'Science, Technology, Engineering and Mathematics' – a designated priority area for Australia's National Curriculum.
2 For international readers, the 'yarning' is an Indigenous method that focuses on conversational approaches to get to the truth of things.

References

Archer, M. 1995. *Realist Social Theory: The Morphogenetic Approach.* Cambridge: Cambridge University Press.
Bhaskar, R. 1998. *The Possibility of Naturalism: A Philosophical Critique of the Contemporary Human Sciences.* 3rd ed. London: Routledge.
Bhaskar, R. 2008. *A Realist Theory of Science.* 2nd ed. London: Routledge.
Bodkin-Andrews, G., and B. Carlson. 2014. "The Legacy of Racism and Indigenous Australian Identity within Education." *Race Ethnicity and Education* 19 (4): 33–39.
Fletcher, A.J. 2017. "Applying Critical Realism in Qualitative Research: Methodology Meets Method." *International Journal of Social Research Methodology* 20 (2): 181–194.

Foley, D. 2003. "Indigenous Epistemology and Indigenous Standpoint Theory." *Social Alternatives* 22(1): 44–52.

Foley, D. 2019. "Indigenous Methodology: Is It Invented or Is It Legitimate?" *Journal of Australian Indigenous Issues* 21 (3): 20–39.

Gorski, P. 2017. "Human Flourishing and Human Morphogenesis: A Critical Realist Interpretation and Critique." In *Morphogensis and Human Flourishing, Social Morphogenesis*, edited by Margaret Archer, 29–43. Cham, Switzerland: Springer International Publishing.

Office of the Chief Scientist. 2016. *Australia's STEM Workforce: Science, Technology, Engineering and Mathematics*. Canberra: Australian Government.

Pearson, L. 2018. "Once Again the Daily Telegraph Prefers a Culture War to Facts." *The Guardian Australia*, 2 November. Retrieved from https://www.theguardian.com/commentisfree/2018/nov/02/once-again-the-daily-telegraph-prefers-a-culture-war-to-facts.

Rigney, L.I. 2006. "Indigenous Australian Views on Knowledge Production and Indigenist Research." In *Indigenous Peoples' Wisdom and Power: Affirming Our Knowledge Through Narratives*, edited by N. Kunnie & I. Goduka, 32–50. Hampshire and Burlington: Ashgate.

Sarra, C. 2011. *Strong and Smart – Towards a Pedagogy for Emancipation*. New York: Routledge.

9

THE SPATIALITY OF SCHOOL CHOICE

A Critical Realist Quantitative Geography of Education?

Anna-Maria Fjellman

In this chapter, I do three things. First, I discuss the possibility of asking critical questions in quantitative research and how it is related to critical realism. Second, I discuss my ongoing journey of finding and grappling with critical realism and why critical realism as a philosophy of science attracted me from the beginning. Third, I re-imagine and explore the assumptions of an analysis of the spatiality of school choice in Swedish upper secondary education through a critical realist rationale.

Asking Critical Questions in Quantitative Research

The main challenge with a critical quantitative approach is how the characteristics of quantitative data, measurements, and analytic processes appear to be incompatible with the objective of critical inquiry (e.g., Stage and Wells 2014, 3). The methodological mismatch between critical epistemology and statistical analytical practices and conventions (e.g., generalisability, sampling, causal inference, probability, and bias) is substantial and needs to be bridged (Hernández 2015). Sayer further challenges the usefulness of statistical analysis on an ontological basis and poses the problem with quantification: "What must objects be like for it to be possible to quantify them?" (2010, 177) and follows up with another question: what are quantitative measures *actually* measures of? (2010, 178). Yes, qualitative research is the heart of critical inquiry, but if these differences and difficulties can be bridged, critical quantitative scholarship could be a valuable and important companion to qualitative research (McLaren 2017). The social transformative dimensions of research are not completely lost just because quantitative research (often but not always) does not engage directly with individuals or a community during the research process. There are important processes where a production of quantitative knowledge can influence these processes in socially just ways

(Fjellman, Yang Hansen and Beach 2019, 519), reveal, and attempt to change power structures (Stage 2007).

Throughout my PhD, I predominantly worked with analysing population-based register data through statistical and spatial techniques and measures, such as multiple regression analysis, propensity score analysis, and hot spot analysis together with global and local measures of spatial autocorrelation. The aim of the thesis was to analyse "the spatialities of the Swedish school choice in upper secondary education using a socio-spatial framework" (Fjellman 2019a, 22). Delimiting, understanding, and analysing the 'school markets' that emerged on national, regional, and local levels in the post-choice educational system was an important part of my analyses. Contrary to popular belief, my appreciation for 'quant' has nothing to do with a love for the application of mathematical statistics (that seems common enough among stats-inclined researchers) but everything to do with a fascination of the potential of large-scale and longitudinal statistical analyses of societal structures and institutions. The notion of trying analytically to capture and understand social change and the relationship between time and space was especially intriguing. The fascination in conjunction with trying to ask critical questions to reveal inequities in the education system had me contemplating their joint applicability since the two desires prompted intellectual conflicts I could not solve.

A middle ground was necessary between traditions and conventions: "the fact that critical realism is a balancing act between extremes" (Aligica 2011, 614). Quantitative methodologies based in a positivistic paradigm implies both an ontological and epistemological foundation that would be antithetical to critical analysis; however, a philosophical underpinning of critical realism could be an alternative route where both the quantitative analytical process and interpretations could be overhauled (e.g., Sablan 2019). Similarly, as Sayer wrote, "realism offers a third way between polarities" (1993, 321). A critical realist philosophy with a different approach to reality, context, causality as well as agency and structure could mitigate some methodological 'extreme' differences between critical epistemology and traditional inferential statistics in education science and in the following section I try to exemplify this based on my own experiences.

Trying to Find My Place

At first, when I was finding my way through my doctoral studies, I mainly concentrated on passing courses and trying to learn how to write articles (and suffering through 'reviewer 2' for the first time). I admittedly did not focus on the ontological implications of my thesis project (explicitly anyway). As an additional challenge, my perception was that the communities I participated in consisted of a large part of methodological purists, and it made it harder for me to grasp and cultivate a more pragmatic attitude regarding paradigm belongingness (i.e., McEvoy and Richards 2006). Moreover, it stifled creativity in data analysis as I was taught to respect theoretical boundaries and statistical conventions.

Obviously, my lack of thinking about ontology also involved several important implicit binary assumptions of ontological and epistemological character on complex phenomenon that fuelled difficulties that eventually appeared down the line: "The latter issues become particularly important when the 'methodological cart' often comes before the 'philosophical horse' in geographic research" (Yeung 1997, 51).

The first problem consisted of having difficulties fitting explanatory models to the changes I thought I could see in my data material. Capturing educational and economic restructuring by school choice through statistical analysis of population-based register data proved difficult, specifically pertaining to an investigation of causal relations through quantification over time and fitting parametric tests (i.e., Sayer 2010, 192–193). The implementation of school choice and the accompanying reforms of vouchers and enabling private providers to make profits on education prompted several important changes and transformations of educational institutions, actors, and practice. However, prior research grounded in rational choice theory and economic modelling of choices and privatisation seemed incapable of explaining system functionality and the relations between processes of urbanisation, educational reforms, and school and residential segregation. The ideologically charged concepts of markets also remain ill-defined in economic research and while economic theory agrees on *how* markets should work there is little agreement and explanation to how they actually work (Kirzner 1997). For example, what is a school market? It is definitely not a 'free market' based in a consumer-seller equilibrium nor is it a geographical territory where its organisation overlap well with the administrative borders of, for example, regions, municipalities, cities, or neighbourhoods (e.g., Fjellman 2019b). What *is* a school market? How is it constituted? What are the structures and relations that make up a market? What is change or place in school markets? How does it change over time as the system processes advance (e.g., when the administrative limitations of the school mechanism transformed multiple times)? What is the relationship between choices being made by students, the market structures, and their simultaneous and continuous interaction? Finally, what is the relationship between all of these and my population data?

Approximately around the midpoint, a crossroads of sorts appeared as I combatted both an academic identity crisis (is this what I am supposed to do with my life?) together with severe methodological difficulties as the traditional statistical analyses that had been planned for the project were unsuccessful in modelling the data (how can I fix this when *nothing* works?). It was from that point that I started to engage with the concepts of space (i.e., Massey 2005) and spatial justice (i.e., Dikeç 2001) in addition to abandoning the multilevel modelling I had been struggling with using. The nature of, what I called, 'school market areas' was not homogenous enough for those methods and the nature of this variability impacted the reliability and robustness of a longitudinal analysis. Nevertheless, important things were transforming at different levels of the Swedish educational system and these processes impacted the national goals and provision of equitable schooling and educational opportunities for children and youth (Svensk Författarsamling 2010). So, what now? Instead of trying to fix the analytical complications as a single issue, I started to think a bit more about the nature of 'what' rather than the just 'how' hoping that one might aid the other. A senior colleague advised us during a lecture to 'find our people' and as I went searching for 'my people' after my PhD (trying to find my way); I started to discover other perspectives and an alternative to the traditional philosophies of positivism and interpretivism, namely, critical realism.

This philosophy of science offered a new ontology – there was still a tangible reality and a possibility of causal explanation, albeit not grounded in a successionist causal inference (Mingers and Standing 2017). Rather it was focused on generative mechanisms: "Realism seems like the only way forward if one wished to call off the search for 'general laws' without simply abandoning the goal of causal explanation" (Gorski 2013, 659). The open system perspective was important as well, because there seemed to be no good or reasonable method strategy that could offer causal explanation through trying to isolate the mechanisms and processes that operated in the educational post-reform market:

> The key realist insight here is that the natural world consists in mechanisms that generate actual events and situations. While these may be conceptualized as facts (transitive and subject to revision or rejection), the real objects of experimental (or more broadly, scientific) work are structures and mechanisms. They are not experiences, events or their conjunctions.
> (Banfield 2015, 85)

Critical realism seemed to offer a different reality, where the emergence of markets could be understood as wholes instead of in isolation – to cultivate a comprehensive system-level understanding (e.g., Ehret 2013). The existence of the markets and their contingency on place and time seemed to not fit a comprehensive statistical model and it could not causally explain structure and agency within their operation through regularity or universal laws (e.g., Mingers and Standing 2017). Nevertheless, causality and explanation could be predicated on something other than epistemological shortcomings:

> It is the natural necessities consisting in things themselves (i.e., existing independent of mind and explanation) that direct the practice and establish the possibility of science. Only in virtue of the causal order and the real stratification of the world can the progressive accumulation of scientific knowledge be explained.
> (Banfield 2015, 87)

Those arguments are what attracted me the most to critical realism and it appeared to 'solve' some of the conflicts of the existence of reality and problematic implications for methods in trying to capture the temporality of a mutable phenomenon. It pointed me in a new direction where there is: "a place for both statistical analysis and meaningful interpretation" (Mingers and Standing 2017, 175) although I continue to grapple with what this can mean practically for future analyses and how actually to fully cross the aforementioned methodological bridge (i.e., Hernández 2015; Sayer 2010). Some of the problems are undeniably methodological in nature and there are critical realist-inspired ideas to build on in terms of how to design measures and perform statistical analyses (e.g., Sablan 2019). However, as critical realism is compatible with a range of methods, an important point could be to shift the focus from methods all together to the nature of the object of study (Sayer 2000) and stop identifying 'the problem' as quantitative versus qualitative. Sayer makes a distinction between 'intensive' and 'extensive' research as an alternative:

> As the name suggests, extensive research shows us mainly how extensive certain phenomena and patterns are in a population, while intensive research is primarily concerned with what makes things happen in specific cases, or in more ethnographic form, what kind of universe of meaning exists in a particular situation. Note, however, the extensive/intensive distinction is not identical to the survey-analysis/case-study or ethnography distinction: extensive approaches might be used within a single case study; intensive approaches do not have to be limited to single cases and can use other methods besides ethnographic ones.
>
> (Sayer 2000, 20–21)

The main advantage with emphasising that distinction would be an argument for the complimentary nature of these two approaches and recognition for how different kinds (both qualitative and quantitative) of methods can be used in either depending on research questions, relations, and groups being studied (Sayer 2000). Naturally, the new divide will carry over into the premises for generalisability and causality, specifically for large-scale studies of populations and in the next section, I explore some of it through an empirical example.

Re-imagining the Spatiality of School Choice and the Geographical Availability of Education: The Emergence of School Markets

Questions of equity and justice should be central to educational inquiry, and the spatial organisation of education impacts the possibility of a fair and equitable consumption of schooling in different places. The geography of education represents an attentiveness to how educational processes can develop differentially over space (Thiem 2009). Spatial justice is related to social justice where the spatiality of justice emphasises the process that produces space and how it is organised (and re-organised) through social, economic, and political relations (Dikec 2001). Sayer wrote: "It seems obvious enough that space makes a difference"

(1985, 50) and examining the organisation of spaces helps us understand who belongs there (Massey 2004). Following the intellectual process of contemplating a critical philosophy of education I described above I wanted to explore and re-imagine the ontological underpinnings and conceptualisations of a previous study that involved an analysis of the spatial organisation of Swedish upper secondary education after a school choice mechanism was implemented. The aim of the study was to identify, substantiate, and discuss:

> The possible causal mechanisms and future implications of these problems in relation to the restructuring of upper secondary education in Sweden between 1997 and 2011. A socio-spatial framework, which recognizes the importance of how we think about and organize space, is used to understand the development of the Swedish upper secondary school marketization.
>
> (Fjellman, Yang Hansen and Beach 2019, 519)

The study relied on Doreen Massey's theoretical concept of space and a heterogeneous functional regions model based on student commuter patterns to define regional and local school market areas. These market areas were argued to be the spatial materialisation of the "market on the ground" (i.e., Berndt 2015), which was defined as a geographical outcome originating from educational restructuring and the ensuing interactions between educational policy, the choices of students, and the available upper secondary school provisions. These elements co-constitute the school market, though, in understanding uneven developments, the mechanism and process need to be thought of separately when understanding socio-spatial change (Hsu 2019). The student commuter patterns (i.e., rates, direction, and origin) were analysed for spatial autocorrelation utilising Global Moran's I. In this context, spatial correlation was related to the presence of market formation, that is, the close proximity and significant concentration of similar student commuter rates compared to values further apart. These rates were also used in a hot spot analysis, which meant analysing the proximity of similar values and if this related to location in an attempt to find significant formations with intensified commuter rates and clusters of low and high values. Mapping out provisional patterns of schools and educational provider establishment patterns by municipality types (i.e., metropolitan, urban, rural, sparsely populated municipalities) over time was also an important secondary part of the analysis.

In the original article, successive 'regularity' in temporal events was used as the base for the concluding inferences on the presence of market failure where effects were attributed to time and market functionality: "Students' choices today affect future educational opportunity… while market adjustments push the schools out and force large quantities of the students to seek education elsewhere" (Fjellman, Yang Hansen and Beach 2019, 536). When trying to understand spatial variations in the consumption of schooling through choice, the spatial materialisation of the school market and the geographical availability of education retained within it are the keys. Questions around what is chosen, what is available, what is on offer and by whom – and how these are maintained, reproduced, and restructured over space and time – become crucial. However, causal inferences, as founded on empirically observable event regularities (Mingers and Standing 2017), in this case, the observations of changes in student commuter patterns and establishment and closure patterns of schools, cannot explain why things happen or fully explain how the school market function. However, a critical realist approach to educational markets might offer advantages, in relation to causality and macro-level theories, such as an open-system perspective, a clarification of the interaction between social structures and actors and an important approach for examining the emergent properties of a market that produces other qualities not possessed by its constituents (Ehret 2013). In this sense, observations and predictions of regular events are less emphasised:

> The central idea of causation within critical realism is easy to state. [...] Events that is changes, that occur do so as a result of the interaction of relatively enduring mechanisms that have particular properties or causal powers. The mechanisms are not necessarily physical but could be social, psychological or conceptual, and may or may not be observable.
> (Mingers and Standing 2017, 175)

The emergent properties of markets as social structures, that is, the characteristics that transcend individual interactions, are according to Bhaskar "the emergent powers of an entity are possessed by it conceived as a whole and make the entity 'capable of acting back on the materials out of which' it was formed" (Zahle and Kaidesoja 2019, 2). These kinds of causal powers can generate effects in certain conditions. Individual actions and market structures are still distinct, as structures can exist even though individuals are substituted (ibid) – which the exemplified school market continuously do from year to year, although students finish upper secondary education on a yearly basis and new students start school. Even if critical realism considers reality as 'tangible', the world is perceived as stratified and this stratification consists of (1) domain of the real (mechanisms), (2) domain of the actual (events), and (3) domain of the empirical (human experience) (Banfield 2015, 87). The strata of reality organises individual experiences in relation to influential relationships we are unaware of, but researchers can investigate these actual and empirical events in trying to identify mechanisms that reside in the real. This enables causal explanation on other premises, which is especially important in the example of school market functionality, that is highly dependent on place and time, and possesses powers in a reciprocative relationship with students and families:

> So far we have been primarily concerned with what might be called "upward causation", i.e., the manner in which the structure of a mechanism,

its components and their relations, generate the properties and powers of the whole. But in many systems, especially social systems, there appears to be "downward" causation as well – that is the structure of the whole can affect the behaviors of the components.

(Mingers and Standing 2017, 178)

The possibility of underpinning macro-level theories of markets and causal explanations through critical realism (Ehret 2013; Mingers and Standing 2017) seemed exciting as it furthers the opportunity of trying to gain a system-level understanding how the school market functions but importantly how systematically unjust geographies and context-dependent inequities are reproduced through the market, where the effects are emergent on multiple levels.

Conclusion

When it comes to trying to bridge the mismatch between critical inquiry and quantitative methodology, several arguments are brought forward in this chapter to how this can be approached. First, reframing the 'problem' as not founded in methods primarily (since critical realism is compatible with different methods), but rather shifting from epistemological concerns to an ontological discussion on the nature of the object of study creates a good opening for the complimentary nature of intensive and extensive research (e.g., Sayer 2000). Second, the recognition of a tangible reality and the open system perspective within critical realism enables causal explanation outside of quantitative analyses framed around successionist causal inference attempting to isolate observable mechanisms through data in a chaotic world. Third, but most importantly, the discussion of the empirical example demonstrates the significance of how the critical realist approach can develop the possibility of using large-scale analysis and quantitative data to reveal systematic perpetuations of inequalities (e.g., Stage and Wells 2014) in a complex and irregular process as the regional and local school markets where traditional statistical analysis and causal inference have proved to be inadequate. In the end, beyond important implications for my own intellectual journey and future studies, my hope is that the chapter inspires more scholarly work and discussions on critical realist quantitative research in education.

References

Aligica, P.D. 2011. "A Critical Realist Image of the Future Wendell Bell's Contribution to the Foundations of Futures Studies." *Futures* 43 (6): 610–617. doi: 10.1016/j.futures.2011.04.011.

Banfield, G. 2015. *Critical Realism for Marxist Sociology of Education*. London: Routledge.

Berndt, C. 2015. "Ruling Markets: The Marketization of Social and Economic Policy." *Environment and Planning A* 47 (9): 1866–1872. doi: 10.1177/10.1177_0308518X15598324.

Dikeç, M. 2001. "Justice and the Spatial Imagination." *Environment and Planning A* 33 (10): 1785–1805. doi: 10.1068/a3467.

Ehret, M. 2013. "Emergence of Business Markets—A Critical Realist Foundation." *Industrial Marketing Management* 42 (3): 316–323. doi: 10.1016/j.indmarman.2013. 02.014.

Fjellman, A.M. 2019a. "School Choice, Space and the Geography of Marketization-Analyses of Educational Restructuring in Upper Secondary Education in Sweden." PhD diss., Gothenburg University.

Fjellman, A.M. 2019b. "School Choice, Private Providers and Differentiated Mobilities in Swedish Metropolitan School Markets: Exploring through a Counterfactual Approach." *International Journal of Educational Research* 98: 171–191. doi: 10.1016/j. ijer.2019.08.006.

Fjellman, A.M., K. Yang Hansen, and D. Beach. 2019. "School Choice and Implications for Equity: The New Political Geography of the Swedish Upper Secondary School Market." *Educational Review* 71 (4): 518–539. doi: 10.1080/00131911. 2018.1457009.

Gorski, P.S. 2013. "What Is Critical Realism? And Why Should You Care?" *Contemporary Sociology* 42 (5): 658–670. doi: 10.1177/0094306113499533.

Hernández, E. 2015. "What Is "Good" Research? Revealing the Paradigmatic Tensions in Quantitative Criticalist Work." *New Directions for Institutional Research* 2014 (163): 93–101. doi: 10.1002/ir.20088.

Hsu, J.Y. 2019. "Process-ing with Mechanism: The Renaissance of Critical Realism in Human Geography?" *Dialogues in Human Geography* 9 (3): 262–266. doi: 10.1177/2043820619875330.

Kirzner, M.I 1997. *How Markets Work: Disequilibrium, Entrepreneurship and Discovery*. London: Institute of Economic Affairs.

Massey, D. 2004. "Geographies of Responsibility." *Geografiska Annaler: Series B, Human Geography* 86 (1): 5–18. doi: 10.1111/j.0435-3684.2004.00150.x.

Massey, D. 2005. *For Space*. Thousand Oaks: Sage.

McEvoy, P., and D. Richards. 2006. "A Critical Realist Rationale for Using a Combination of Quantitative and Qualitative Methods." *Journal of Research Nursing* 11 (1): 66–78. doi: 10.1177/1744987106060192.

McLaren, L. 2017. "A Space for Critical Quantitative Public Health Research?" *Critical Public Health* 27 (4): 391–393. doi: 10.1080/09581596.2017.1326214.

Mingers, J., and C. Standing. 2017. "Why Things Happen – Developing the Critical Realist View of Causal Mechanisms." *Information and Organization* 27 (3): 171–189. doi: 10.1016/j.infoandorg.2017.07.001.

Sablan, J.R. 2019. "Can You Really Measure That? Combining Critical Race Theory and Quantitative Methods." *American Educational Research Journal* 56 (1): 178–203. doi: 10.3102/0002831218798325.

Sayer, A. 1985. "The Difference That Space Makes." In *Social Relations and Spatial Structures*, edited by Derek Gregory and John Urry, 49–66. London: Palgrave.

Sayer, A. 1993. "Postmodernist Thought in Geography: A Realist View." *Antipode* 25 (4): 320–344. doi: 10.1111/j.1467-8330.1993.tb00222.x.

Sayer, A. 2000. *Realism and Social Science*. Thousand Oaks: Sage.

Sayer, A. 2010. *Method in Social Science*. 2nd ed. London: Routledge.

Stage, F.K. 2007. "Answering Critical Questions Using Quantitative Data." *New Directions for Institutional Research* 2007 (133): 5–16. doi: 10.1002/IR.200.

Stage, F.K., and R.S. Wells. 2014. "Critical Quantitative Inquiry in Context." *New Directions for Institutional Research* 2013 (158): 1–7. doi: 10.1002/ir.20041.

Svensk Författarsamling. 2010. Skollag [School law] 2010:800. Stockholm: Utbildningsdepartementet.

Thiem, C.H. 2009. "Thinking through Education: The Geographies of Contemporary Educational Restructuring." *Progress in Human Geography* 33 (2): 154–173. doi: 10.1177/0309132508093475.

Yeung, H.W.C. 1997. "Critical Realism and Realist Research in Human Geography: A Method or a Philosophy in Search of a Method?" *Progress in Human Geography* 21 (1): 51–74. doi: 10.1191/030913297668207944.

Zahle, J., and T. Kaidesoja. 2019. "Emergence in the Social Sciences." In *The Routledge Handbook of Emergence*, edited by Sophie Gibb, Robin Hendry and Tom Lancaster, 400–407. London: Routledge.

10

REAL MEN, REAL VIOLENCE

Critical Realism and the Search for the Masculine Subject

Ben Wadham

Introduction

Across the West, men and masculinity are under scrutiny as much as they are in revolt. Donald Trump recently led the movement (at least symbolically) of recuperative white men massing across western democracies rallying against diversity, lamenting a lost culture, and demonising others as agents of disintegration amongst our communities. Fascism and right-wing forces are on the rise across the globe, a movement that reifies white masculinities and their predicate of survival of the fittest and extinction of the weak. The #MeToo movement has called out some men's predatory behaviours in the media professions, and our major institutions like the Police and the Military have faced organisational challenges to their gender orders. As I write, the predatory masculinities of some Australian male parliamentarians, their staff, and their cultures are under intense scrutiny after the now former Attorney General was accused of the alleged rape of a childhood acquaintance. Beyond these actualities the broader question stared back at me: how can we understand and reduce men's use of violence on the streets, against their families and upon themselves? How can we change the way men and the culturally produced masculinities embody violence from the local to the global? To do this I turned to critical realism to reassess what the journal-based literature had talked about these things so far.

I was recently leading a primary violence prevention project for young men. The project aimed to work with young men around their ideas of manhood, to question the dominant narratives of masculinity in their lives, and to widen their sense of compassion and respect for others. If you are going to produce change programmes for men, a complex understanding of structure and agency is central. If we overdetermine men's masculinities as natural, biological, or even God-given, then our understanding of men's agency is diminished. If we tend towards

DOI: 10.4324/9781003193784-10

voluntarism, we neglect the structural and cultural conditions in which they identify and practise manhood. To produce change there must be an analysis of the structural and cultural conditions within which masculinities are produced, consumed, regulated, and reproduced as well some focus on the self and other – the primordial dialectic of identity and being. A key question is 'what are the generative mechanisms of men's violence?'.

What follows below is an initial critical realist underlabouring of existing approaches to understanding men, masculinity, and violence. The original task outlined by the research team was to undertake a systemic literature review from 1990 to 2018. However, it soon became evident that: "rather than looking for an additive model of evidence, which is what systematic review does by counting up the number of 'quality' studies that report positive or negative results, a critical realist approach would define evidence as work that can give insight into the structures, powers, generative mechanisms and tendencies that help us understand the concrete worlds of experience" (Clegg 2005, 421).

I anticipated that by reviewing all peer reviewed journal articles on men and their violence towards other men we would employ judgemental rationality to assess those approaches that best articulate the "structures, powers, generative mechanisms and tendencies" (Clegg 2005, 442) behind men's violence towards other men. This was a narrative literature review informed by critical realism. It is worth noting that we did not find any explicit critical realist journal articles on men, masculinity, and violence at the time of the review. The key element of the review highlighted the relationship between the psychosocial and sociohistorical. It also outlined the growth of discourse analysis of men and their use of violence. This discourse analysis was wide and varied and often employed historical and dialectical materialist forms of understanding the subject matter. This chapter focuses on the relationship between the psychosocial masculinity studies and what is predominantly a social historical approach. Equally a paper on how critical realism can underlabour discourse analysis in critical masculinity studies would be valuable.

The chapter begins by outlining the field of men masculinity and violence and my reasons for working in this field. It then takes some of the fundamental definitions of masculinity in order to identify the ways in which the field of masculinity and violence/crime constructs the possibilities of men, violence, and change. The ensuing discussion covers the tensions between the psychosocial, the ethnographic, and the structural focus on masculinities and violence. From a critical realist vantage point, the ways that structure and agency, voluntarism/determinism, and epistemology/ontology have been framed are highlighted. This chapter is restricted to that scope but recognises the much wider opportunities for engagement with critical realism. It identifies the importance of identity and difference in rethinking Australian manhood. I use the discussion of the literature review to move to questions of the relations of culture, identity, and reflexivity through Connell's masculinity politics, Adornos' logic of identity, and Archers four modes of reflexivity. I argue that Adorno and Connell both demonstrate an engagement with dispositional realism that isn't fully realised. In doing so, I identify how critical realism can partner these other theoretical approaches by bringing clarity to the study of men, violence, and change. I make the point that critical realism is a meta-philosophy whose power lies in underlabouring the many existing theoretical framings of these social concerns.

On Violence and Men

During the late 1990s, I was researching race and gender relations in Australia and searching for an approach to social research. As an early career researcher, I was captured by the idea that truth was relative, mutable, and constructed within different cultural and discursive foundations. As a military veteran I had been shaped cognitively to see the world in instrumental terms, to assess the world through dualisms, and to effectively expect that 'what you see is what you get'. This was an identitarian way of being that lived by the assumption that the concept corresponded to the object. This was a mark of violence on my being and identity – the mark of militarisation. This led me to the work of Theodor Adorno of the Frankfurt School and his negative dialectics, logic of identity, and dialectic of enlightenment. Adorno gave me a form of depth ontology within a frame of dialectical materialism. Importantly, Adorno maintained the existence of the thinking and practicing subject which was being disavowed by the sociohistorical and critical forms of social construction I was engaging with. My recent engagement with critical realism has done what critical realism intends to do – underlabour – and, while I remain indebted to Adorno, I have come to recognise some limitations in his philosophy. Norrie first drew my attention to Bhaskar and Adorno's common commitment to a realist ontology and, as such, to the realisation that a productive engagement of the two might be fruitful for my research. Norrie observes in "comparing and contrasting Dialectical Critical Realism with Theodor Adorno's negative dialectics [it is negative dialectics] which probably comes closest to Dialectical Critical Realism" (2004, 23). Grasping this connection had a twofold benefit. Not only did it raise the possibility that critical realism could be useful in understanding the benefits and limits of negative dialectics but also heightened my curiosity about critical realism.

My principal interest in this project was to consider primary prevention that promotes open and relational forms of masculinity – logics of identity that were not identitarian. I came to the project with the questions: how is violence understood, and what does the field of men's violence towards men's scholarship identify as the *real* characteristics of men's use of violence towards other men? How has the field addressed questions of men, culture, structure, and agency over time? How do I as an educator, conceptualise men, manhood, and change? How do I educate to effect gender change? In addressing these questions, I found three distinctive features of original (i.e.,1M) critical realism useful: (i) reality is differentiated, stratified, and emergent, (ii) that we can observe and understand causality in the human sciences, and (iii) that knowledge and practice are transitive and intransitive. However, critical realism did not address the practical and educational substance of this research: "what is hegemonic masculinity, how can we affect gender change and what is an open and empathic masculinist subjectivity? Critical realism engagement with critical masculinity studies is sparse and not always precise in its conceptualisation of the key ideas in the field" (see Irfan and Wilkinson 2020).

I began writing in critical masculinity studies in the 1990s when the field was moving more deeply into a social constructionist approach through the use of discourse analysis. Adorno's (1996) notion of identitarian thinking draws upon a critical reading of psychoanalysis which brought to life the inner world of the subject and their disposition to totality, certainty, and control – three characteristics of dominating masculinities and masculine privilege. I became interested in the work of Adorno because his development of critical psychoanalysis attempted to describe the conditions of possibility – the relationships of self to others, the logic of one's identification with the world and others around them and the potential for not dominant ways of being.

I was also interested in Adorno because of his critique of positivist philosophy and authoritarian ways of being. This was principally through the framing of consciousness as a dialectical process between self and other within social and historical contexts. The self, according to Adorno (1996, 146), attempts to understand its place within its environment by generating knowledges of, and categorising and classifying, naming and determining the other. Determining the other is a fundamental strategy used to generate mastery and control, to help one find their place in the world. For Adorno, the process of determining the other in order to determine the self is marked by the striving for Enlightenment, for an end to alienation between man and his environment, for harmony and reconciliation, between self and other. In other words: for unity, cohesion, and ultimately control. The dyad then, of self and other, is always determined with a final point – a telos – in mind; a striving for control, mastery, and ultimately a particular conception of freedom. In the context of western modernity, the instrument for attaining this final/reconciliation, of achieving Enlightenment has been a historically and culturally specific conception of Reason (Lloyd 1984; Seidler 1994). The self is a key element of the debates within the literature, coupled with the debate over the cultural (re)production of masculinities. Adorno was important to my thinking because he sustained the thinking-doing subject but recognised the wider social conditions that inhibited the full expression of the human condition, as well as the minutiae that supported its persistence.

This discussion highlights the importance of understanding men, masculinity, and possibilities of change and why critical realism – as an alternative meta-philosophy to positivism, interpretivism, and social constructionism (Gorski 2013) – can bolster our educational attempts to generate forms of empathic and relational masculinities. Critical realism underlabours these theoretical movements by recognising that structure and agency are "two radically different kinds of things" (Bhaskar 1998, 33). Primary prevention around men's violence is significantly about changing knowledge assumptions, beliefs, attitudes, and expectations in men about men, and women and their cultural and material roles in the world. If masculinity as a notion is narrow and reified then that must be liberated. That means enhancing the meta-reflexivity of the subject which is an educational project. So, an understanding of the potential for changing men, rewriting masculinity, and understanding identity and identity politics is crucial. The theory of change upon which this sits discerns the world in its intransitive (the physical and social world we inhabit) and the transitive (the discourses that shape our understanding of the world). When our theories of the world change so do the ways we act and be in it. The political embrace that we find ourselves in is informed by a focus on power, social justice shaped by critical feminist, and critical masculinities studies.

In assessing the men and violence literature, critical realism provided me with a frame for making sense of the different theory struggles in the field over the decades. These struggles predominantly include structure and agency, but also extend to voluntarism and determinism and epistemology/ontology. Archer (1995) describes these vagaries of mutual constitution in terms of conflation – upward (voluntarism), central (interdependency of structure and agency), and downward (determinism). The scholarly debate in the reviewed journal articles largely moves around the issue of recognising the power of the psyche and the capacity for human agency in response to claims of overdetermination. To me, it was clear that the 'psycho social turn' (which I will describe below) seeks to recover the subject and the psyche but, in doing so, engages in an upward conflation of structure and agency. Significant here is that Connell holds to a dispositional realism that recognises structure and agency as two different kinds of things in virtue of their distinct causal powers. His focus on life history interviews interrogates the power and, in particular, the many reconciliations between self and other across the life course. He demonstrates that it is not only the powers of particulars that generate reality but the cultural cognition of the subject in engaging in that world. Within the reviewed literature the key paradigms are the socio-historical, the psychosocial, and discourse analysis. I will outline these philosophical movements and argue for the value of Archers four expressions of reflexivity (the process through which agents consider and choose a particular course of action), Adorno's logic of identity, and Connell's theory of masculinity politics promote dispositional realism to differing extents.

Within the field of critical masculinity studies Jefferson explained that there was a continuing need to situate crime in relation to broader social relations and a continuing need to develop and grow the emerging literature "implicating masculinities in the commission of all sorts of crime" (1996, 337). Connell is a leading scholar among those who have tried to describe the evolution of masculinity studies as one field where considerations of violence have been central. The relationship between masculinities and violence, or at least, men and violence, has been well regarded for some time. Edwards (2004) explains that these approaches to men and crime provided the foundation for stronger critical masculinity studies that developed in the early 1990s onwards.

Edwards (2004) describes the emergence of the second wave of critical men's studies in this late 1990s. This approach is multidisciplinary drawing upon sociology, history, and media studies. For example, feminist analysis has been particularly salient since the 1960s with the development of radical feminism and its focus on men's violence towards women. Feminist scholars have illuminated the structures of social and power relations, and sociology the ethnographic focusing on the particular and the local in relation to the macro and global: "The patterns of conduct our society defines as 'masculine' may be enacted in the lives of individuals, but they also have an existence beyond the individual. Masculinities are collectively defined in culture, and are sustained in institutions" (Connell 1998, 4).

In this early work, Connell (1996) demonstrates an emergent understanding of masculinity where individual subjectivities produce cultural forms that, in turn, are shaped by forces in other social strata. Pointing to a stratified, emergent ontology of men's violence towards other men, Connell makes three observations that are relevant here. First, men's use of violence is structural and an authentic cultural expression in its own right. This meant that social researchers need to "consolidate the analysis in relation to class, race and ethnicity and other forms of power" (Connell 1998, 6). Second, there is a need for research to move beyond the ethnographic as its main game. This implies incorporating the micro, the meso, and the macro into a theory of gender relations. Consequently, Connell champions the life history method for its capacity to draw attention to the emergent powers of particulars in framing possible expressions of masculinity. Finally, Connell noted the corporeality and cathexis of gender relations. These concepts provide the basis for a focus on affect, emotion, and desire. Here we see Connell's commitment to a dispositional realism of embodied powers: capacities that exist beyond the transitive construction of what it means to be a man. Connell however argues that rather than focusing on the biology of man, which can result in an unnecessary search for origins, we can understand the cultural powers of biological foundation by studying it within the reproductive arena.

The different strata of social reality within critical realism are very helpful in under labouring biological and culture in gender relations:

> The 'real' refers to objects, their structures or natures and their causal powers and liabilities. The 'actual' refers to what happens when these powers and liabilities are activated and produce change. The 'empirical' is the subset of the real and the actual that is experienced by actors. Although changes at the level of the actual (e.g., political debates) may change the nature of objects (e.g., political institutions), the latter are not reducible to the former, any more than a car can be reduced to its movement. Moreover, while empirical experiences can influence behaviour and hence what happens, much of the social and physical worlds can exist regardless of whether researchers, and in some cases other actors, are observing or

experiencing them. Though languages and other semiotic structures/systems are dependent on actors for their reproduction, they always already pre-exist any given actor (or subset of actors), and have a relative autonomy from them as real objects, even when not actualised.

(Fairclough, Jessop, and Sayer 2004, 25)

An analysis of the men's violence literature identifies the focus that has been taken with regard to the actual and empirical domains. Behind these actual sites of men's violence there are generative mechanisms of the violence which the field attends to in varying ways. The actual and empirical expressions of men's violence according to the field include the night time economy and bar room violence, gang or group violence, college and school violence, violence in the workplace, men and sport and men's violence towards men in rural settings. Many studies attempt to grasp the generative mechanisms of men's use of violence and the field generally would benefit from engagement with the underlabouring capacities of critical realism. A historical analysis of the literature demonstrated how the theory struggles in the field set the conditions for what we know and use today.

These points above are important in considering change programmes for men. To overdetermine men and masculinity leads to primary prevention that shames 'bad masculinity' and conflates masculinity with men. Shame is a destructive force that works to generate disconnections for men and the project of gender equity. I am looking for a way to describe structure and agency while liberating men to see the value of an ethics of care for their families and communities. A clear sense of structure and agency dispels the idea that men cannot change and opens up the potential for liberating their sense of empathy for themselves and those around them. A stratified and emergent sense of men, masculinity, and violence permits an understanding of the way structural forces are expressed in the minutiae and cultural forces of everyday life. This focus on the power of particulars gives the researcher and educator the capacity to identify the collective shaping, and individual expressions of masculinities.

The Developing Field

Significant theorisation of men, masculinities, and violence occurs through the 1990s and into the 2000s, reducing in the last decade or so. During this period the work of Connell (2005) predominantly becomes staple theory in other disciplines including law, public health, and psychology. The notion of hegemonic masculinity becomes a moniker for men, masculinity, and violence and the idea is heavily utilised as well as heavily contested. Hegemonic masculinity is characterised by identarian thinking – the desire to have others live their lives on the terms of the self. British researchers Jefferson (1996), Hall (2002), and Hood-Williams (2001) mounted a challenge to Connell and to a lesser extent Messerschmidt's (2000) growing orthodoxy in the field. They argue that hegemonic masculinity is a structurally deterministic theoretical approach. However, hegemonic masculinity is recognised as a social project rather than a character type – it is not a psychological condition, but it does involve particular forms of cultural cognition. Hegemonic masculinity should not be valorised at the expense of Connell's other relations of masculinity – complicit, subordinate, and marginalised masculinities. In this sense Connell progresses to the power of particulars in shaping different cultural forms. It is here too that Adorno's identitarian thinking represents authoritarian ways of being and doesn't engage with more relational and open forms of masculinities.

Jefferson revived a turn to the psychosocial in 1996. He and his colleagues argue that Connell's critical version of realism were overly sociological, structurally deterministic, and neglected the psychosocial (Gadd 2003; Hood-Williams 2001; Jefferson 1996, 2002; Winlow 2014; Winlow and Hall 2009). Across their review of the literature, this theoretical challenge re-established psychoanalytical research as a means of making sense of men and their use of violence. The theoretical ground that was established leading up to the new millennium picked up the key themes of determinism versus voluntarism and structuralism and the psychic lives of men. While not specifically called for by any author there is a clear anxiety around ontology in masculinity studies, and the question of men's agency. As a researcher who had already discovered a critical form of psychoanalysis, aligned it with the historical and social conditions in which men developed their sense of masculinity over their life course and retained a commitment to depth ontology I was drawn to this literature. But ultimately, I was disappointed because the attempts by these authors tended towards under realising structure at the expense of re-finding agency. To my mind there the underlabouring capacity of critical realism would clarify and render much of the developing theory with more precision.

Jefferson (1996) argued that we must pay attention to the reality of the psyche conceived of as an irreducible domain with its own determinations. The psyche in this field is an intransitive phenomenon with powers. Hood-Williams claimed that "the central term 'masculinities' is tautological and that the arguments linking masculinity to crime are implausible and logically flawed" (2001, 2). A common refrain among Jefferson, Gadd, and Hood-Williams is that Connell and Messerschmidt's sociological thesis over-reaches. Jefferson maintains some connection to structure, at least through the notion of discourses of masculinities supplemented with reference to psychoanalysis. However, this attempt is confused by the emphasis of epistemology upon the subject. This illuminates a confounding of epistemology and ontology. His work can be described as a psychoanalytic interpretive approach which rather than focusing on generative mechanisms emphasises the context in which masculinities are constructed. Hood-Williams appears to lose structure altogether, along with Gadd who argue that psyches are somehow independent of the social context – that the cause and effect of social discourse on the psyche is not straightforward: "psychic experience is not a simple product of social discourses, and therefore masculinity cannot be straight forwardly read off from what men say" (Gadd 2003, 1). I read this as a reaction to the social constructionist move that has been read as overdetermining – a downward conflationism rendering men and their use of violence as merely an effect of language. Philosophically this was useful to understand although in practice of research the field *is* engaged in many of the same questions as critical realism, without the meta-philosophical guidance that critical realism provides. What critical realism offered for me was a way to bring clarity to these processes and formations as a partner and meta-theory, but critical realisms value was mainly realised in the meta-theoretical infrastructure not the substantive theory of critical masculinity studies.

A principal critique of the sociological masculinities by these psycho-social researchers is that big structures do not descend into the depths of biography and identity – there is not enough nuance in understanding how men become male, and the extent to which it is an expression of the wider social relations. Critical realism argues for dispositional realism which would facilitate an analysis of the power of these particulars (Engelskirchen 2004). Social structure is read as an overwhelmingly oppressive force that denies men agency to negotiate their gender and sexuality and other axes of identification. For example, the discursive approach which the authors Wetherell and Edley (1999) represent is critiqued as failing to produce an inner world producing research subjects that are artificially unitary, rational, and coherent. It is this point that points to Archer's reflexivities, Adornos identitarian thinking, or Connell's relations of masculinities. Gadd (2003) is more generous than Jefferson and Hood-Williams recognising the manner in which Connell and colleagues have engaged with the psychoanalytic and attempted to develop a depth analysis of masculinities: Carrigan, Connell, and Lee (1985) identified psychoanalysis as "a more complex and powerful tool" (580) for thinking through the "psychodynamics of masculinity", psychodynamics that should "not been seen as a separate issue from the social relations that invest and construct masculinity" (598).

The key point I take from this is that these different approaches favour the biographical element in understanding how men become different kinds of men. They are, however, confounded by structure and agency, voluntarism and determinism and epistemology and ontology.

Dispositions and Differentiation: The Power in Particulars

Kenway and Fitzclarence (1997, 119) explain in the late 1990s that "It is now fairly well understood that the social, cultural and psychic construction of masculinity is related to violence and that some kinds of masculinity are more directly associated with violent behaviour than are others". Similarly, Tomsen (1997) and Polk (1999) have both emphasised the role of dominating forms of hegemonic masculinities in public, male-male violence. However, the focus on hegemonic masculinity demonstrates a failure to engage with the diversity of masculinities and the particularities which generate them. This is part of the psychosocial critique. The literature highlights the tensions of different research collectives to be precise about structure and agency and epistemology and ontology. Critical realism permits the researcher to take these competing approaches to men and violence and illuminate their strengths and weaknesses. It permits us to retain the masculine subject, and to work with the psyche over the life course within the social and historical conditions which men's subjectivities are produced and reproduced.

The psychosocial turn to the subject was an attempt to understand the authentic biographical complexities of men who use violence towards other men. As such it represents a desire for ontology. Life history methodologies have been the staple of the critical masculinity researchers described above. As a method it is also about connecting but not conflating epistemology and ontology and structure and agency. The discussion above highlights the struggles the field has had in articulating this. Connell (2005) explains that life history research gives rich accounts of "personal experience, ideology and subjectivity" (89). Life history presents an expression of cultural relations, both in history and in the present. However, these relations of masculinity do not describe the culturally produced cognitive dispositions that produce the open or closed subjectivity, or the dominating or relational subject.

In this context I found myself returning to Adorno's identitarian thinking. Attending to the dialectics of structure/agency and determinism/voluntarism Adorno and Horkheimer (1973) introduce us to the notion of the dialectic of enlightenment. The notion of self and other is considered a foundation of human experience. The subject and their identity are produced through this dynamic of me and you, me and the other, and me and the environment which I experience. Here Bhaskar's (1998) duality of identity/non-identity is important for my thinking. In the dialectical materialist tradition, the self seeks identity through correspondence between the concept and object. This emergence generates multiple masculinities – those that overdetermine their being by striving for identicality with the world and others around them (hegemonic masculinities), and those that seek to 'be with' the world. I see this as a tension between identicality and alterity. This is the basis of hegemonic masculinity and the violent disposition. For the gendered being who recognises non-correspondence between the concept and object the disposition to violence is diminished, balanced by the recognition that the world is not what it seems and that recognising non-identity is a key element of the human condition. The attempt to produce oneself in the worlds we inhabit is a form of reconciliation. We can, across our lived histories, choose to reconcile others to our presence, reconcile with others or recognise their alterity and difference, permitting the presence of a different sovereign subject. Fredric Jameson (1990) describes this in terms of the open and closed self.

However, Adorno's depth ontology has its limitations. While his philosophy works against the essentialisation of women and the violation and subversion of the Jewish community, it fails to recognise that his bourgeois subject is more accurately a description of the white, masculine, heterosexual subject and hegemonic masculinity. By focusing on identitarian thinking he also does not recognise other subjectivities within social relations. The power of Adorno and indeed the Frankfurt School's insights are diffused by their failure to differentiate the relations of dominance. But alongside Connell's ontologies of masculinity (relations of masculinity), the search for totality, certainty, and control is able to be differentiated. The identitarian thinking that Adorno (1996) outlines is a hegemonic and dominating cognition and way of being, it is dominant and domineering. In gender change programmes we develop pedagogies of empathy to dismantle this impulse for identicality. We seek to build subjectivities of alterity. While Adorno retains the thinking-doing subject it is hard to find in Adorno objects, other than human subjects, that are themselves bearers of the power to change (Engleskirchen 2004: 4).

Margaret Archer's (1995) work on reflexivity is also significant in this sense. Her critical realism outlines four forms of reflexivity that also work to make sense of the dispositions of particular forces on the subject:

- communicative reflexivity – where the subject is moved to action through and with others;
- autonomous reflexivity which is sustained autonomously and lead directly to action;
- meta-reflexivity demonstrates a critically reflexivity about the world and their deliberate action in society;
- Fractured non-reflexives – for these people the experience of reflexivity leads to distress rather than to courses of action.

Reflexivity is the subject's mediation of structure and agency. In an Adornian sense it is also a reconciliation between self and other. This framework permits a differentiated construction of the masculinised subject. Hegemonic masculinity can be described as sustaining itself through the principal expression of autonomous reflexivity. To engender change in young men education must scaffold an understanding of the work in terms of historical and cultural formations as well as individual responsibility and choice. This asks for the development of the meta-reflexive disposition which inhibits the logic of identitarian thinking and the closed self. Archer's (1995) reflexivity doesn't provide this avenue to political disposition but is enhanced when it is considered in line with Connell's (2005) masculinity politics which includes hegemonic, complicit, subordinated, and marginalised masculinities.

Conclusion

The second turn in field of research onto men's violence towards other men has consistently produced research and theorisation over the last 20 years or so. The field has developed from the strong sociological approaches to men, masculinities, and violence, practised through life history interviews and critical ethnographies, in different social settings. A principal understanding of this research is that men engage in crime and violence as a way of negotiating their place in the world as men. The life history method, used by Messerschmidt and Connell, attend in great detail to the individual subject, and while they may not use psychoanalysis explicitly, they are equally encouraging about its value in this research field. The turn to the psychosocial however has fundamentally neglected the social, arguing that the psyche does not correspond to the cultural relations of manhood in society. Connell and Messerschmidt are more precise and coherent in their theorisation of men, masculinities, and violence. The psychosocial turn did serve to highlight the need for greater precision in key ideas like structure and agency, ontology and epistemology, and the biographical and psychic complexity of the male subject. This turn however could be clarified by the underlabouring of critical realism which as demonstrated has given us the ability to understand that men and masculinity are relatively enduring; there is a deep realism to men and their use of violence. This has been a highly contentious position in gender scholarship because the mere mentioning of a realism to men – read essentialism of foundationalism – denies the possibility of change and gives succour to men's right and positivist science interactions in the field. Connell's work does align with critical realism.

I think that one clear piece of evidence is that the wider field described uses the sociological approach, and ideas like hegemonic masculinity, far more than the psychosocial. Psychoanalysis has had a decade of resurgence but decline in the last five years and has failed to be taken up by the host of other allied researchers in public health, legal studies, or education. The attempt to get at this complexity is an attempt to rediscover ontology. There is no doubt that Jefferson, Hall, Gadd, and Winlow are seeking to apprehend the underlying factors of men, crime, and violence. However, there is a fundamental confusion about structure and agency and epistemology and ontology which could be mediated by critical realism's understanding of a stratified reality and the deep real.

In this chapter I have outlined the development of the field of research into men's violence towards other men and outlined how a critical realism can underlabour critical masculinity studies, developing precision and avoiding the conflation of key ideas. While the argument that there is a crisis in global gender relations has persisted across the decades there appears to be a coexisting tension in critical masculinity studies of men's violence – it is a tension around ontology. The psychoanalysts desperately seek their subject, as does critical realism. Connell leads a collective of researchers that do utilise precision in their articulation of structure and agency, epistemology and ontology, and other key dialectics. But the opportunities of critical realist meta-philosophy provide a strong platform greater precision in these matters. The notion of reflexivity which mediates between structure and agency is another way of reformulating this desire for biographical complexity without compromising the value of social structural accounts on men, their masculine identity, and their use of violence. This is fundamentally a psychosocial reconciliation between men and their communities and environments, which is demonstrated by the tendency to control and dominate or reflect and relate. Critical realism has become a useful partner to me in understanding these theoretical matters and has reasserted the theoretical complexity and precision of the work by Connell and associated researchers. I have learnt in this process that there is great richness in critical feminist and masculinity studies that are only strengthened by the underlabouring that critical realism provides.

References

Adorno, T. W. 1996. *Negative Dialectics.* London: Routledge.
Adorno, T. W., and M. Horkheimer 1973. *Dialectic of Enlightenment.* London: Verso.
Archer, M. S. 1995. *Realist Social Theory: The Morphogenetic Approach.* Cambridge: Cambridge University Press.
Bhaskar, R. 1998. *The Possibility of Naturalism: A Philosophical Critique of the Contemporary Human Sciences.* London: Routledge.
Carrigan, T., B. Connell, and J. Lee. 1985. "Toward a New Sociology of Masculinity." *Theory and Society* 14 (5): 551–604.
Clegg, S. 2005. "Evidence-Based Practice in Educational Research: A Critical Realist Critique of Systematic Review." *British Journal of Sociology of Education* 26 (3): 415–428.
Connell, R. W. 2005. *Masculinities.* Cambridge: Polity.
Connell, R. W. 1995. "New Directions in Gender Theory, Masculinity Research and Gender Politics." *Ethnos* 61 (3–4): 157–176.
Edwards, T. 2004. *Cultures of Masculinity.* London: Routledge.
Engelskirchen, H. 2004. "Powers and Particulars: Adorno and Scientific Realism." *Journal of Critical Realism* 3 (1): 1–21.
Fairclough, N., B. Jessop, and A. Sayer. 2004. "Critical Realism and Semiosis." In *Realism, Discourse and Deconstruction*, edited by J. Joseph and M. Roberts, 23–42. London: Routledge.
Gadd, D. 2003. "Reading Between the Lines." *Men and Masculinities* 5 (4): 333–354.
Gorski, P. S. 2013. "What Is Critical Realism? And Why Should You Care?" *Contemporary Sociology* 42 (5): 658–670.
Hall, S. 2002. "Daubing the Drudges of Fury." *Theoretical Criminology* 6 (1): 35–61.
Hood-Williams, J. 2001. "Gender, Masculinities and Crime: From Structures to Psyches." *Theoretical Criminology* 5 (1): 37–60.
Irfan, L., and M. Wilkinson. 2020. "The Ontology of the Muslim Male Offender: A Critical Realist Framework." *Journal of Critical Realism* 19 (5): 481–499.
Jameson, F. 1990. *Late Marxism: Adorno or the Persistence of the Dialectic.* London: Verso.
Jefferson, T. 2002. "Subordinating Hegemonic Masculinity." *Theoretical Criminology* 6 (1): 63–88.
Jefferson, T. 1996. "Introduction: Masculinities, Social Relations and Crime." *The British Journal of Criminology* 36 (3): 337–347.
Kenway, J., and L. Fitzclarence. 1997. "Masculinity, Violence and Schooling: Challenging' Poisonous Pedagogies." *Gender and Education* 9 (1): 117–134.
Lloyd, G. 1984. *The Man of Reason: 'Male' and 'Female' in Western Philosophy.* London: Methuen.
Messerschmidt, J. W. 2000. "Becoming "Real Men" – Adolescent Masculinity Challenges and Sexual Violence." *Men and Masculinities* 2 (3): 286–307.
Norrie, A. 2004. "Bhaskar, Adorno and the Dialectics of Modern Freedom." *Journal of Critical Realism* 3 (1): 23–48.

Polk, K. 1999. "Males and Honor Contest Violence." *Homicide Studies* 3 (1): 6–29.
Seidler, V. 1994. *Unreasonable Men*. London: Routledge.
Tomsen, S., 1997. "A Top Night: Social Protest, Masculinity and the Culture of Drinking Violence." *The British Journal of Criminology* 37 (1): 90–102.
Wetherell, M., and N. Edley. 1999. "Negotiating Hegemonic Masculinity: Imaginary Positions and Psycho-Discursive Practices." *Feminism & Psychology* 9 (3): 335–356.
Winlow, S. 2014. "Trauma, Guilt and the Unconscious: Some Theoretical Notes on Violent Subjectivity." *The Sociological Review* 62: 32–49.
Winlow, S., and S. Hall. 2009. "Retaliate First: Memory, Humiliation and Male Violence." *Crime, Media, Culture* 5 (3): 285–304.

11
THE CRITICAL REALIST TOOLKIT

Ellenah Mackie

Introduction

This chapter presents critical realism as a toolkit for anyone seeking to understand complex real-world problems. I use critical realism as a philosophical framework that can link ways of thinking to ways of doing, to enhance my understanding of the world, and to provide the impetus for positive change where various forms of oppression exist. In my work and research, I found critical realism provides me with a toolkit of resources to understand and explore complex sociopolitical problems to mobilise action. Bhaskar (2008a) delivers a way of working on and in the world that illuminates our understanding and appreciation of our core universal humanity whilst attending to the mediations or stratifications that make us concretely singular (Norrie 2010). This is what I have come to understand as a 'loosening'. It affirms the possibility of utopic imaginings on the path to eudaimonia and universal flourishing. I share my loosening by reflecting on the journey I took to critical realism and, in the process, outlining some of the conceptual tools I have found most relevant.

Coming to Critical Realism

I was first introduced to Roy Bhaskar's work 12 years ago by my dear friend and mentor Dr Gary MacLennan. One morning over coffee I was sharing my frustration over the way Australian public policy seemed to continually fail Aboriginal and Torres Strait Islander children. Gary proceeded to draw a diagram of concentric circles. At the centre was, what he referred to as, the 'concrete universal' (Figure 11.1). Surrounding it were outward facing circles representing various structural and emergent properties.

122 Ellenah Mackie

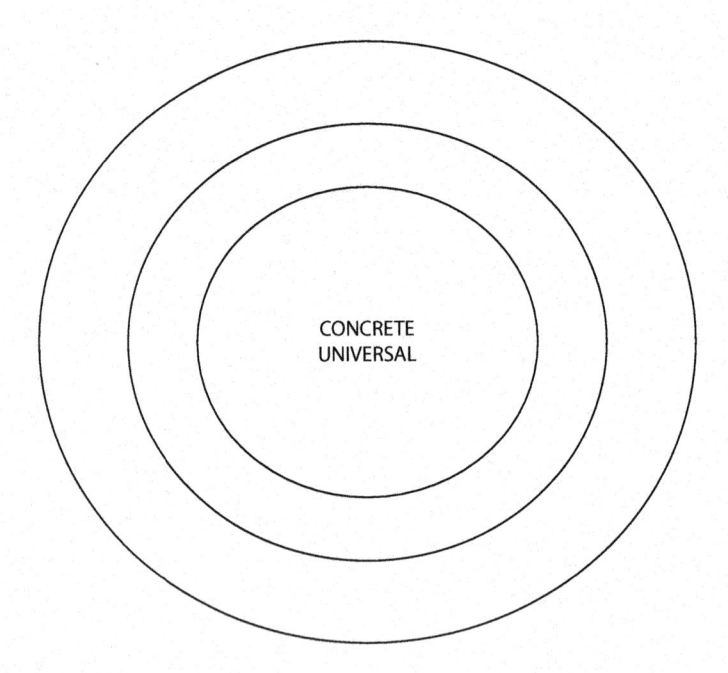

FIGURE 11.1 Sketching the Concrete Universal

Gary's purpose in sharing the diagram was to demonstrate how the oneness of humanity is best understood as enfolded. He left me with a copy of *Dialectic the Pulse of Freedom* (Bhaskar 2008a). I tried to engage with the work for many years. It was the version with the black cover. I thought it looked sexy and sophisticated. Despite wanting to have a mind that could turn to the text, I could not get into it. In honesty, I found it complex; I was not ready for the enormity of Bhaskar's writing and what it would mean in my future. Years passed, I had my third child, capitalism and individual possession seemed to be in full swing and neoliberalism entered a phase I refer to as demagogic neoliberalism (Mackie 2020): a time characterised by manipulation of prejudice and emotion over objectivity and rational discourse, where the irrational is dominant and there is a plague of post-truth demagoguery. As a consequence, I was feeling rather dismayed about the world my children were to inherit. I started disengaging from political discourse, finding it uninspiring. The news, national and international politics, and my twitter feed made me feel despair. I now reflect on this time and recognise this feeling as *alienation*, I was unable to work through the duality or split I was experiencing in my interactions. I felt like Hegel's 'beautiful soul': "the pure agent who will not reconcile herself to the norms of, and so is alienated from, her community" (Bhaskar 2002a, 167).

Again, I turned to Gary looking for answers. I did not (and do not!) want my children to grow up in a world where, if they fail to realise the capitalist dream, they would in turn be punished for it. Frankly, I do not want them to grow up in a world where humanity is a luxury and where full freedom isn't a freedom for all. It is from this that I came to the power of placing the critical realism concept of the *concrete universal* alongside the notion of *utopias*: they combine to present a way for understanding the world and ourselves. I have come to liken the concrete universal to a strong marriage. There are two key contributors to the marriage: universals and particulars. These are what make us unique and, at the same time, identical. Like marriage our concrete universality is mediated by and through process, space, and time. These influence the experience of the marriage and indeed the realisation of its potential. At this time Gary returned me to the concepts of concreteness and singularity. We then talked about the necessity of utopia and what resources we have for hope. Upon reflection we were confirming the importance of possibility and imagination, agency, desire, and a shared commitment to action in order to realise our humanity. He gave me a copy of the book – *Philosophy of Meta-Reality* (Bhaskar 2002a) and again urged me to attempt to engage with Bhaskar.

This book was my true entry point into critical realism. For me, philosophy of meta-reality showcased critical realism as a whole system of deepening understanding that was underpinned by concepts that resonated with me: love, creativity, and spontaneous right action. As I have come to see it, the first four moments of critical realism present a system for understanding the world and appreciating the 'other' and the final three moments a system for understanding self. The system in its totality underpinned by possibility and pluralism – two notions that have been fundamental to my research in stipulating for the necessity of utopic imaginings when planning for the future (Mackie 2020). Through philosophy of meta-reality, I was able to make sense of the connection between universality, singularity, social being, and utopia. I could almost feel the pulse of freedom as I read and re-read the text; there was energy in the book. I think the reason philosophy of meta-reality resonated with me was threefold. I had matured, I had a real-world problem I wanted to understand – and I was searching for meaning. In philosophy of meta-reality I found the resources for hope, I had a platform from which to understand and work through my feelings of alienation. This inspired me. I found what I was looking for in those pages. In critical realism I found a system that helped me make sense of the world. I knew that I couldn't ignore or mute the world by turning off the news and that I could not give up on emancipatory projects. Critical realism gave me the toolkit for actively working on myself, working through duality across a "multiplicity of determinations" (Norrie 2010, 114) so that I could work towards my utopic imaginings. Philosophy of Meta-Reality is such a beautifully elegant book. For me, it has been one of the most significant texts of my life. It changed how I engage with life. I had never read a philosophical text cover to cover before philosophy of meta-reality, so I credit Bhaskar (and Gary) for introducing me to philosophy.

I will be frank here in that my path into critical realism was somewhat idiosyncratic. I did not engage directly with the early Bhaskar (1975, 1979) work until after I had confronted the later texts. If I were to mentor someone into critical realism, I would not necessarily recommend the path I chose unless this more alternative track is something that seems appealing. You might access the introduction of Philosophy of Meta-Reality and, if it doesn't appeal immediately, then try beginning with the discussions Bhaskar held with Hartwig (Bhaskar and Hartwig 2010) where a narrative of the development of critical realist thought is given. Perhaps the key early texts such as *A Realist Theory of Science* (Bhaskar 1975) and *The Possibility of Naturalism* (Bhaskar 1979) could then be tackled. I would strongly suggest reading the Hartwig introductions in the later Routledge editions of those texts (Bhaskar 1998, 2008b). From here I would proceed to *Dialectic the Pulse of Freedom* (Bhaskar 2008a). Again, I suggest using Hartwig's introduction to enable you to navigate the text. From *Dialectic* it is a relatively easy path (in my opinion!) to the Philosophy of Meta-Reality.

The reason I really immersed myself in philosophy of meta-reality is because it not only gave me hope at a time I felt desperate for it but also it provided me tools to live a meaning-filled life. This is how I use critical realism, as a toolkit to make meaning and to understand complex real-world problems. It is a philosophical framework that links ways of thinking to ways of doing to enhance our understanding of the world. The holistic consideration of the critical realism toolkit as a single and integrated system allows me to approach the research process and my life with the fluidity required when undertaking analysis, seeking explanations, and making decisions. As Bhaskar views *Dialectic* as a 'great loosener', I view critical realism as a toolkit that delivers an approach that allows the research process, and its application to evolve, as the analysis does. Reflecting most purely the complexity of research in open and stratified systems reinforces how critical realism is a practical philosophy for understanding the everyday (Bhaskar 2008a). I will next outline the critical realism concepts or 'tools' I find most useful.

My Critical Realism Toolkit

For understanding problems

Critical realism presented me as a researcher with a useful philosophical system for examining and understanding complex or "wicked problems" (Crowley and Head 2017; Rittel and Webber 1973). Of course, it is also relevant that I was working in the public service where often the requirement is to act and understand complexity quickly. This was a clear instance for the role of utilising theoretical frameworks for generating practical solutions. It was of benefit to me that I could grasp in critical realist terms that a wicked problem is a problem with ontological depth and multiple causalities at many strata of reality. It is complex, and it challenges us to think differently. As such, the lure of the magical solution or silver bullet can be resisted. A critical realism researcher undertakes a process of thinking about the world so they can understand it and take an active role in it – not unlike the role of the public servant. This requires an examination of the 'fine structures' underpinning the world and a commitment to reflexive practice

(Bhaskar 2002a). Positioning methodology within critical realism Philosophy presents an ontological framework that is orientated to the real-world application of philosophy to understand an urgent and pressing problem. It demonstrates the need for the human sciences to directly address philosophical questions in order to demonstrate their relevance to 'everyday work' (Shipway 2011, 128).

For realising possibility

My recent research argued for the necessity of utopia and highlighted the importance of imagining as a means to inform futures-based planning. Bhaskar, when referring to utopia, always prefaces it, as 'concrete'. For instance, he states that "the moment of concrete utopianism, which identifies 'the positive in the negative', must always be grounded in real possibilities-in-process" (2008a, 274). Mumford distinguished between Utopias of escape and Utopias of reconstruction. The utopia of escape is "raised and it collapses and it is built up again almost daily" (Mumford 1962, 18). It is dangerous, Mumford (1962, 20) argues, "to remain in the utopia of escape for … to remain there is to lose one's capacity for dealing with things as they are" (1962, 21–22). Bhaskar negates this danger by distinguishing his utopian thought from fantasy. He does this by orientating the process towards flourishing in daily praxis and balancing possibility, alongside natural necessity, ethical possibility and considering the domain of limits (Bhaskar 2008a). I understand the value of a critical realism approach to underlabouring for utopian thinking by turning to Jameson's remarks on the link between fantasy and utopia. He wrote: "But the truth value of fantasy, the epistemological *bon usage* or proper use of daydreaming as an instrument of philosophical speculation, lies precisely in a confrontation with the reality principle [emphasis added] itself" (Jameson 2005, 74).

If Jameson had worked with the threefold critical realism ontology of the real, the actual, and the empirical, he would have grasped that the confrontation is not between daydreaming and reality but between imagination and the actual. Indeed, to see imagination as breaking from actualism is the key to understanding the role of utopia in critical realism thinking. What imagination does is to liberate us from the grasp of the actual and to release the "Not Yet" (Bloch 1986) that is contained within the real. It is not only in its provision of a threefold ontology that critical realism's contribution to utopian thinking lies. Within Bhaskar's notion of the dialectical relationship between what he called the 7 E's and the 6 T's we have, arguably, the nucleus of a critical realism map of utopia and a way to achieve it; what a toolkit for making meaning and working on the world!

For understanding relationships

In examining sociopolitical problems along with understanding relationships, systems, and structures a grasp of depth ontology and Bhaskar's four-level dialectic are particularly useful. If we take the concrete universal, as Gary depicted for me all those years ago, we can think about depth ontology as influencing the mediations or stratifications that surround or enfold one's own core humanity. When I consider the concrete universal as nested within the domains of Bhaskar's stratified reality for four planar social being, I can appreciate how one experiences the world and the role of structures, mechanisms, and events in that. When I have this appreciation, it supports me to make better decisions informed by knowledge of real-world complexities which is necessary for human beings to interact as moral agents with trust and solidarity. In philosophy of meta-reality terms, we see each other in non-judgemental identity. There is a purity that comes through co-presence. We can work through and across difference that shape identities. This process I am describing is a way of moving from the abstract to the concrete, between the universal and the singular to achieve a unity of theory and practice. This part of the toolkit solves the problem of the one and the many by asking whether underpinning variety is an essential oneness – or concrete universal.

Norrie (2010) explains that we can understand the concept of the concrete universal by understanding four planar theory of being. Through the dynamic of structure and agency, we can orient ideas of identity mediated in space and time. Four planar being "illustrates the very different rhythmics that may engage an individual at different levels of being" (2010, 115). As such, the four-level dialectic or four planar being is one of the key tools in my critical realism toolkit for deepening my understanding of the world. Dialectical Critical Realism allows the deployment of the four-level Bhaskarian dialectic in its original four-level form. At 4D we are introduced to the concepts of human agency conceived as four planar social being. These are: the plane of the intra-personal, the plane of the inter-personal, the plane of our interactions with social structures, and the plane of our interactions with nature (Bhaskar 2008a). The four planes of social being have been important for me as they offer an understanding of structure and agency and transformative practice. This level (4D) is one of the defining features of Bhaskar's dialectic offering a resolution to the inconsistencies and complexities or crisis within open social systems and can be thought about as a social cube for praxis (Bhaskar 2016, 130). The application of four planar being deepens our understanding of the concrete universal (Norrie 2010). We can approach this process by embodying our ground states, offered to my toolkit by Bhaskar's final moments in philosophy of meta-reality.

For understanding self

Philosophy of Meta-Reality is derived from Bhaskar's ethical critique of the antinomies of post modernity. The philosophy itself goes beyond the four-level dialectic (see Figure 11.2). It drives much of the emancipatory impulse for my

MELDARZ(A) or 7A>6R>5A>4D>3L>2E>1M

FIGURE 11.2 Beyond the Four-Level Dialectic and MELDARZ(A)

research and provides the longed-for 'resources for hope'. Essentially through philosophy of meta-reality, Bhaskar delivers a complete system to understand ontology that I use daily and I believe requires practice as it is a pursuit in what I think can only be termed as purity.

As I have said earlier, the four-level dialectic (1M–4D) provides the tools to understand the underlying structures and tendencies within open ontology, through non-identity or absence. However, in *The Philosophy of Meta-Reality, Volume 1*, Bhaskar (2002a) gives us the tools to work through ourselves to understand what is beneath the dual world we experience every day. He provides an additional three levels to his system. I employ these to understand the fine underlying structures that may be at play within an open ontology and through identity or unity. In turn, this turn has influenced how I view myself – not just the world or my role in it. It is almost as if these last three levels were the tools, I needed to realise the importance of my agency, how to be a more considered agent, and how to sustain a level of passion and engagement in a world that can be challenging. Such as when the systems and structures are not changing (or not changing fast enough!) or the progress is swinging in the direction of loss rather than gain. Philosophy of meta-reality gives hope that if we as agents stay focused and toil in these moments, through our ground states we progress and grow sparking a *silent revolution*. A revolution that will have so much power, the systems and structures of oppression must fall or at a minimum bend. The key that unlocks this universal flourishing is the work required to access one's ground state/s which require us to consider Gary's first concept to me – the concrete universal.

Again, if we think about the concrete universal through these additional three levels of Bhaskar's system, we can understand how we need to attend or work through the duality underpinning the non-dual world, here we see reality as enfolded. At the core of reality there is a ground state/s, a spirituality that Bhaskar identifies as qualities implicit within humans such as love and creativity. Secondly, there is transcendence, which could be thought of as a type of emergence. Transcendence is unity in its totality, in consciousness, agency, self, and ingredient. To understand the non-dual world is to understand "the fine structure or what we could call the deep interior of any moment or aspect of being or consciousness" (Bhaskar 2002a, xi) it is at its core our fundamental humanity, our sameness, we are at this level enfolded.

I believe this process that I am describing commences at 5A, the spiritual aspect that presupposes emancipation. I understand this to be the aspect that connects us, that brings us together through a process of reflexivity and inward contemplation. 6R, the sixth realm, is re-enchantment. This is a process of shedding, a process of growth. This is about the realisation of being and meaning grounded in self-love. Where the realities of duality and demi-reality are collapsed, the world, text, values, and structures within everyday life all have meaning. At 7Z/A, the seventh zone or awakening of non-duality, we find the state of inner bliss and unity or what I believe could be referred to as utopia. It is the transcendence to our ground state and complete totality within the cosmic envelope. This is where the concept of the concrete universal flourishes. The seven levels of being present a continuous process that involves self, other, and structure across stratified reality and across the three domains of the real. Together they are necessary for the abolition of master-slave relationships, the realisation of freedom and the actualisation of eudemonistic society. Bhaskar (2002a, xvi) writes: "we need to draw back the curtains of our mind to lift the illusory web of time to roll back the technologies and systems we have produced to unveil the creative, loving, right-acting ground state activity which sustains them but has nothing in common with them".

Essentially, as philosophy of meta-reality enabled me to realise the limitations of the world of duality, it provides the processes and tools that empower one to breakdown and shed the opposing forces and structures, which block the realisation of emancipation. This theory, based on a spiritual dialectic, moves one from alienation and split to emancipation and unity based on us all having a ground state of universal love, solidarity, and compassion. In turn, this provides a foundation for all that we do (Bhaskar 2002a, 2002b). As Bhaskar points out, even a phenomenon such as war depends on acts of love, "The horror of war presupposes all the peaceful acts necessary to keep it going" (Bhaskar and Hartwig 2010, 172). It is, indeed, love that is essential and not hatred (Bhaskar 2016, 80). The premise that love is primary and hate is parasitical means that we can only exist in a world with love. A world of only hatred is a logical impossibility. Such a world would have no capacity to reproduce itself. The jewel in the toolkit here is that with one stroke debilitating pessimism is disarmed and the great motivator, hope is given its proper place. So, one can see how in the despair I talked to earlier, Bhaskar's final moments shed light on a different way of thinking about what I was feeling, experiencing, and seeing in my every day that I could then apply to a research problem and context I was struggling with.

Summary

This chapter positioned critical realist philosophy as a practical toolkit that I have used in my everyday life and research for understanding the world. I came to the philosophy somewhat unconventionally and I think my notion of critical realism as a toolkit with the resources for hope reflects this. The critical realism toolkit enables one to deploy the system in its full form or engage with key ideas and concepts as needed based on where one may be in their own research or personal journey. Here I provided a brief exploration of key realist concepts that have been most impactful on my journey; depth ontology, four-level dialectic, and the final three levels of Bhaskar's system through the Philosophy of Meta-Reality that I believe link back to the concept of the concrete universal and the importance of utopic imaginings in terms of their importance to my pathway to philosophy. Research underlaboured by critical realism delivers a system of thinking about the world that can assist researchers to take on a role of agency in the pursuit of emancipatory projects or matters of utopian endeavour, like it did with me. The critical realism system offers a suite of resources or a 'toolkit' that when applied either as individualised components or as a system in its totality is an effective way to bridge theory to practice, to understand self and other. May the silent revolution begin.

References

Bhaskar, R. 1975. *A Realist Theory of Science*. Leeds: Leeds Books.
Bhaskar, R. 1979. *The Possibility of Naturalism: A Philosophical Critique of the Contemporary Human Sciences*. Brighton: Harvester Press.
Bhaskar, R. 1998. *The Possibility of Naturalism: A Philosophical Critique of the Contemporary Human Sciences*. 3rd ed. London: Routledge.
Bhaskar, R. 2002a. *The Philosophy of Meta-Reality, Volume 1, Meta-Reality: Creativity, Love and Freedom*. New Delhi: Sage.
Bhaskar, R. 2002b. *Reflections on Meta-Reality – Transcendence, Emancipation and Everyday Life*. New Delhi: Sage.
Bhaskar, R. 2008a. *Dialectic – The Pulse of Freedom*. 2nd ed. London Routledge.
Bhaskar, R. 2008b. *A Realist Theory of Science*. 2nd ed. London: Routledge.
Bhaskar, R. 2016. *Critical Realism in a Nutshell*. London: Routledge.
Bhaskar, R. and M. Hartwig. 2010. *The Formation of Critical Realism – A Personal Perspective*. Milton Park: Routledge.
Bloch, E. 1986. *The Principle of Hope* (N. Plaice, S. Plaice, & P. Knight, Trans. Vol. 1). Cambridge : MIT Press.
Crowley, K. and B. W. Head. 2017. "The Enduring Challenge of 'Wicked Problems': Revisiting Rittel and Webber." *Policy Sciences* 50 (4): 539–547. doi:10.1007/s11077-017-9302-4.
Jameson, F. 2005. *Archaeologies of the Future: The Desire Called Utopia and Other Science Fictions*. London: Verso.
Mackie, E. 2020. *Future Ready Queensland: The Role of the State: A Philosophical Position on Public Policy for the Fourth Industrial Revolution*. (PhD), Southern Cross University.
Mumford, L. 1962. *The Story of Utopias*. New York: The Viking Press.
Norrie, A. 2010. *Dialectic and Difference; Dialectical Critical Realism and the Grounds of Justice*. London: Routledge.
Rittel, H.W.J. and M. M. Webber. 1973. "Dilemmas in a General Theory of Planning." *Policy Sciences* 4 (2): 155–169. https://doi.org/10.1007/BF01405730.
Shipway, B. 2011. *A Critical Realist Perspective of Education*. London: Routledge.

12

JOURNEYS TO CRITICAL REALISM

A Conversation about Spirituality, Love, and Human Emancipation

Loretta Geuenich, Celina Valente, and Grant Banfield

Introduction

Over two evenings in October and November of 2021, the authors of this chapter met to share memories of their journeys to, and with, critical realism. In what follows, we present our recollections in dialogical form. Our stories are told using our actual spoken words – whether these be taken directly from the recordings of our initial conversations or from subsequent reflective dialogue between us.

Our journeys are both individual and collective. They are bound by the fact that two of us (Loretta and Celina) were recent postgraduate research students at an Australian university who shared the same research supervisor (Grant). Grant introduced critical realism to both Loretta and Celina.

Celina's project enquired into the possibility of academic activism in the contemporary neoliberal university. Drawing on the work of critical realist sociologist, Margaret Archer (1995, 2003, 2012), Celina employed theory-driven interviews with selected Australian academic activists to explore the kinds of reflexive capacities academic activists possess and draw upon in their activist work. In the broadest of terms, her research was about the fundamental capacities of human beings to transform the world and transform themselves.

In a similar way, Loretta's research looked at the possibility of building ethical and social capacities in a changing higher education landscape. She explored the use of 'contemplative practices' in higher education – predominantly within the global North (USA and Canada) – as a vehicle for self-enrichment and the cultivation of an ethical social 'response-ability'. Loretta recognised a strong synergy with critical realist philosophy and her own Buddhist practice that underpinned what is called 'Contemplative Higher Education'. To explore the potential of Contemplative Higher Education Loretta knew she needed a realist ontology of human nature to underpin her research. Critical realism provided this. Her research focused on key Contemplative Higher Education academic practitioners and what motivated, constrained, and enabled their practice. Data was collected through multiple in-depth interviews with educators in North America. Archer's internal conversation and morphogenetic sequence shaped the research design (Archer 1995, 2003).

Grant's journey to critical realism also began with his PhD. Unlike Celina and Loretta his interests rested in coming to a better understanding of Marxist praxis. Critical realism became the philosophical underlabourer to the project. Where Celina and Loretta's inclinations rested in Bhaskar's latter works, Grant's work had its primary origins in Bhaskar's early critical realism. We discuss the reasons for and implications of this difference in our conversation. It is central to our dialogue consolidating around the importance of love and spirituality for human emancipation.

We now invite you into our conversation. It begins with Loretta and Celina reflecting on the challenges they faced in tying down what their research projects were to be about.

LORETTA: Celina, I can remember when you were going through the process of thinking about what you were going to do – the different pathways you could take. It took time. Getting started took time.

CELINA: Yes, it was a long process. Deciding on the best way to tackle it was not straightforward.

LORETTA: A 'long process' and 'far from straightforward' definitely resonate for me. However, I wonder if the reasons for our struggles were different? Having arrived with a clear research project, my long process was encountering critical realism and coming to a methodological framing that reflected a nuanced understanding of ontology. It took about 8 months of reading and wrangling. But I recall you coming to yours quicker than I did. You seemed to know of critical realism early in your candidature whereas I didn't know it existed until I was well into my time.

CELINA: Yes, that is right. For me, critical realism was there almost from the beginning.

GRANT: This is interesting. You remind me of something I had forgotten. You each brought very different starting points to your postgraduate study and research. Celina, you came with a reasonably clear methodological path in your mind. With your background in social science and having serious questions about its internal (and debilitating) philosophical tensions, you saw the underlabouring potential of critical realism very early. It was obvious to you. I think I simply pointed you in a direction and let you go. Your issue was not methodological but empirical.

Loretta, things were different for you. I recall when you first approached me to supervise your research you had a clear view of the substantive nature of your project.

LORETTA: Yes, in my mind I had a clear research problematic – a real world problem to research. My concern was with how we, as educators, were to prepare students for this already tumultuous 21st century. I was curious about how Contemplative Higher Education might support a socially oriented agency. The movement to 'mindfulness' worried me.

GRANT: In what way?

LORETTA: Mindfulness is orientated to Actualism, i.e., towards the amelioration of the effects of an ontology of lack (personal, societal, and increasingly global). It often presents as a fix: a remedy to the imperfect self, mind, etc. Mindfulness frequently, but not always (depending on whose hands it is in), sets out to soothe the symptoms of an alienated and alienating world. In contrast, contemplative education nurtures a fuller range of human capacities for agency and transformation – both inner and outer. So, the question underpinning my research was: Could contemplative education help heal our alienation within ourselves, from others, and from our living breathing world?

GRANT: OK. I understand. You mention capacity building for 'inner and outer' transformation. This says something important about how your path to critical realism was different to mine. My coming to critical realism was via revolutionary Marxism. This meant that, in both my head and my practice, transforming the 'outer' was prioritised to the exclusion of the 'inner'. For me, the inner was 'spiritual' – quasi-religious – and to be rejected as bourgeois idealism.

I don't think this would have been the kind of early conversation we would have had when we were discussing your project. So how and when did critical realism come into the picture and how did it stick?

LORETTA: No, you are right. We did not discuss Marx. Well, not much. However, I can remember that first meeting when you suggested critical realism. Something sparked. This was after months of wrangling with research paradigms and not being able to locate my ontological commitments within any of them.

GRANT: What 'wrangling' are you referring to?

LORETTA: I need to start by saying that I had been struggling with methodological and conceptual issues throughout my undergraduate degree and into my Master's thesis. I was leaning to poststructuralism. However, I was not completely satisfied. At the same time, my path of training and practice in Tibetan Buddhism was deepening and broadening. There came a point where I consciously realised that things didn't fit. There was an obvious theory-practice inconsistency. I made a little turn towards constructivism which seemed to satisfy some epistemological questions I had.

GRANT: Your formal studies seem to have presented poststructuralism and constructivism as the only alternatives.

LORETTA: Yes, but neither of them were completely satisfactory. Ontology was missing. It did not sit with my practice which was about cultivating the capacity to get in touch with, what I was to learn later Bhaskar calls, the 'Real'. I was committed to developing capacities to get yourself out of the way enough so you experience things 'are *as* they are' – rather than you might '*think* they are'. This requires a shift from seeing the self as a solid unchanging entity engaging with an objective outer world, to one that experiences that world as impermanent, aggregated, and constantly shifting: arising in a state of 'inter-being'. That 'self' may, or may not, bear any resemblance to who we tell ourselves we are – through our opinions, storylines, and beliefs. We do not exist in isolation. As the Vietnamese meditation master Thich Nat Hanh says we 'inter-are' with our world. So, all of this was going on.

CELINA: You make a deeply humanist point Loretta. We become more 'human' the more we get in touch with, what Bhaskar (2002a) referred to as, our 'ground state'. For me, getting 'ourselves' out of the way refers to learning to see through and beyond the mental structures – the incessant chatting of the mind – that prevent us from accessing the ground state. Meditation is all about that.

GRANT: In reading Bhaskar's personal account of the evolution of critical realism (Bhaskar 2010) I found it very interesting the central place that mediation had in initiating the move to Transcendental Dialectical Critical Realism. Bhaskar recalls a time in the mid-1990s when he had just completed *Plato Etc* (Bhaskar 1994) and *Dialectic* (Bhaskar 1993). Exhausted and very run down, he caught a heavy cold. Instead of taking his usual path to western medicine he turned to Reiki, massage, and meditation. As a result of the experience, he says

> It occurred to me that everything I had been doing referred to the world of external objects and material things, [… Reiki and meditation] put me in touch again with a deep inner world: what was happening, as it were, in myself behind – or rather in the deep uncharted interior of – the world of physical bodies and material objects.
>
> (Bhaskar 2010, 146)

Through experience – not abstract reflection – Bhaskar touched what he saw as the 'unchartered interior': an "alternative world that I had forgotten about or repressed" (Bhaskar 2010, 146). I think this is what both of you are expressing. Am I correct?

LORETTA: Yes, we mostly don't acknowledge or even believe that it is possible to go beyond mental structures and experience deeper realities. Yet, we constantly have insights and experiences of this – whether we recognise them or not. Bhaskar talks about how our everyday life is "underpinned by a barely noticed but deep spiritual … infrastructure" (2016, 170–171). In our daily lives, we are entwined in our own thoughts and projections. We solidify those ways of thinking, being, and doing in the world. Meditation and other deep contemplative practices help disrupt those habitual tendencies which keep us imprisoned – exiled and alienated from ourselves and others. They also offer a portal to connection our underlying human capacities that are inherent and yearn for greater expression. Capacities that are available in every moment. We can learn to let that 'other stuff' fall away. Understand that nothing, in its nature is fixed and unchanging. Rather, everything is constantly 'in-becoming' – in ways that are fresh, immediate, not lacking anything. We experience the 'Real', this deep infrastructure. Yet, as soon as we try to put language to this, it is necessarily partial and thus fallible. This is what I couldn't find in any of the academic books I was reading at the time. Critical realism changed that.

CELINA: My experience is similar but, as we have said, my path was different. Like you, I was looking to explore the inner lives of human beings that social science ignores. I wanted to explore that aspect of human beings from a sociological vantage point – or, as I now understand it, a *naturalist* vantage point where inner lives are understood as one of the strata from which social structures emerge. This invites the asking of very important questions around, for example, the relation between social structures and our inner lives. Or, more practically: for social change to be possible what work must we do on ourselves?

GRANT: In working with both of you over time I became aware of how your experiences and the ways you saw the world around you were, in significant ways, different to mine. Both of you were intuitively drawn to the study of inner lives. I wasn't. This gave me pause to consider how I was intellectually socialised and the mechanisms operating behind my back that this entailed. Through our many conversations, you reminded me of my own socialisation into the discipline of sociology. Or, might I say, you pressed me (without perhaps knowing it) to reflect on how I was disciplined by sociology.

LORETTA: I know. I was a bit relentless. So many questions!

GRANT: Yes, there were! But I enjoyed that. No, it is more than that. Let me put it this way: the kind of relentless seriousness that both of you brought is necessary for ruthless 'internal' and 'external' critique. Therefore, by necessity, this demanded I confront my own disciplining. This began with the obvious: acknowledging that the object of the field, society, was to be grasped unproblematically as something 'out there'. Of course, there are arguments within the field of sociology rejecting strong structuralist accounts residing within its own ranks. However, from my experience, the concept of 'society out there' weighs heavily on the field and reinforced at sociology conferences, in the writing of research grants, and in collegial exchanges. These are, in critical realist terms, real mechanisms generating a taken-for-granted suspicion of any reference to life 'in here'. I must say that, along with both of you, Bhaskar did his degree of pushing. His second chapter in *The Possibility of Naturalism* came to my brain like a bolt of lightning. Simply entitled 'Societies', it offered a critique of western social thought as a failure to adequately grasp the 'person/society connection' (Bhaskar 1993, 25–79). After reading and rereading the chapter over some time, I began to question most of what I had absorbed in undergraduate sociology texts and played with in postgraduate explorations.

CELINA: This is sounding like my experience!
GRANT: Like you Celina, the unresolved tensions in sociology troubled me. However, I did not have the conceptual means to unpack them before they were laid bare in Bhaskar's three models of Weberian voluntarism, Durkheimian structuralism, and Bergerian dialecticism. As the three of us worked through and discussed many times, while the first two modes present the person/society relation as one where either the person or society was more fundamental to the connection the latter fuses them in what Bhaskar referred to as an 'illicit identification' (1993, 32). This was the individual-society problem to which introductory sociology texts routinely refer but offer no solution. Bhaskar's way out of the problem was via a naturalist path: a return to ontology. Simply put, people and the societies they make "refer to radically different kinds of thing" (Bhaskar 1993, 33). Sociology (and Marxist sociology in particular) suffered from, what I would later come to refer to as, 'ontological shyness' (Banfield 2016).
LORETTA: I must say that your articulation of ontological shyness was a great breakthrough point for me. In my practice, ontology has always been right up front. But, in the academy, it seemed that people were fearful of it. Everything had to be reduced to language. This was a shock to me.
GRANT: For me, it was more of a frustration. By the time I began reading Bhaskar's work I had been in the academy for some years. None of my postmodernist or interpretivist colleagues disagreed that an 'external' reality existed. They simply insisted it couldn't be known – and that was the end of the matter. Vital questions around, for example, what it is to be human are conveniently jettisoned. Why ponder the impossible? It wasn't until I had some critical realist tools that I was able to unpack some of these kinds of problems for myself.
LORETTA: And what were those tools?
GRANT: That's a good question. My introduction to critical realism was via, what might be called, the traditional path. It begins with Original critical realism where Bhaskar developed his arguments for transcendental realism, critical naturalism, and explanatory critique. So, it was in 1M that I found the tools I needed. I began to see that, if Bhaskar's naturalist path was correct, then this leads to tackling questions of human nature of the possibility of radical human transformative agency – all very important matters to a humanist Marxist like myself.

However, in moving through Dialectical Critical Realism and Transcendental Dialectical Critical Realism, I was forced to confront matters of spirituality. To be honest, this was territory I was reluctant to traverse. In this regard, I suppose I would have qualified as realist who, in Archer's terms, holds to a realism that doesn't "go all the way down" (Archer 2004, 70). To my mind, the spiritual carried strong religious undertones. For a Marxian sociologist, the spiritual was a 'no go' zone. As the great man put it: religion is the opium of the people (Marx 1975, 243).

CELINA: I understand what you are saying Grant. My background is also social science and Marx is very familiar to me. However, I have a different view of spirituality and religiosity. Let me explain.

When I was at university at home in Argentina I was told: 'We are going to use these tools to describe what is happening, but values are not something that we will consider. If you are a scientist, you have to leave your values at the door'. But I said: 'It was my values that brought me here!' That was a big disappointment for me because I knew leaving your values at the door was impossible – and therefore must be unscientific!

I believe that, as children, we all have a more direct access to the ground state. As we grow up, we are socialised out of making that natural connection. In my case, however, it was a bit different. I grew up with my Mum who was a very spiritual person and always fostered that aspect of my being. There were always 'spiritual' kinds of books around the house – books about meditation, Buddhism, and different aspects of spiritual life. But that part of my life was separate from my life as a student and my formal studies. When I went to university, I did sociology because I wanted to do something good for the world. I thought that social science could be the way to put what I believed into action. I wanted to do something about poverty, inequality, and racism.

GRANT: I can see some resonance with my experiences. I understand your frustration with positivist science and its dominance in the academy. But I can see that your familiarity with a spiritual life is very different to mine. Let's explore the resonances first and divergences later.

CELINA: OK. That makes sense.

GRANT: When you decided to pursue a PhD, and that was in Australia, did you have in your mind that you would use it to push against the value-free positivism of 'normal' social science?

CELINA: Yes, I wanted to go deeper into social science. Upon reflection, I found it hard to keep my life separate from my study life. I had this spiritual side – a curiosity about that dimension of life. But bringing them together was difficult, they never seemed to touch each other.

LORETTA: Exactly my experience.

CELINA: This is where critical realism came in. I remember you talked to me about critical realism – and I got very curious. So, I started Googling things like who Bhaskar was and what critical realism was about. I found some of his material online. I remember one of the first works of Bhaskar I looked at was *The Formation of Critical Realism* (Bhaskar 2010). In this work, I was struck by Bhaskar's quest to explore the world outside science and philosophy. It resonated with me. Grant, this is where our divergences begin.

GRANT: I agree.

CELINA: Grant, you mentioned earlier Bhaskar's experiences with Transcendental Meditation and Reiki. His experiences were familiar to me. I had done all those things as a 'seeker'. Like Bhaskar, I think that that seeking of a path (which, in the end, is an exploration of and an underlabouring for 'truth') is a natural inclination of human beings. Bhaskar's idea of religion as something contingent to spirituality also struck a chord for me. I have never been involved in any kind of religious practice. However, 'secular' spirituality, as Bhaskar calls it, has been a constant in my life (Bhaskar 2000, 2010, 145–166).

GRANT: Thank you for bringing up the idea of secular spirituality. I suspect our divergences might not be as wide as we first thought. Reflecting on what you have said, I am taken back to my struggles with religiosity and spirituality. My critical realist journey has taken me to the understanding of spirituality, as Bhaskar put it, "as a presupposition both of religious and of emancipatory projects … [and that of] everyday life". Here, Bhaskar insists that spirituality is ontologically deep: it sits deeper than religion and religiosity. This means, as Bhaskar makes this abundantly clear when he continues, "that there is no necessary connection between spirituality and religiosity, that the ways in which religion is practised are not just distorted manifestations of spirituality, and that you can have a completely secular spirituality" (2010, 152).

LORETTA: Earlier you described spirituality as bourgeois idealism. This does not match with what you are saying now, Grant.

GRANT: Spot on. It does not match. My thinking about spirituality, Marx, and Marxism has shifted. Some critical realist underlabouring along with your gentle persistence to get me to consider inner work as revolutionary praxis has had effect.

LORETTA: That's good! I'd be interested in hearing what critical realist underlabouring you did.

GRANT: That's a huge task! However, it is salient to be reminded that Bhaskar's "most important motivation" in developing the 'spiritual turn' was "to strengthen the cultural resources of the left" (Bhaskar 2010, 148). For Bhaskar, the 'spiritual turn' was always a project for socialism. Reflecting on the world as he saw it at the end of the last century, Bhaskar understood the struggle for socialism as a project of solely transforming the plane of social structures to the exclusion of the other three planes in his '4 Planar Social Being' (Bhaskar 1993, 160): material transactions with nature, interactions between people, and interactions with the self. Within western Marxism, it was the latter that was most notably absent. "This was despite Marx's injunction in the third thesis of Feuerbach that the educators – those who would usher in a new society – must themselves be educated, that is, must educate themselves" (Bhaskar 2010, 148–149).

LORETTA: Now you mention this Grant, you remind me how powerful Marx's injunction and his provocation of 'who will educate the educators?' was in my early exploration of Contemplative Higher Education vis-à-vis mindfulness. In my interviews, I quickly learned that the educators were practiced at 'educating themselves'. They had developed a rich range of human capacities in tune with Bhaskar's Four Planar Social Being. This enabled them to practise a kind of 'full education' that opened their lives and that of their students to the related complexities of material transactions with nature, social interactions between people, social structure, the embodied personality (Bhaskar 1993,160, 1986, 130), and their own deep spiritual infrastructure.

GRANT: I like your reference to a 'deep spiritual infrastructure'. It brings an ethic to the ontological or, what Bhaskar would call, the 'self-structuration of being' (2002a, 117). This is where Marx's provocation in the third thesis takes Bhaskar.

CELINA: I now see that it is no accident that you finished your book on a critical realist underlaboured Marxist sociology of education with Marx's third thesis on Feuerbach (Banfield 2016).

GRANT: Yes, in that final chapter I tried to make the argument for a sensuous materialist pedagogy. Spirituality is base to that. Contrary to my earlier view, spirituality is not opium of the people – in the way religion can be. It is not the sigh of the oppressed. Rather, it is the will of the oppressed for self-emancipation. To actualise that will, we must educate ourselves recognising the spiritual expresses materially real human powers of inner necessity. Spirituality is, in dialectical terms, the pulse of freedom: the unfolding potential of "our causal powers to flourish" (Bhaskar 1993, 385). Here we have clearly presented in the most obvious way, the centrality of spirituality to being human. In contrast, religion, in all its forms, expresses historically conditioned and socially emergent moral postulates. Spirituality is the base to a materially grounded, sensuously materialist, ethical naturalism that demands distinguishing 'ought' (moral postulates) from 'is' (the ontologically real).

CELINA: Yes, we have no divergence here. But I must stress that any distinction between 'is' and 'ought' can only be *analytical*. A complete distinction followed by a rejection of values takes us to positivist science. As I have said, this is one of the issues that brought me to critical realism in the first place. The distinction – or *relation* I should say – must be grasped dialectically.

GRANT: Certainly! Stressing an analytical distinction is most important. The separation of fact from value for the purpose of analysis is necessary for explanation. But this can only be momentary. For they must be put back together again to see them, as you stress, in their relation.

CELINA: Of course, an analytical distinction is not a severance. As we know, Bhaskar's critique of positivism involves the rejection of the fact/value split which then forms the basis of his explanatory critique (Bhaskar 1986, 181–200, 1993, 258–270). It seems we agree!

GRANT: We do. And what is more, I now realise that I have always lived and yearned for the spiritual. To give one example: solidarity presupposes spirituality. Solidarity is a connection (intangible as it is real) with others that you may never have met – or ever will. Bhaskar goes further and recognises a universal solidarity such that "in principle any human being can empathise with and come to understand any other human being" (2016, 172). Celina, it is clear to me that you embarked on a sociology degree in an act of solidarity.

CELINA: You are right.

GRANT: The conversations the three of us have had over time have critically informed my reflections on spiritualty. As I have said, both of you (in your various and gentle ways) pushed me in this direction. This has been a good thing. Can I ask to what degree I pushed you? Behind this question, I am really asking: did I push you into critical realism and this was *not* a good thing?

LORETTA: You did not push. I saw it as an offering: an invitation. You said: 'What about critical realism?' It came out of general conversations we had early on in which I shared with you the struggles I was having around the thinking through my project. When I started my studies, I thought I had found a suitable supervisor with expertise in the area. But it didn't work out. Whether they had an interest in my project I don't know. I came to see that they were unable to guide me through the rigorous methodological work I knew I needed to do. I wanted guidance in developing a philosophically informed methodological frame.

GRANT: I clearly remember you had a general understanding of the *kind* of philosophy you thought you needed. This knowledge arose from your experience and your practice. Your challenge was to bring all that into alignment with the demands of doing empirical social research.

LORETTA: That's right. I knew this alignment was going to be important. It would be essential in directing me to wisely choose appropriate concrete theories and research methods for my project. And this brought me to another problem – or absence – I had to address. Given the *nature* of what I was interested in exploring, I knew I'd be needing social theory of some kind in my project. I had studied visual arts and had done some politics in my Master's degree. However, I knew I needed more. I needed a supervisor with a background in social theory or sociology. As I understand it now, I needed some underlabouring assistance with how to think through and define and express my ontological commitments that would then lead to a methodological frame. At the time, I wouldn't have known how to articulate that – or what that even meant. All I knew was that I needed help to get some grounding in philosophy and sociology 101 and 102!

So, Grant, I came to you. You put critical realism on the table, it was an offering. You just said: 'What about critical realism?' And I thought: 'What's that?'.

GRANT: How did you go about exploring 'What's that'? Where did you first dabble? How and where did you initially get your toes wet? Did you jump into a book? Go to YouTube?

LORETTA: I did all of that – and more. I came at it from every direction. I simply read everything I could get my hands on. I read and read – even thought I didn't always understand what I was reading or immediately saw the implications for my research project. Nevertheless, it was compelling. I kept at it. To begin my deep dive into critical realism you gave me a copy of José López and Garry Potter's *After Post-Modernism* to read (López and Potter 2001).

GRANT: I did that so you would begin to unpack some of the postmodern assumptions you came with.

LORETTA: Yes, I know. Your motivations were obvious!

GRANT: Was I that transparent?

LORETTA: You were! I then picked up Andrew Collier's introduction to critical realism (Collier 1994). I found a series of You Tube videos entitled 'An Introduction to Critical Realism' which were very helpful. In them, Roy Bhaskar was interviewed by Gary Hawke about critical realism. Seeing and hearing Bhaskar talk plainly about his work assisted me in my developing understanding. It also gave me a sense of him as a human being; how he was, his disposition – experiencing that was important. Those virtual talks have been published in a book (see Bhaskar 2017). I should also mention – and recommend to people new to critical realism – Philip Gorski's concise article enticingly entitled 'What is Critical Realism? And Why Should You Care?' (Gorski 2013).

GRANT: Yes, you read and read. And you came back with more and more questions. Where did all the reading and questions take you?

LORETTA: In my deep dive, I quite quickly came to see the congruence with what I was studying and practising in Tibetan Buddhism. I was reading that there is an independent reality that is knowable – even though it can only be grasped partially. I read that reality is not unchangeable and fixed. Nothing in my formal postgraduate studies offered me the theory-practice connections I was looking for. The social science paradigms we were directed to consider were silent on the things that I knew mattered. Critical realism offered me hope.

CELINA: Just like you Loretta normal science did not provide the explanatory lens I needed. I wanted to convey this in my thesis. How I would do it didn't come to me until I had nearly completed the final write-up. I decided to open my thesis with an account of a conversation I had with friend of mine. My friend speaks:

> I was sitting towards the back of the lab and looking out the second level window at the trees, feeling a bit hot and distracted. Our teacher was discussing the topic of Thermodynamics. As the teacher briefly described the Laws of Conservation of Matter and Conservation of Energy, I experienced one of the most profound embodiments of deep understanding of my life. Looking down at the old lab benchtop, scarred from 50 years of graffiti and repainting, I UNDERSTOOD that the surface was timber. It had been a tree. That tree had taken carbon from the atmosphere to incorporate into the trunk. That same carbon had come to the atmosphere from the breath of some other creature who had eaten a plant, fertilized by manure of another creature, and broken down by microorganisms. I felt a profoundly physical embodiment of deep understanding, of the shared and interconnected nature of existence. I felt and saw the infinite interconnections in an instant. Looking

down at "My" hands, it was irrefutable that this collection of recycled atoms was not really "Me". Those molecules had been trees, space dust, dinosaur poo and immeasurable things before. They were merely borrowed by me and only for a short time! Many of them would no longer be with me by the end of the year! The interconnection and shared nature of the Stuff of Our Universe, of the Energy and Matter, escalated my strong sense of personal justice to a life of embodied activism. My friend's story was a way of explaining the 'aboutness' (Collier 1999) of my research. It was in critical realism that I found the tools I needed. For me, as a philosophy for everyday life, critical realism holds the promise of explaining experiences like that of my friend. Critical realism gave me the conceptual means to explore the inner realities of human beings and their interconnections with the wider social and natural worlds. What was characteristic of the activists I spoke with was they had some understanding of 'ground state'. Once it is comprehended that we are all connected, actively engaging in the struggle for a world in which all living beings are free to flourish becomes the only conscionable choice.

LORETTA: I completed my degree and left our university before the last part of your research journey Celina. So, I missed what was probably the most intense part. Listening to you now, I find it very interesting that our projects have strong similarities – of deep real ontological and ethical commitments.

CELINA: Yes, we both shared a recognition of the importance of inner-reflective processes of human beings in self and social transformation. For me, I focused on academics who were reflexively engaging in the historically conditioned world in which they were working. I tried to bring Dialectical Critical Realism and the Philosophy of Meta-Reality to the task. It was obvious in the interviews that I did with academic activists that they were all underlabouring their own reflexive processes. They were very clear that they did not see their activism as a struggle of simple dualities: 'us against them', for example. Rather, they saw themselves and the others around them in a broader process of connected historical struggle. Most had a well-developed spiritual understanding. They were aware of the demi-reality created by neoliberal discourse, structures, and practice – along with its alienating drive to separate people and set them in competition with each other.

LORETTA: So, in the end, their struggle was *for* connection and interconnection. Was that surprising to you?

CELINA: That's hard to answer. I suppose you can't help having preconceived ideas of what you might find or hear. However, I was surprised that *all* the academic activists I interviewed had some connection with their 'ground-state'. There was a recognition that we – human beings – cannot experience ourselves as separate from nature and from other human beings if we were not, at a fundamental level, one with everything that exists.

GRANT: Do you think you could call that awareness and experience of fundamental interconnectedness 'love'?

CELINA: Certainly. It was clear to me – and clear in the words and emotions of the academic activists – that their values were rooted in deep sense of interconnected love and kindness. And they brought that into their everyday practice in the university.

GRANT: You stress the centrality of emotions. This makes sense to me. Without it we have little *reason* to care for anything. The reason-emotion split that we get in, what we have been calling, 'normal' science leads to an explanatory void. The bringing together of reason and emotion is the basis of Bhaskar's ethical naturalism that he simply and aptly describes as "the art of living well" (1993, 15).

CELINA: In my thesis I make the point that the etymological origin of the word 'emotion' comes from the idea of movement. Emotions are what gets us moving. They are powerful causal mechanisms at the root of our capacities to put our thinking into concrete transformative actions. In other words, emotion is a sine qua non for human agency.

But, more than this, critical realism has shown me that the importance of emotions goes deeper. We cannot sever emotions from reason. In their connection, we find the possibility of living well. Collier (1994) first brought this to my attention when he emphasised that, by underlabouring our emotional worlds, we liberate ourselves from *heteronomous elements*. In this way we begin to touch our 'ground-state' wisdom. This is, as I see it, an important – and usually overlooked – dimension of activism.

LORETTA: Emotions are also overlooked in higher education. Rather than seeing emotions as intrusive or corruptive, educators highlighted them as valuable for inclusion into academic learning journeys and vital aspects of relational being. Asrael and Bialek (2016) say that it is in the messiness and discomfort of emotions, that compassion is both born and expands. It is through the sitting practice of meditation that we learn to recognise and understand our embodied *and* discursive selves. While psychology emphasises 'emotional regulation', traditional Buddhist methods of practice and inquiry teach us to move beyond habituated responses and instead harness emotion's inherent energy and movement. I liked how you have talked about this Celina. It highlights how compassion is simultaneously an inner and outer transformation and thus a type of activism.

CELINA: Exactly.

LORETTA: Through intimate knowledge and befriending of our own emotional landscape, deeper inquiry into social suffering and structural injustice become possible. As emotion and reason ('heart-mind') join, compassion is agentic movement towards 'living well'.

CELINA: I see this as an example of the openness of critical realism. It offers us a way to overcome the fear of exploring certain areas of human life – like emotions and spirituality – that have been a 'taboo' in western social science and life in general.

LORETTA: For me, the power of critical realism is that it offers a secular language and philosophical frame which is inclusive of non-western ways of knowing and being. As such it is powerful in my everyday personal and professional life as a bridge and conduit for two-way understanding and translation – a tool of ontological and epistemological soft diplomacy.

CELINA: Our conversations have reminded me of the importance of having good support while walking the critical realist path. Loretta and I had you, and we had each other. In my case, I couldn't have achieved what I did without the support, space, and time required to deeply reflect and think that I had. My worry is that in the neoliberal university such necessities are being absented – rapidly. My research brought me face-to-face with that reality and with academic activists who – with love, solidarity, and spirit – were fighting to absent the absences.

Critical realism demands we think deeply about, and act ethically for, the world. Is that possible in the historical context we live in? Now, in my non-academic work, I try to push some boundaries to create spaces for thinking and acting deeply because, as I learned on my PhD journey, there is no other conscionable choice. To my surprise, I have found a good appetite for that outside the University. Maybe critical realism needs to push its way out of the academic world?

GRANT: Or maybe it is the historical moment for the ultimate project of critical realism: socialism. A project, Bhaskar insists, is mobilised by "the wisdom of universal human emancipation" and, following Marx, finds its expression in a society "in which the free flourishing of each is a condition for the free flourishing of all" (1993, 98).

LORETTA: Yes, I agree. Reflecting on our three journeys, I wonder if engagement with critical realism itself always involves a journey of alone-together? We alone can take it, and very often it feels lonely and overwhelming. What is simultaneously confounding and heartening is that in our journeys we are working with what already exists. As Bhaskar puts it, it is 'enfolded within us' as part of "a *basic dialectic of learning that applies when we are coming to learn anything*" (2016, 165). This is the 'unfolding the enfolded' (Bhaskar 2002b, 299–318). We do not start from nothing – and this includes ourselves. Grant and Celina, you both spoke to this unfolding process in terms of the free flourishing of causal powers, of a yearning for the spiritual, and of irrepressible love and kindness in the face of neoliberal demi-reality. Part of what we share is that critical realism aligns with and brings forth our own personal commitments. Bhaskar's critical realism is not just a philosophy or a movement, it points to things 'as they are' – to reality 'as it is' and to human yearning.

GRANT: Critical realism's gift then is bringing ontology back – an invitation to take ontology seriously?

LORETTA: Yes, this is what resonates most strongly with me.

CELINA: And with me. Without ontology we have no ethic for action – no emotion to get us moving. Without ontology, what is the point? What are we *about*? What do we stand *for*?

LORETTA: Exactly. In this way, critical realism is not just a tool for research, but a reminder to us all that we must absent all that clouds and constrains our own flourishing. It also reminds us of our human responsibility to embrace (and not to deny) our inherent irrepressible movement of love towards the free-flourishing of all.

CELINA: The struggle for human emancipation is an act of love.

References

Archer, M. S. 1995. *Realist Social Theory: The Morphogenetic Approach*. Cambridge: Cambridge University Press.

Archer, M. S. 2003. *Structure, Agency and the Internal Conversation*. Cambridge: Cambridge University Press.

Archer, M. S. 2004. "Models of Man: The Admission of Transcendence." In *Transcendence – Critical Realism and God*, edited by M. S. Archer, A. Collier, and D. V. Porpora, 63–81. London: Routledge.

Archer, M. S. 2012. *The Reflexive Imperative in Late Modernity*. Cambridge: Cambridge University Press.

Asrael, D., and P. Bialek. 2016. "No Hidden Corners: Compassion Training in Counselor Education." In *Shadow & Light (Vol. 2: Talks & Reflections): Theory, Research, and Practice in Transpersonal Psychology*, edited by F. J. Kaklauskas, C. J. Clements, D. Hocoy, and L. Hoffman, 91–118. Colorado Springs: University Professors Press.

Banfield, G. 2016. *Critical Realism for Marxist Sociology of Education*. London: Routledge.

Bhaskar, R. 1986. *Scientific Realism and Human Emancipation*. London: Routledge.

Bhaskar, R. 1993. *Dialectic – The Pulse of Freedom*. London: Verso.

Bhaskar, R. 1994. *Plato Etc. – The Problems of Philosophy and Their Resolution*. London: Verso.

Bhaskar, R. 2000. *From East to West: Odyssey of a Soul*. London: Routledge.

Bhaskar, R. 2002a. *The Philosophy of Meta-Reality, Volume 1 Meta-Reality: Creativity, Love and Freedom*. New Delhi: Sage.

Bhaskar, R. 2002b. *From Science to Emancipation: Alienation and the Actuality of Enlightenment*. London: Routledge.

Bhaskar, R. 2010. *The Formation of Critical Realism – A Personal Perspective*. Milton Park: Routledge.

Bhaskar, R. 2016. *Enlightened Common Sense – The Philosophy of Critical Realism*. London: Routledge.

Bhaskar, R. 2017. *The Order of Natural Necessity – A Kind of Introduction to Critical Realism*, edited by Gary Hawke. Published by the author.

Collier, A. 1994. *Critical Realism: An Introduction to Roy Bhaskar's Philosophy*. London: Verso.

Collier, A. 1999. "About Aboutness." *Alethia* 2 (1): 2–5.

Gorski, P. S. 2013. 'What Is Critical Realism? And Why Should You Care?' *Contemporary Sociology: A Journal of Reviews* 42 (5): 658–670.

López, J., and G. Potter. 2001. *After Postmodernism – An Introduction to Critical Realism*. London: Althone Press.

Marx, K. 1975. "A Contribution to the Critique of Hegel's Philosophy of Right – Introduction." In *Karl Marx – Early Writings*, 243–257. London: Penguin.

13
A KIND OF CONCLUSION
Against Full-Stops and Bookends?

Alpesh Maisuria and Grant Banfield

Introduction

Given the intention of this edited collection is to capture the stories of students, researchers, and academics grappling with critical realism, as the Editors, we thought it appropriate for at least two reasons that we do the same. First, if reasons are causes, as Bhaskar insisted, then our stories will (hopefully) give some causal context to the book. Second, and more importantly perhaps, is that our particular stories might be useful to others – especially those, like us, who draw on the work of Marx or are open to the possibilities that Marx might offer. In this chapter, we narrate our respective critical realism journeys (and their intersections) from our PhDs and beyond. This e-dialogue draws from a conversation that has been ongoing for more than 13 years. We offer this as a conclusion to the collection of works. But we are wary of closure, full-stops, and bookends. So, in the spirit of both the Marxian and Bhaskarian dialectic, the conclusion, we hope, serves as an invitation to others to come and explore critical realism.

GRANT: Well, Alpesh, we have set ourselves the task of writing the final chapter. As you know, I was not completely comfortable with us having the final say. To position us at the beginning and end of the collection – like bookends keeping all between in order and in place – didn't represent what the project had become for me.

ALPESH: Yes. I understand what you say. And, to a certain extent, I share your reservations. The project – and if we define 'project' as this edited collection – has become more than what either of us anticipated.

GRANT: Exactly. For example, in the process of working closely over time with all the contributors in the crafting of their chapters, I learned a lot. This was certainly the case in relation to theoretical issues and matters of applying critical realism across disciplines and contexts. But there was more to it

DOI: 10.4324/9781003193784-13

than this. The back and forth we had with everyone in the writing process together with the phone calls and video calls hook-ups gave a life to the project that is more than what appears on these pages.

ALPESH: I get it. Our conversation and this final chapter could not be what it is without the exchanges we have had with the contributors. So, there is something wrong with us writing the 'full stop'. However, we must get *real* about this…

GRANT: I know where you are going with this. We know each other too well! And I will agree with what you are about to say.

ALPESH: OK, the first reality check is to recognise that *we* brought the project (the book) into being. And, with that comes certain responsibilities.

GRANT: Agreed! And that means that, while all contributors are authors *in* this project, we are the authors *of* the project. So, in critical realist terms, we are different *kinds* of authors.

ALPESH: With different responsibilities.

GRANT: Exactly. This is simply a 1M critical realist acknowledgement of difference. I can now say to myself: 'Get on with it, Grant, and begin putting in the full-stop'.

ALPESH: Ha, ha. Now *I* know where *you* are going! In giving attention to your suspicion of bookends and full-stops you are really working your way to a couple of points that are appropriate to a concluding chapter like this one. First, as we have seen, Bhaskar's *dialectic* (with Marx) insists that we be wary of closure. However, we have transformative agency to act *in* and *on* the world, which requires making a mark. And wasn't this a reason why we and all the other authors turned to critical realism in the first place? Full-stops and bookends are necessary and unavoidable if we are to get things *done* in the world – and this includes absenting absences.

GRANT: You are right. Am I really that transparent? All of us, in the end, have no choice but to 'get on with it' – but only with the best knowledge available to us. So, what do you think my other point is?

ALPESH: I would say it has something to do with collaboration. The two of us have noted how much we have gained from working with the contributors.

GRANT: Spot on. Social life is thoroughly collaborative. Or, I might say, a fully human life is necessarily a life *with* and *for* others. We must all be underlabourers not overlords. Eudaimonia rests on the realisation that the full flourishing of each depends on the flourishing of all. I was thinking of collaboration in this light. And this is not possible in a class society.

ALPESH: To be ruled by the logic of capital is to be condemned to a world of demi-reality.

GRANT: Yes, a logic that Marx exposed in his three volumes of *Capital*. This draws us to the very thing that brought us both to critical realism and began our conversations nearly 15 years ago. We can now fulfil our responsibility to tell our story and stories. Our coming to critical realism has been through a desire to better *know* Marx and Marxism. Would this be fair?

ALPESH: I think so. For quite a while now we have been discussing the potential uses of critical realism to strengthen our scholarship and practice in what might be broadly described as the field of Marxist Sociology of Education, Critical Education, and ethnography (Maisuria and Beach, 2017). For me, it has taken the form of a comradely solidarity with very different types of collaborators that has been so important in the development of my appreciation of critical realism.

GRANT: I agree Alpesh. Likewise, your involvement in my journey through Marxism, critical realism, and education has been significant. If this journey had a track, you helped me stay on it – or at least hold onto some vague sense that I knew where I was going! The value in having someone to bounce ideas off, share frustrations, and celebrate the little wins along the way cannot be overstated. We are fellow travellers. Both of us carry a commitment to radical and transformative education strongly influenced by Marx. However, it was our mutual interest in critical realism that brought our paths together. There have been many phone calls and Skype sessions between London and Adelaide over the years as we made our ways through and eventually beyond our PhDs. And, in those times, when we were on the same continent and in the same city, we continued those conversations – often over a curry and always with a little bit too much beer and wine if I recall. But fellow travellers do what fellow travellers must do.

Before we talk about the critical realism content of those conversations, can I ask you if you remember our first meeting and its context?

ALPESH: Ha – there's a question. You were in England, Institute of Education in London, to speak at the inaugural *International Conference on Critical Realism and Education*. I came to your session mainly because I had to! What I mean is that My PhD supervisor, Tony Green, was a co-organiser and also presenting at the session where you gave your paper. I'm glad I did though. I recall you presented on *Critical Realist Impulses in Paul Willis' Learning to Labour: Towards an Emergent Marxist Ethnography*.

ALPESH: Given where we are now, and where critical realism is after Bhaskar's passing, it's interesting to check back to reflect on that conference. There was a clear emphasis on education and also Marxism. But critical realism was nowhere near the mainstream. Let me read you the blurb:

> This conference is designed to lay the basis for the development of an *International Centre for Advanced Studies in Critical Realism and Education*. In recent years there has been growing interest in the interface between critical realism and education, which makes this conference especially timely. Education is central to the critical realist project. On the other hand, critical realism is still, relatively speaking, a newcomer in the field of education and education studies, and only too rarely explicitly utilised in research or thematised in teaching. … The bulk of the conference will address the development of a mediating level of theory and description between philosophy and the day-to-day concerns of educational practice. Throughout, the conference will attempt to initiate, develop, and enrich a two-way interaction between critical realist philosophy and educational research and practice.

At the time, I'm not sure that I had grasped the profound nature of what Roy was trying to achieve – it was brave and momentous. Let me explain: Marxism was (and still is) widely perceived as some sort of quirky hobby of a few eccentrics who were in schools of education, so those of us who synthesised Marxism and education were not taken very seriously at all; secondly, in my experience of readings groups and events, mainstream philosophy tended to be very conservative by sticking to theory and the classics concerning questions of knowledge rather than reality and the world. They probably would have seen critical realism as a rival. So, Roy was stepping on people's toes right from the start and ironically at a place called the *Institute of Education*!

ALPESH: Yes, really interesting. I am thinking that, if critical realism is to have an underlabouring role for Marxist science then critical realism's relationship to Marxism must be examined. However, fissures have emerged among subscribers to critical realism, how would you characterise these?

GRANT: When you talk of 'fissures', I take it you are referring to something like 'disagreements' within both critical realism and Marxism as well as to the nature of the relationship between the two. As I mentioned earlier, critical realism and Marxism do not provide doctrines for the faithful to blindly follow. Disagreement is a sign of life. Consistent agreement leads ultimately to death. Harmony is not unison. Life is not a search for 'balance'.

To me, the important point rests in understanding the nature of the fissures (i.e., what those disagreements are *about*) and the weight they carry in moving forward with what, in the end, is an ethical project (i.e., what such 'fissure work' is ultimately *for* and *what* is at stake). I take this to be the nub of your question. It is, as I have said, what brought me to critical realism in the first place: I wanted to know and better understand the nature of the fissures in Marxism.

It is worth reminding ourselves that Bhaskar's critical realism project (at least as it relates to the human sciences) was built on the resolution of what he identified as a number of persistent fissures or debilitating splits in the philosophy of the human sciences. As critical realists well know, these include: collectivism/individualism, structure/agency, cause/reason, mind/body, and fact/value (Bhaskar, 1998, xiii–xiv). According to Bhaskar, the fundamental split underlying all was the positivism/hermeneutics 'antinomy'. It is this fissure that someone like myself who had had more than a little postgraduate dabbling in social science methodology was well aware. And I can say that, in the process of my studies, I was schooled to take the hermeneutic side of that fracture. Not that I was subjected to overt indoctrination. It was just the times.

ALPESH: That time still exists. In my experience, most social science students at all levels are told they are not positivists so they are told that they MUST be working in the interpretivist paradigm or within constructivism. This is the default advice I see given to novice and emerging researchers.

GRANT: It is interesting that this is not the case for the contributors to this book. Of course, they are a self-selecting group but the default, as you describe it, is not hegemonic. All of our accounts tell stories of dissatisfaction in one way or another with the positivism/hermeneutics split.

ALPESH: So, there is hope.

GRANT: I think so – or would like to believe so. As far as my story is concerned – which begins with my time as a postgraduate student – the post-positivist push was in full swing. The only show in town was hermeneutics. We were to hold heavy structural and functional sociology at arm's length (for good reasons of course). As a young sociologist brought up on the 'Founding Fathers' approach I could see Durkheim and Weber slotting easily into the neat structural-interpretivist scheme of things. But Karl didn't seem to fit so easily. This bothered me. I was told he was a 'conflict theorist', and this was supposed to explain something. To me, it didn't explain much – only that he didn't fit. The bigger lesson I learnt for all this was that, if you don't fit, you'll have a new category invented for you so you will. The old scheme remains in place, nothing really changes, and the show rolls on. I was later to learn that making and trying to live in rigid boxes was not a good idea. Derek Sayer (1987) aptly called it the 'violence of abstraction'. So maybe you can see why Willis was such a revelation for me. It was a coming together (a resolution?) of hermeneutics (via ethnographic method) and Marxist theory (via a radical humanism).

ALPESH: I really like that phrase – bravo to Sayer for capturing the zeitgeist. While there were, of course, some orthodox Marxists who mistakenly did try to advance an economic/historical determinism and/or a rigid base super-structure model, equally I do think that perhaps, some anti/non-Marxists were intent on creating a strawman of all Marxist theory and its apparent lack of application to the real world. All of this was powerful and ubiquitous in the academy, and I almost got lost in trying to avoid structuralism while paying heed to culture, agency, and change; and, like many others, I briefly had an interest what *discourse* could offer, this was until critical realism came into my thinking while doing my PhD. Before critical realism, I was opening the door to one intellectual rabbit hole before quickly closing it only to find myself in another, and doing the same thing over and again. Tell me more about your journey to steer through the conundrums that we've mentioned above.

GRANT: OK, let me begin by fleshing out in a little more detail what brought me to critical realism in the first place. Like you, it was part of my PhD journey. My first PhD supervisor introduced me to critical realism. She insisted that Bhaskar's early work would provide an understanding of the materialist (and, more generally, realist) grounding to Marx's thinking she believed I needed to grasp. Her strategy was to set me on a course of intense reading. I was to suspend all reading that I thought was important and read selected works of Bhaskar. I was thrown into the critical realist deep end. Without a background in philosophy this was hard going: a steep climb! I am not sure how much of those works I got through in the time I was given. I am not even sure how much I understood! Whatever the case, this started a long process of reading Marx through Bhaskar and Bhaskar through Marx.

ALPESH: Ah yes, my experiences were similar with *Realist Theory of Science* and *The Possibility of Naturalism* (Bhaskar, 1975, 1979), and then later *Scientific Realism and Human Emancipation* (Bhaskar, 1986). It's therapeutic to hear you say you found them a slog too!

GRANT: Yes, it certainly was a slog at times, but nonetheless rewarding. I wouldn't wind back the clock. This includes the long periods where I had no supervisor. Through intermissions and periods of non-enrolment I continued to read and to develop a growing respect for the underlabouring capacity of critical realism. I have to add that I did manage to formally complete a PhD. While I would have been quite happy continuing to craft my own (non-credentialed) intellectual journey, times in Australian universities were changing. Neoliberalism was biting and its managers had a different view of 'academic freedom' to the one in which I was socialised. It was time to 'get it done'. What about you?

ALPESH: Well, like you – and many of the contributors to this book – I was guided (read coerced!) to take-on critical realism. I say 'take-on' because it has been – and continues to be – a challenging encounter!

GRANT: I whole-heartedly agree. And your honesty resonates with the ethos of this book – a project to encourage newcomers to critical realism. And the hard conceptual work that engaging with critical realism demands needs to be recognised and embraced. We must also support each other in this.

ALPESH: In the early days it was definitely a struggle – and I'm not afraid to admit that. The crop of introductory and intermediate books that are now available didn't exist back then. Your *Critical Realism for Marxist Sociology of Education* (Banfield, 2016) is very accessible. ... Just before I go on, are there any that you particularly recommend?

GRANT: In my early 'slog', I found Andrew Collier's introductory text, *Critical Realism*, indispensable (Collier, 1994). It put Bhaskar's transcendental realism and critical naturalism into a language I could understand. Collier was one of my early critical realism/Marxian guides and it is to him that I still direct my students today. I'd also suggest two of Sean Creaven's books *Marxism and Realism* and *Emergentist Marxism* (Creaven, 2000, 2007). Furthermore, I would add the edited collection by Andrew Brown, Steve Fleetwood, and John Michael Roberts, *Critical Realism and Marxism*, as essential reading (Brown et al., 2002). Indeed, for those looking to see whether they wish to weigh into the field of critical realism in order to understand or clarify some of the persistent problems within Marxist thought then this could be a good first-off source.

ALPESH: Good shout. To add to that, I think Tom Fryer's *A Short guide to ontology and epistemology* is superb. Anyway, back to your question ... I began my journey during my undergraduate being taught by Dave Hill who is a well-known Marxist professor within Critical Education. I was greatly influenced by his and others' scholarship, which gave me a lens to understand myself, the world around me, and also myself in this world. Itching for more Marxism – which was largely absent at Goldsmiths University of London where I was reading my Masters – I started to attend at the *Marxism and Education: Renewing Dialogues* (MERD) seminar series convened by Glenn Rikowski and Tony Green in 2002 at the Institute of Education (IoE).

Tony became my PhD supervisor in late 2007 and, crucially for me, was influential in bringing Ram Roy Bhaskar to the IoE in 2007/8 as a *World Scholar* – a newly established title to recognise eminence. Tony had an emerging interest in critical realism to make Marxism more philosophically sophisticated. In my first months he introduced me to Roy who had moved into the office next door. Serendipity is kind!

GRANT: Now you are really rubbing it in! I've always felt terribly jealous of your easy access to major players in critical realism – not to mention Roy Bhaskar himself – and the opportunities open to you to attend regular critical realist and Marxist seminars. Being in Adelaide felt like being on the moon. Efforts were made to form an Australian critical realist network. But nothing came of it. Enough of my complaining. What was your PhD about?

ALPESH: It focused on social class in a social democracy where inequality levels were relatively lower and presumably social class more hidden. I used the case of Sweden. My concern was with exploring the way that class was in consciousness and practice, or not. This concern was investigated both in terms of how my participants reflected on themselves as classed beings and how they felt this articulated with their own actions; I was equally interested in how they perceived other people to situate themselves as classed beings in consciousness and practice. I was clearly working at the level of the empirically real and actual domains, and my supervisor was ushering me towards depth ontology – the deep laying mechanisms and structures that generate tendencies for social class to materialise in consciousness and practice in the form that my participants described to me. This intellectual excavation through explanatory critique of the deep real is now what I firmly believe ought to be the aim of social scientific research, which is unfortunately widely unacknowledged, especially in strong versions of interpretivism and constructivism. It means that most mainstream social science researchers stay at the level of events and that what is apprehended in experience through observations and interview methods. At best they acknowledge epistemological relativism but miss the importance of ontological stratification, and this includes the likes of Michael Young and his Social Realism (Young, 2008).

ALPESH: I think Young was trying to deal with ontology in some way. In a private correspondence, he wrote that:

> ***social realism*** does not imply asserting a difference from critical realism, at least not in principle. ... It was explicitly developed to counter the

various social constructivism's that had pervaded sociology of education since the 1970s. It has two aspects- first it refers to the **reality of the social** as external to our everyday perception of it and is in opposition to those such as Steve Shapin who assert that 'it is ourselves and not reality that are responsible for what we know'. Secondly social realism refers to the **reality of knowledge** that has emergent properties not dependent on or reducible to the practices or interests of knowers or the contexts in which it is acquired or produced.

(original emphasis)

I think there's a danger lurking in what he says. The primacy he gives to knowledge, risks falling foul of the epistemic fallacy.

GRANT: There is nothing a critical realist would necessarily disagree with in what Young said to you. His 'first aspect' expresses 'common sense realism' such that "objects exist (and endure) independently of them being perceived" (Psillos, 2007, 399). This is fine. There is no critical realist quarrel here. However, to his 'second aspect', a flag of caution must be raised. From a critical realist vantage point, knowledge is real in its effects and is of the transitive dimension of science. Bhaskar's transitive-intransitive distinction is important here. Knowledge is *about* something. If this is what Young means then there is, as he claims, no difference, in principle, between social realism and critical realism. If not, then the path is open to reducing ontology to epistemology or conflating the transitive and intransitive domains of science. As you suggest, a danger is lurking.

ALPESH: For Marxist science and praxis, recognising the intransitive domain is crucial. Without it, depth explanation of mechanisms and structures is impossible. In the absence of a *real* response to the question of *what conditions enable the possibility of X to be realised*, emancipatory possibilities are thwarted. This is what critical realism brings to my Marxist research. And this started with my PhD.

I recall one early supervision meeting in 2008 where Tony led me next door to Roy's office. I talked to Roy about my interest in class, social democracy, and Sweden. Given Roy's Scandinavian affiliations and his self-identification as a socialist our interests aligned. The conversation that ensued was instrumental in cultivating my curiosity of critical realism. Roy instructed me (he was helpful and forceful simultaneously) to come to his reading group.

GRANT: You are doing it again Alpesh! You are making me jealous!

ALPESH: I must say that I admire you coming to critical realism largely by yourself – these readings groups were so very helpful because most of us were novices, and also, meeting people like Bushra Sharar, Par Engholm, Birendra Singh, Rachel Rosen, and Sharon Tao was instructive for me to work out that critical realism could be productively deployed specifically as a meta-theory *with* Marxism for emancipatory practice. I reflect now on the value of this reading group. This approach characterised in the spirit of our ongoing video call *dialogues* and through this book is a continuation and the epitome of my point. It was at this time, around 2009 that I began my serious engagement with the Marxist method, utilising critical realism's depth ontology. Now before we elaborate on that and some of the critical realism toolkit, let me put a direct question to you stemming from criticism that I've encountered. Roy made it clear that critical realism is an aid to progressing socialism – hence the focus on Marxism at the first conference we talked about above. But let me play devils-advocate – should any Marxist be afraid of critical realism?

GRANT: My short response would be that no Marxist should be afraid of critical realism. It is crucial to understand that critical realism is a theory about theories. We can describe critical realism as a meta-theory or, as Steve Fleetwood has put it, a 'full-blown' philosophy of science (Brown, Fleetwood and Roberts, 2002, 3). There are two important points from Fleetwood's observation that help me explain my short and confident response to your provocation. The first picks up on critical realism as a full-blown *philosophy*. We take from this that critical realism operates, conceptually, at higher levels of abstraction than do more concrete conceptual systems like Marxism. In other words, critical realism is a different *kind* of conceptual system than Marxism and, as such, cannot replace it. Nor does critical realism set out to do so. It is in virtue of this difference that a critical realism-Marxism relation is possible. And that relation is one where critical realism acts as an underlabourer to Marxism. Critical realism takes a humble and respectful role in working with – not on or against – Marxism. This also means that Marxist theorists and practitioners are not obliged to blindly accept all that critical realism purports to offer (see Banfield, 2022; Bhaskar and Callinicos, 2003; Brown, Fleetwood and Roberts, 2002; Creaven, 2011).

The second point is that critical realism is a full-blown philosophy *of science*. While Marxism is a science, it does not have a fully developed philosophy of science.

ALPESH: Yes, the missing methodological fulcrum in Marx's work, this is the role of critical realism as Bhaskar put it.

GRANT: Exactly. Marx did not attempt a philosophical explication of his scientific realism as he did for his materialist view of history. Historically, this has not only led to internal confusions within Marxism around the development of praxis but also provided grist for mill of external challenges to the relevance and coherence of Marxist theory. It is to the clearing up of these confusions and challenges that critical realism can claim to be of use. In this regard, it is important to register that Bhaskar not only believed there to be "an elective affinity between critical realism and historical materialism" (1991, 143) but also expressed the founding intent of critical realism "to support the science of history that marks had opened up" (2010, 134).

ALPESH: Critical realism provides the philosophy of science to Marxism's science for the purpose of explanatory and emancipatory leverage. At the time of coming to critical realism, I was grappling with tensions within Marxism that you have put a spotlight on. I found that critical realism could help Marxism reject abstract utopian idealism and naïve empiricism. This would come via the revindication of ontology. The notion of underlying generative mechanisms that have the causal power to create a tendency towards acting on empirical and actual reality is perhaps the one that I attached the most value.

Critical realism has helped me unpack some of the history of Marxist theory. I am thinking of the young Hegelians and utopian socialists who posited an abstracted utopian idealism and reduced ontology into epistemology. It seemed that empirical reality and the deep real escaped them – they were at operating at the level of the actual, they had flattened reality. I began to be struck by how often I observed this epistemic fallacy. The issue of reality, existing and available to obtain, as well as being stratified and differentiated, and also changing is important in scientific research. All of this about the importance of what Roy called *seriousness*. My interest is advocating for a Marxism serious about bringing an alternative world into being. This means having an account of the world as it *really* is – which makes it possible to conceive of new worlds.

GRANT: Indeed: getting serious in a *concrete* utopian sense. As Bhaskar has forcefully argued throughout his work, there is something fundamentally unserious about contemporary philosophy (which subsequently infects social theory and practice). Just as he showed how the early Greek philosophers were not immune to the influence of aristocratic power$_2$ relations of domination (Bhaskar, 1994), contemporary philosophy remains unserious about, as you put it, 'the world as it really is'. As it generates more unserious questions, philosophy can say little about the real (personal, social, and ecological) grounds of our existence.

ALPESH: And Bhaskar lays blame firmly at the feet of Hume in this regard. In a reading group I recall him explaining what he meant by seriousness. While chuckling, Bhaskar ridiculed Hume who suggested that there is no better reason to leave the building he was in by the ground floor door than by the second-floor window. This is preposterous. If Hume really believed what he said, then he would, when convenient, exit the building by the second-floor window. Of course, Hume never did because he *knew* he would encounter the actually existing force of gravity and suffer real material consequences of his unseriousness. Roy continued his offensive suggesting that Hume had no better reason to prefer the destruction of his little finger to that of the whole world. Again, preposterous. Destroying the world would also destroy his finger. Hume's finger is in the world. With ontological realism absent from Hume's philosophy it is fundamentally unserious.

GRANT: So, we have Humean empiricism and its substantial influence on the philosophy of science. No wonder Bhaskar said that, for an emancipatory social science to be possible, "philosophy has to be thoroughly ex-Humed" (1993, 359).

ALPESH: Yes, ex-Hume-ing for a Marxism that is serious about revolutionising the exploitive social relations of capital that negate human flourishing. Of course, this has been – and remains – a long struggle and we need a philosophical base to our praxis that is serious about the world (natural and social). This is the struggle against forms of exploitation and alienation.

GRANT: Struggle – yes. How can such work be anything else? A struggle to be human. After all, as Marx reminds us via his famous adage of "the worst of architects and the best of bees" (1976, 284), it is the capacity for critical thought and consciousness that, at least in part, makes us human. So, to labour both *as* a human being *for* humanity is an act of love i.e., it is to live and, in doing so, realise the possibility of human life. Conversely, to have this capacity (read: potential, power) diminished or thwarted is to be condemned to a less than human life, like you say, an alienated existence. Given that it is our burden to be human, we are compelled to struggle for our collective fulfilment – which includes our (class) struggle for the material realisation of non-alienating social relations. Or, as Bhaskar might put it, this refers to our struggle to negate, to absent, social ills. However, the conditions upon which the possibility of a non-alienated life depends may not be within easy reach. Or, indeed, we may actually conspire – wittingly or otherwise – to deny ourselves such conditions and such a life. However, we must recall that it is the nature of capitalism to mystify and obscure the way it systematically degrades human life along with the very natural ecology upon which our material existence rests (Maisuria, 2022).

So, I have no problems with shouting loud and clear that it is a labour of love to work towards the demystification and the ultimate transcendence of social relations that injure us all. Love is struggle. It demands uncovering and getting to know with great clarity the nature of those things that would deny us our humanity. Otherwise, how are we to absent them? Marx knew this well. This was his purpose in writing *Capital*: his greatest scientific work. This was an act of love. It was also hard work – as it must be: "There is no royal road to science, and only those who do not dread the fatiguing climb of its steep paths have a chance of gaining its luminous summits" (Marx, 1976: 104).

ALPESH: Viva la revolucion! And we benefit from a critical realism's philosophy of science to underlabour a serious Marxism.

GRANT: Indeed! Intellectual work is a revolutionary act and vital to revolutionary action.

ALPESH: We're returning to my question earlier regarding the fear that some Marxists have of critical realism. I've been involved with critical realism since Roy came to the Institute of Education in 2007, and I feel as strongly as ever that critical realism is helpful for the raison d'être of the Marxist project of revolution for human flourishing. I feel like this because, as history through pandemics, wars, political trajectories, and irreversible environmental doom, we are brushing with the probable annihilation of our very existence; but simultaneously, we are also traversing the possibility of positive change too. We've got to grasp this reality through the philosophy of science that critical realism offers in conjunction with classics, such as Trotsky's *Permanent Revolution* and his *The Revolution Betrayed* (Trotsky, 2004, 2020). I suppose this is what you profoundly said earlier: 'Marx through Bhaskar and Bhaskar through Marx' to find our way through to hope and struggle for a different world – a socialist world – in which, as Bhaskar has put it echoing Marx, "the free flourishing of each is the condition of the free flourishing of all" (Bhaskar, 1993, 98).

GRANT: With these words, we are forced to look beyond difference. They bring us to consider the reality of identity – or more specifically, perhaps, synchronic identity. Here we have the 1M–4D rhythmic or movement. I don't know how many times I have mouthed 'free flourishing of each is the condition of the free flourishing all'. However, in all honesty, for most of those times I don't think I really grasped the dialectical significance of the words. I hope my conversations with Celina and Loretta captured in Chapter 12 reveal this. I was schooled in sociology which entailed the erection of particular conceptual bookends around my thinking. I got the sociological 'flourishing for all' bit. That was comfortably 'out there'. However, the significance of the 'flourishing of each' passed me by. That was uncomfortably 'in here'. I also hope the chapter shows how Celina and Loretta (who came to critical realism with different histories, interests, and motivations) played a significant part in bringing me to new realisations.

ALPESH: I get a sense of on-going open-ness in what you are saying.

GRANT: Definitely. And this takes us back, I think, to where we began this conversation. Bookends are just convenient things that allow us to present other things in certain ways. They are not – and should not be – final or ultimate frames.

ALPESH: I get that. Marx agonised and spent years wondering how to present his critique of capital. The way he eventually set it out in Volume I was not how his research proceeded. Rather, he began his presentation where his analysis (or retroductive abstractions) ended – with the commodity.

GRANT: That's a good example. And, in his presentation, he retraced (retroductively) his steps back to where he started – in the concrete world of emerging capitalist life.

ALPESH: And full-stops?

GRANT: They are simply pauses. They allow us to take a breath, reflect, and move on. Might I say: 'get on with it'? But above all, full-stops allow for the possibility – and offer the promise – of more to come.

ALPESH: Absolutely, practically this could be returning to our contributors in some years to circle back on their *stories of methodological encounters* published in this volume. …

References

Banfield, G. 2016. *Critical Realism for Marxist Sociology of Education*. London: Routledge.
Banfield, G. 2022. "Critical Realism." In *Encyclopaedia of Marxism and Education*, edited by A. Maisuria, 147–166. Leiden: Brill.
Bhaskar, R. 1975. *Realist Theory of Science*. London: Routledge.
Bhaskar, R. 1979. *The Possibility of Naturalism – A Philosophical Critique of the Social Sciences*. London: Routledge.
Bhaskar, R. 1986. *Scientific Realism and Human Emancipation*. London: Verso.
Bhaskar, R. 1991. *Philosophy and The Idea of Freedom*. Oxford: Basil Blackwell.
Bhaskar, R. 1993. *Dialectic: The Pulse of Freedom*. London: Verso.
Bhaskar, R. 1994. *Plato Etc. – The Problems of Philosophy and Their Resolution*. London: Verso.
Bhaskar, R. 1998. "General Introduction." In *Critical Realism – Essential Readings*, edited by M. Archer et al., ix–xxiv. London: Routledge.
Bhaskar, R. 2010. *The Formation of Critical Realism – A Personal Perspective*. Milton Park: Routledge.
Bhaskar, R., and A. Callinicos. 2003. "Marxism and Critical Realism – A Debate." *Journal of Critical Realism* 1 (2): 89–114.
Brown, A., S. Fleetwood, and J. M. Roberts, eds. 2002. *Critical Realism and Marxism*. London: Routledge.
Collier, A. 1994. *Critical Realism – An Introduction to Roy Bhaskar's Philosophy*. London: Verso.
Creaven, S. 2000. *Marxism and Realism*. London: Routledge.
Creaven, S. 2007. *Emergentist Marxism – Dialectical Philosophy and Social Theory*. London: Routledge.
Creaven, S. 2011. *Against the Spiritual Turn – Marxism, Realism and Social Theory*. London: Routledge.
Maisuria, A. 2022. Chapter 30: "Neoliberalism and Revolution: Marxism for Emerging Critical Educators." In *Encyclopaedia of Marxism and Education*, edited by A. Maisuria, 483–500. Leiden: Brill.
Maisuria, A., and Beach, D. 2017. "Ethnography and Education." *Oxford Research Encyclopaedia of Education*. Oxford, UK: Oxford University Press.
Marx, K. 1976. *Capital – A Critique of Political Economy. Vol. 1.* London: Penguin.
Psillos, S. 2007. "Realism." In *Dictionary of Critical Realism*, edited by M. Hartwig, 397–100. London: Routledge.
Sayer, D. 1987. *The Violence of Abstraction – The Analytic Foundations of Historical Materialism*. Oxford: Basil Blackwell.
Trotsky, L. 2004. *The Revolution Betrayed*. New York: Pathfinder Press.
Trotsky, L. 2020. *The Permanent Revolution and Results and Prospects*. London: Wellred.
Young, M. 2008. *Bringing Knowledge Back in: From Social Constructivism to Social Realism in the Sociology of Education*. London: Routledge.

INDEX

abduction 8, 14, 18–21, 26, 35, 65, 66–67, 69, 73, 85
abstraction *see also* abduction; retrodiction; retroduction; vantage point 8, 15–18, 22–26, 32, 34–35, 65, 85, 149, 153, 156
activism xii, 9, 52, 60, 130, 141–142
Actual *see* Actualism; Domains of Reality 5, 18, 22, 24–26, 32, 35, 44–45, 55, 70, 72, 80, 91, 93, 97, 99–101, 103, 107, 112–113, 125, 128, 130, 151, 154
Actualism 5, 125, 132
Adorno 10, 108–117
Agency 6–9, 12, 30, 36–39, 47, 53–56, 60, 69, 85, 98, 100, 107–111, 113–118, 123, 126–128, 132, 135, 142, 146, 148–149
Alienation 56, 59, 94, 110, 122–123, 128, 155
anti-naturalism 6
Archer, Margaret iii, 6, 11, 51, 117, 130

Bhaskar, Roy iii, xi, xii, xv, 2, 14, 51, 79, 84, 121, 140, 148, 151–155

CAIMeR 68–70
Causality *see also* causal power; mechanisms; *also see* reasons as causes 2, 5, 7, 9–10, 14, 30–35, 57–58, 60, 98, 100–101, 103, 109
causal power iii, 3, 6–7, 9, 15, 24, 26, 31, 33–36, 38, 44, 46, 55, 57, 72–73, 78, 103, 111–112, 138, 142–143, 154
CMO 65, 68

Collier, Andrew 11, 140, 150
concrete universal 11, 35, 121–128
consciousness raising 70
constructionism iii, 9, 80, 110
constructivism 8, 42, 44, 47–48, 78, 132, 148, 152
contemplative education/practices xiv, 130–133, 137
counselling xv, xvi, 9, 67, 69–70
Critical Discourse Analysis 78, 80, 82–83, 85–86, 108, 110–111, 114
critical naturalism 6–7, 12, 43, 48, 53, 58–59, 95, 119, 124, 129, 134–135, 138, 142, 150

Danermark, Berth iv
depth ontology 4, 9, 33, 64, 77, 78, 80, 86, 109, 114, 125–126, 128, 151, 153
determinism 6, 108, 111, 114–116, 149
Dialectical Critical Realism *also see* Four Level Dialectic; MELD iii, 3–4, 7, 109, 126, 133, 135, 141
Domains of Reality 5, 32, 44–45, 126, 128
DREI(C) *see also* retrodiction; retroduction 66, 73

Education I, ii, iii, xi, xiii, xiv, xv, 9–10, 41–47, 49, 51–60, 77, 79, 83, 85, 89–92, 94–95, 97, 98–104, 110–111, 117–118, 130–132, 137–138, 142, 147–148, 151–152, 155
Elder-Vass, Dave 39

Index

Emancipation xi, xii, 10–11, 48–49, 91, 93, 127–128, 130–131, 138, 143–144, 150
Emergence iv, 7, 100–101, 112, 116
Empirical Domain *see also* Domains of Reality; Empiricism 5, 18, 21, 25, 32–34, 44–45, 103, 113, 151
Empiricism iii, 4, 154
Epistemology 4–5, 10, 22, 41, 47, 49, 51–52, 67–68, 74, 79, 91, 97–98, 108, 111, 114–116, 118, 150, 152, 154
epistemological relativism 46, 151
eudemonia 128
evaluation research *see also* CMO xiv, xv, 15, 29
explanatory critique 7, 32, 78, 135, 138, 151
extensive research 101, 104

families 10, 21, 29, 30, 33, 35, 37, 48, 103, 107, 113
feminism 64, 112
Four-Level Dialectic 4, 125–127
Four Planar Social Being 37, 126, 137

Gorski, Philip 83–84, 93, 100, 110, 140
ground state 11, 126–128, 133, 136, 141–142

Hegel, Georg Wilhelm Friedrich 6–7, 122, 154
Hermeneutics 6, 148–149
Homelessness xi, xiv, 8, 29–38
Hume, David 2, 4–7, 154–155

Identity xv, 4, 7–8, 10, 60, 62, 93–95, 99, 108–109, 111, 115–116, 118, 126–127, 156
Indigenous xiii, 10, 89–92, 94–95
Indigenous research methods 10, 89, 91, 95
Induction 68, 70
intensive research 101
interdisciplinarity 36–37
internal conversation 38, 131
interpretivism 6, 44, 53, 151

judgemental rationality 43, 46, 73, 108

Kant, Immanuel 4–6

Marxism i, ii, 11, 132, 137, 146–148, 150–155
Marx, Karl i, ii, xii, 7, 11–12, 72, 131–132, 135–138, 143, 145–156

Masculinity 10, 107–119
mechanisms *see also* Domains of Reality xv, 5, 7–10, 14–18, 21–24, 26, 32–36, 38, 41–49, 55–59, 63, 65, 67–71, 74, 78–82, 84–85, 90–91, 100, 102–104, 108, 113–114, 126, 134, 142, 151–152, 154
MELD 4, 126
MELDARZ(A) 126
meta-theory 4, 10–11, 43, 49, 64, 72, 78, 86–87, 115, 152–153
Morphogenesis (morphogenetic, morphostatic) *see also* morphogenic sequence iii, 6, 54, 93–94, 131
morphogenic sequence 37

naïve realism 96
naturalism *see also* anti-naturalism 6, 48, 58, 124, 134, 138, 142, 150
neoliberalism 82–83, 122, 150

ontology *see also* depth ontology; ontological realism iii, 3–5, 7, 9–10, 14, 30–31, 33, 36–37, 44, 47, 49, 51–54, 59–60, 64, 67, 71, 74, 77–81, 86, 88, 91–92, 94, 99–100, 108–109, 112, 114–116, 118, 125–128, 130–132, 135, 143, 151, 153–154
ontological realism 43–44, 154
open ontology 127
open system 5, 22, 52, 72, 100, 104

parent engagement 8, 41–46, 48–49
philosophy of metaReality *see* MELDARZ(A) iii, xii, xv, 3, 7, 10–11, 14, 49, 109, 118, 123–124, 126–128, 141
Popper, Karl 57
Porpora, Douglas 11
Positivism/post-positivist iii, 2, 4–7, 9–10, 12, 32, 43, 47–48, 51–53, 57–58, 78–80, 87–98, 100, 110, 118, 136, 138, 148–149
Postmodernism 9
power iii, xiv, xv, 3, 6, 7, 9, 11, 15, 17, 22–24, 26–27, 31, 33–36, 38, 44, 46–48, 52–53, 55, 57, 71–73, 77–78, 81, 91, 98, 103–104, 108–109, 111–115, 117, 123, 127–128, 137–138, 142–143, 149, 154–155

quality xiv, 9, 30, 48, 77–78, 80–84, 86

racism xi, 10, 90, 92, 136
Real Domain *see also* Domains of Reality 34, 44–45

realist evaluation xiii, 8, 14, 16–17, 65, 69, 73
reasons as causes 145
reform xiv, 9, 77–78, 80–83, 86, 100
retrodiction 8, 14, 24, 35, 65–66, 70–71, 73
retroduction 8–9, 14, 18–19, 21, 24, 26, 35, 65–66, 70–73, 81–82, 85–86
RRE *see also* retroduction 81
RRRIREI(C) *see also* retrodiction; retroduction 65–67, 70, 72

Sayer, Andrew 33–34, 36, 38, 44, 52, 55–56, 67, 71, 81–82, 97–99, 101, 104, 113, 149
school choice 10, 97–99, 101–102
school markets xiv, 98–99, 101, 104
sexual assault xv, xvi, 9, 63, 67, 73
sociological imperialism 53
social constructivism 152
social work xiii, xv, 8, 15–25, 36, 65, 68
Socialisation 134
Spirituality *see also* spiritual turn; Transcendental Dialectical Critical Realism 4, 7, 11, 127, 131, 136–138, 142

spiritual turn 4, 7, 10, 127
stratification 33–34, 36–37, 73, 100, 103, 121, 126, 151
structure-agency 6
structuration 6, 138

template analysis 65–68
tendencies 18, 47, 52, 58, 70, 73, 108, 127, 133
Transcendental Dialectical Critical Realism 133, 135
transcendental realism 4–6, 135, 150
Transformational Model of Social Activity (TMSA) 6, 37

Underlabouring i, 3–4, 8, 41, 43–44, 46, 49, 52–53, 58, 60, 64, 108, 113–114, 118–119, 125, 131, 137, 139, 141–142, 148, 150
Utopia 11, 123, 125, 129, 154

vantage point 37, 108, 134, 152
violence xi, xv, 10, 63–64, 67, 71–72, 107–109, 111–113, 115–118, 149
vocational education 9, 77, 83